INSIDE SERVLE[

INSIDE SERVLETS

Server-Side Programming for the Java™ Platform

Dustin R. Callaway

ADDISON–WESLEY

An Imprint of Addison Wesley Longman, Inc.

Reading, Massachusetts • Harlow, England • Menlo Park, California
Berkeley, California • Don Mills, Ontario • Sydney
Bonn • Amsterdam • Tokyo • Mexico City

The publisher offers discounts on this book when ordered in quantity for special sales. For more information, please contact:

> Corporate, Government, and Special Sales Group
> Addison Wesley Longman, Inc.
> One Jacob Way
> Reading, Massachusetts 01867

Library of Congress Cataloging-in-Publication Data

Callaway, Dustin R.
    Inside servlets : server-side programming for the Java™ platform /
Dustin R. Callaway.
        p.   cm.
    ISBN 0-201-37963-5
    1. Java (Computer program language)   2. Client/server computing.
I. Title.
QA76.73.J38C35   1999
005.2'762--dc21   99–20222
                                 CIP

Text printed on recycled and acid-free paper.

ISBN 0201379635

4 5 6 7 8 9 MA 03 02 01 00

4th Printing   March 2000

This book is dedicated to my wonderful parents, Chris and Lanell Callaway. Thank you for all the years of love and support.

CONTENTS

PREFACE

Future generations will likely rank the Internet alongside the printing press, the airplane, and the personal computer as one of the most revolutionary technologies in history. After seemingly lying dormant for more than two decades, the Internet has emerged from obscurity to capture the interest and imagination of people around the world. One of the primary factors driving this phenomenon is the astounding popularity of the World Wide Web. Globally accessible via the Internet, the Web has forever changed the way information is published and distributed. The first goal of this book is to familiarize the reader with the underlying technologies that drive the Internet and the World Wide Web.

The Java programming language is another emerging technology whose potential is just beginning to be recognized. Due to its platform-independent nature, standard network interfaces, and many other advantages, Java is the ideal language for Internet programming. Although initially popularized by applets capable of running on any client, the true power of Java is being realized on the server. Among other things, server-side Java allows developers to build dynamic Web sites using a powerful, object-oriented language that is completely portable across platforms. In fact, the Java platform runs on top of virtually any operating system and hardware. By writing programs for the Java platform, you are in essence developing applications for all existing platforms. This kind of portability and cross-platform functionality is unprecedented.

The Internet relies on open standards to ensure that all clients have equal access to the vast amount of information it provides. Similarly, standards are essential to the advancement of the Java platform. Sun Microsystems, Inc., in cooperation with many industry partners and other interested parties, has created a standard for developing server-side Java programs that extend and enhance the functionality of the server. Known as the Java Servlet API, this standard ensures that all Java servlets will run properly across all platforms.

By conforming to the Servlet API specification, you can guarantee that all of your server-side programs will run on any platform that fully supports Java. After presenting Web development fundamentals, the second and primary goal of this book is to provide the reader with an in-depth understanding of Java servlets and the Servlet API through discussion and example.

Intended Audience

In general, this book was written for anyone interested in using server-side Java to build dynamic, data-driven Web sites or other networked applications. To this end, *Inside Servlets: Server-Side Programming for the Java™ Platform* presents an in-depth review of the Servlet API as well as advanced programming concepts essential for successful servlet development. These concepts include writing thread safe servlets, session management, and database access.

More specifically, the book is intended for programmers and consultants who desire to learn Web development fundamentals in addition to server-side Java programming. The majority of this audience likely consists of current client/server programmers. After all, in an increasingly Internet-centric world, many client/server programs are being redeveloped as Web applications. This decision is often driven by the fact that Web applications offer significant distribution and maintenance advantages over traditional client/server systems.

Because Java servlets may represent the reader's first foray into Web development, the first part of the book is dedicated to teaching the basics of the Internet and the World Wide Web. Although basic Web concepts are presented, the Java programming language is not taught. This book assumes the reader has a basic knowledge of object-oriented programming and the Java language. If you are not already familiar with Java, I recommend reading the Java primer in *Java in a Nutshell* by David Flanagan. This primer is especially well suited to C programmers. Another personal favorite for learning about Java is *Thinking in Java* by Bruce Eckel. If you do not already know Java, you may want to have one of these books available as a reference while reading this book.

Acknowledgments

Above all, I would like to thank my wife, Erin, for her enduring patience and support throughout this project. Thank you for playing the role of a single parent for the last several months. I would also like to thank my editor, Elizabeth Spainhour, for her help and guidance throughout the publication process.

Finally, I would like to express my appreciation to all of the reviewers at Sun Microsystems and elsewhere for the help and feedback that made this book possible. Specifically, I would like to thank James Duncan Davidson, Harish Prabandham, Todd Gee, Scott Urley, Debbie Fleming, and Christopher Blizzard.

INTRODUCTION

Organization of This Book

This book is partitioned into the following six parts with each part consisting of multiple chapters.

Part I: Introduction to Web Development

Part I introduces basic Web development concepts. These concepts include fundamentals such as firewalls, proxy servers, HTTP protocol, MIME types, and HTML forms.

Part II: Introduction to Servlets

Part II introduces the reader to Java servlets and the Servlet API. The information presented here includes the advantages of servlets over traditional CGI programming, basic servlet structure, writing your first servlet, running servlets, debugging servlets, and a preview of the Servlet API.

Part III: Advanced Servlet Concepts

Part III presents advanced concepts essential for building more complex servlets. These concepts include writing thread safe servlets, HTTP redirects, cookies, session management, server-side includes, request forwarding, and database access.

Part IV: Sample Servlets

Part IV presents several real-world examples of servlets in action. The function of each sample servlet is explained and the entire source code is given. Sample servlets include a Diagnostics servlet, a Form Mailer servlet, and a File Upload servlet.

Part V: Servlet API Quick Reference

Part V provides a comprehensive reference for the Servlet API version 2.1. Every method defined by all classes and interfaces in the Servlet API is presented.

Part VI: Appendices

Part VI provides useful information in the form of several appendices. Additional information within them includes a Java port scanner, a Java HTTP server, HTTP response status codes, HTTP request header fields, common MIME types, Servlet API class hierarchy diagram, and much more.

How to Use This Book

If you are new to Web development, it is recommended that you start with Chapter 1 of Part I and read each chapter in order (skimming or skipping material with which you are already familiar). If you know all about Web development concepts (perhaps you're a CGI programmer), you may choose to skip Part I entirely and proceed to Part II. Finally, if you already have servlet development experience, you may choose to jump directly to Part III, IV, or V to learn advanced servlet concepts or review the Servlet API reference material.

Conventions Used in This Book

A `fixed width` font is used for:

- Anything that might appear in a Java program
- Command lines and other text that should be typed
- Tags that appear in an HTML document
- Any sample program output
- Java class names and packages
- Anything that could appear in an HTTP header or other protocol communication

An *italic* font is used for:

- New terms where they are first defined
- Pathnames, filenames, and program names (except when a program name is a Java class)
- Internet addresses such as domain names and URLs
- Names of user-interface buttons and input fields displayed by an application or HTML page

Contents of the CD-ROM

The CD-ROM that accompanies this book contains the following material.

- The source code and compiled class files for all sample code presented in the text and appendices
- Java 2 SDK, Standard Edition, v 1.2 (formerly JDK 1.2) for Windows and Solaris
- JRun 2.2 and 2.3 from Live Software, Inc., for Windows, UNIX, NetWare, and Macintosh (servlet engine)
- ServletKiller 1.1 from Live Software, Inc. (servlet stress-tester)
- ServletExec 2.0 from New Atlanta Communications, LLC, for Windows, Solaris, HP-UX, Linux, and Macintosh (servlet engine)
- Protocol Explorer application used to examine all types of Internet protocol communications (e.g., http headers, ftp sessions)

Many of the directories that contain the software described here also contain a file called *readme.txt*. This file includes additional information and/or instructions about the software in the current directory. Whenever present, please read this file before using the software.

PART I

Introduction to Web Development

CHAPTER 1

Internet Basics

In virtually any field of endeavor, a sound understanding of the fundamentals is essential before tackling more complex tasks. This "learn to walk before you run" strategy is especially important in the area of Web development. Perplexing problems are often quickly resolved once the underlying concepts are understood. So, before diving into servlet development with both feet, let's review the basics.

This chapter will teach you the basic networking concepts and terminology that you need to know when developing networked applications. The following topics are covered in this chapter:

- Networks
- Protocols
- TCP/IP
- Brief history of the Internet
- Internet addresses
- Ports
- Sockets
- Name resolution
- Firewalls
- Protocol tunneling
- Proxy servers
- Internet standards

Though many important topics are presented, this chapter is only a primer and not intended to replace a comprehensive study of networking. For more detailed information on this subject, excellent resources are the titles in the *Networking Basics Series* from Addison Wesley Longman. On the other hand, if you are familiar with networks and networking concepts, feel free to skim or skip this chapter.

Networks

At its core, a *network* is simply a group of computers and other devices connected in a manner that promotes communication between them. Networked computers are most commonly connected by wire of some sort (often coaxial cable or a twisted pair wire similar to a phone line); however, machines on a network can be linked by virtually any medium. Some networks communicate via radio waves, infrared light, or fiber optic cable. The only absolute requirement of a network is that there must be some way for devices to communicate.

To begin our discussion on networking, let's define a few new words. A *node* is any addressable device connected to a network. This could be a computer, printer, fax machine, or even a network-enabled toaster. In contrast, the term *host* is a more specific descriptor that refers to a networked general-purpose computer rather than a single-purpose device (such as a printer). The relationship between a host and a node is asymmetric. Though every host is also a node, not every node is necessarily a host.

Let's take a closer look at one of the elements in the definition of a node. The definition states that a node must be addressable, but what does that mean? In short, it means that there must be some way to locate each node individually on a network. To facilitate this, a unique address is assigned to every node on a network. Without a unique address, there would be no way to communicate with the device.[1] For example, you cannot send someone a letter unless they have a valid address. Therefore, each node on a network is assigned a unique number to identify it. When a message is packaged and transmitted across the network (this package of information is called a *packet*) the source and destination addresses are included with the message data. This address information is used by network hardware to route the packet to its proper destination. The network hardware, known as *routers,* operates like electronic postal workers that evaluate and forward packets between networks. They may send the packet directly to the addressed node or to another router that will, in turn, pass the packet along. Eventually, the packet will arrive at its final destination. Thanks to unique addressing, it is possible to communicate with every node on the network. We will take a closer look at addresses later on in this chapter.

Now that we have figured out how nodes on a network send each other messages, there is still one more question that needs to be answered. How can we guarantee that a node will understand the messages it receives? Good question! The answer is something called protocols.

---

1. Actually, through something called a *broadcast message* it is possible to send information to all devices on the network without specifically addressing a particular one. However, a device that responds only to broadcast messages (that is not uniquely addressable) is not a considered a node.

Protocols

One of the most fundamental concepts of network communications is the idea of a protocol. Simply put, a *protocol* is a formal set of rules that must be followed in order to communicate. Though you may not realize it, you use protocols every day. Imagine the confusion generated by someone who did not follow commonly accepted protocols for speaking with others.

You approach a stranger in the mall . . .

You: "Excuse me sir, but do you have the time?"
Stranger: "Yeah, it's 1998."
You: "No. I was wondering if you know what time it is."
Stranger: "July."
You: "Uhh, thanks. Goodbye."

Not a lot of communication took place during that conversation because the stranger did not follow a common protocol for exchanging the time of day. Now, let's try it again.

Again, you approach a stranger in the mall . . .

You: "Excuse me sir, but do you have the time?"
Stranger: "Yeah, it's 2:30."
You: "Thank you."

Now we're talking! Once both sides of the conversation were using the same protocol, communication began to take place. A computer protocol is very similar to this example, but a bit more structured. For instance, when you ask for the time, the response could be in any number of formats. A person might say "Yep, it's half past two." They could also use commonly accepted shorthand such as "it's noon." Or they may respond "No, but there's a clock just down the hall." Regardless, you will be able to process the information that is delivered. There is no predefined set of options that must be spoken in response to the phrase "Do you have the time?" Computer protocols, on the other hand, cannot afford to be so loosely structured. Though our minds are perfectly adapted to processing and responding to extremely varied input, computers are not. An extremely complex program is required to process even the simplest natural language sentence. For this reason, networked computers usually converse using an extremely rigid protocol.

For example, when a computer requests a file to download, it either expects the file to be transmitted or an error condition to be returned. The computer would not understand if the host machine responded with "please try back when I'm not so busy" or "it's been a long day, try back tomorrow."

However, a properly constructed error message could be construed as "server busy" by the requesting application. At this point, the application may be programmed to wait for a predefined timeout period and then try again. The computer understands the error condition, but not the randomly constructed sentence.

Within the context of computer networks, there are many levels of protocols. A low-level protocol might define details like the rate at which bits are transmitted or the voltage levels required to interpret a signal as a zero or a one. Alternatively, a high-level protocol defines the format of the data as well as the sequence and syntax of messages. Below is an example of the high-level HTTP protocol in action.

Web Browser: `GET /INDEX.HTML HTTP/1.0`

Web Server:
```
HTTP/1.0 200 OK
Server: Netscape-Enterprise/2.01
Content-type: text/html
Content-length: 70

<HTML><HEAD><TITLE>Example</TITLE></HEAD>
<BODY>It works!</BODY></HTML>
```

The preceding example demonstrates an actual conversation between a Web browser and server. The HTTP protocol defines the format of the requests that are recognized by the server and how the server should respond to these requests. In this case, the browser requested a file called *INDEX.HTML* and the server returned the contents of the file as well as some additional information to help the browser construct the page. We will discuss the HTTP protocol in detail in the next chapter.

TCP/IP

TCP/IP is a collection, or suite, of protocols used to communicate across a network. The entire protocol suite is named TCP/IP after the two original protocols: Transmission Control Protocol (TCP) and Internet Protocol (IP). Typically, the TCP/IP suite is broken down into four layers[2] as shown in Figure 1.1.

Why are the protocols layered? The answer is that layering protocols simplifies the task of communicating over the network and it allows for reuse of layers that are not specific to a particular application. Each layer is responsible

---

2. The most commonly accepted network model, known as the OSI model, actually consists of seven layers. However, very few network implementations strictly adhere to the OSI model. The TCP/IP model, for instance, combines several OSI layers into a single layer.

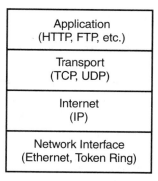

| Application
(HTTP, FTP, etc.) |
| Transport
(TCP, UDP) |
| Internet
(IP) |
| Network Interface
(Ethernet, Token Ring) |

Figure 1.1   The Four Layers of the TCP/IP Model

for a different aspect of the transmission and each layer insulates the layers above it from some detail of network communication. For instance, whether a program is using the HTTP or FTP protocol in the application layer, they both use the same underlying protocols—TCP, IP, and Ethernet. The combination of all layers is referred to as a *protocol stack*. As information is transmitted, data flows down through the protocol stack at the source, across the network, and up the protocol stack at the destination.

As data moves through the protocol stack, each layer attaches its own information. The information added by each layer is called a *header*. Once all layers have attached their header to the data, the package of information that results is called a *packet*. Attaching a header to a packet is similar to putting an envelope inside of another envelope. To illustrate, let's follow this envelope analogy all the way through. Imagine that you have a message that you would like to send to a coworker in one of your company's foreign offices.

First, you print the message that you would like to send (this is analogous to the data portion of a packet). You then place the message inside of an interoffice envelope and address it to your coworker by specifying his name and the office that employs him (the envelope is analogous to a header). When the mailroom receives the envelope, they place it in a larger envelope and address it with more specific information, such as city and street address (this is similar to attaching a second header). This additional information is required to properly route the letter to the Japan office.

Finally, when the envelope arrives at the mailroom of the Japan office, a worker removes the inner envelope (strips off the outer header) and sends it via interoffice mail. When your coworker receives the interoffice envelope, he opens it and removes the message. This exercise is very similar to the manner in which data is transmitted across the network.

Let's take a look at an actual network transmission (see Figure 1.2). A program wants to send some data to an application running on another computer. The data is packaged in the application layer and a header is applied. As the data moves down the protocol stack, each layer adds its own header. Placing the data inside a package of headers is known as *encapsulation*. Once the data has been encapsulated inside a packet, it is transmitted across the network. At the destination, each layer removes its header from the packet and passes it up the stack. This process continues until the data is handed back to the application at the highest layer. The application was not interested in the headers attached by other layers, it was simply looking for data. However, these headers were necessary in order to properly transport the information across the network.

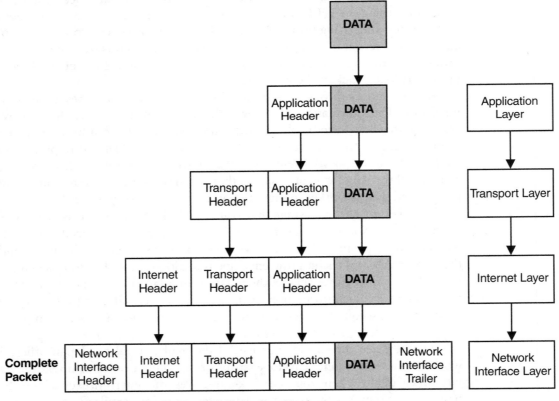

Figure 1.2   Each Layer Adds Its Own Header

Now that we have established that TCP/IP is a collection of layered protocols, let's examine each of the layers: network interface, Internet, transport, and application.

Network Interface Layer

The network interface layer handles the lowest-level details of communicating across the network. This layer consists of the network device driver (software) and the network interface card (hardware). An Ethernet device driver and network card is a good example of an implementation of the network interface layer. Together, these two pieces ensure the proper transmission of data across whatever medium is being used (coaxial cable, twisted pair, fiber optics, etc.). The network interface layer insulates all layers above it from the complexities of interfacing with various network hardware and transmission mediums. It is interesting to note that the network interface layer adds a trailer in addition to the header (see Figure 1.2). The trailer carries CRC (Cyclic Redundancy Check) information used for error detection.

Internet Layer

The Internet layer is responsible for transmitting packets around the network. In the TCP/IP model, the Internet layer uses a protocol called IP (Internet Protocol). This protocol defines exactly how a packet must be structured if it is to be understood by an IP network. The Internet layer's job is to build a packet that conforms to the standard IP protocol. An IP packet, also called a *datagram*, contains a great deal of information. This information includes the length of the header, the total length of the packet, the type of service (Telnet, FTP, etc.), time to live (how many times routers will forward the packet), checksum (for error detection), source address, destination address, and much more.

Transport Layer

The transport layer manages the manner in which data flows between hosts. Though the Internet layer does an excellent job routing network packets, it does not provide any mechanism to ensure their arrival. If guaranteed arrival is desired, that functionality must be provided in the transport layer (or, possibly, in the application layer). Within the TCP/IP model, there are two extremely different transport protocols—TCP and UDP (User Datagram Protocol).

TCP is a reliable protocol that guarantees the arrival of network packets. This guarantee is possible due to the connection-oriented approach implemented by the Transmission Control Protocol. Before any data is sent via the TCP protocol, a connection between the two hosts must first be established. This connection verifies that the destination host is listening and that there is a valid network path whereby the data can reach the destination. The source machine waits for an acknowledgement from the destination host for every packet that is sent. If no acknowledgement is received or the destination requests a retransmission, the packet is sent again. In addition to verifying that no packets are lost, TCP also ensures that the packets are in the proper sequence before passing them up the protocol stack.

To better understand the connection-oriented nature of the TCP protocol, imagine the difference between making a telephone call and mailing a letter. When you speak to someone on the phone, you are sure that they received your message. Why is this? Because you first established a connection with them and they responded to (i.e., acknowledged) your message. Alternatively, consider mailing a letter. Once you address an envelope and drop it in the mail, you have no guarantee that the letter will arrive. In fact, you will actually never know if it does arrive unless you happen to receive a reply. Of course, if a reply does come, there is no telling how long you will have to wait for it.

User Datagram Protocol is the second protocol employed in the transport layer. UDP is an unreliable, connectionless protocol. UDP is referred to as "connectionless" because, similar to mailing a letter, no connection is established between the source and destination when a packet is sent. Unlike TCP, this protocol does not automatically ensure a valid network path through which the packet can be delivered. UDP packets are not guaranteed to arrive at their destination.

It might seem as if an unreliable protocol would be useless. However, this is far from the truth. A connection-oriented protocol like TCP requires much more overhead in order to keep track of packets and manage the connection. Thus, a connectionless protocol is able to transmit information much faster. Another advantage to a connectionless protocol is the ability to broadcast messages without specifying the address of a particular recipient. With UDP, it is possible to send a broadcast message to all nodes on a network without knowing the exact address of any of the recipients.[3] A single message is transmitted over the network and all nodes receive it. Of course, some of the packets may not arrive at the destination, but for a broadcast message, this is seldom a concern. TCP, on the other hand, would be required to establish a connection with

---

3. Fortunately, it is not possible to send a broadcast message to the entire Internet. Broadcast messages are not forwarded by routers and are, therefore, isolated to a local network. Otherwise, the network traffic generated by thousands of broadcast messages could cripple the entire Internet.

each node individually and transmit the information separately to each. The network traffic would be much greater and the performance much worse.

Streaming audio and video is another example of a network application that is well suited to a connectionless protocol. By its very nature, streaming information is time sensitive. The additional performance gained by using UDP is well worth settling for less than 100 percent reliability. In fact, if a streaming audio or video transmission lost a few packets, you probably would not even notice. In addition, even if there was no performance penalty for using a connection-oriented protocol, you would still prefer that lost packets were not retransmitted. If a lost packet was retransmitted while a user was listening to a streaming audio broadcast, the packet would arrive out of sequence. The sound information that the packet carried should have been played long ago and the packet would now be useless. The retransmission would have only increased network traffic.

Application Layer

The application layer is responsible for providing services particular to an application. HTTP is an excellent example of an application level protocol. As we saw before, HTTP defines how a Web client (or browser) communicates with a Web server. In addition to HTTP, some examples of application layer protocols include FTP for file transfers, Telnet for remote login, NNTP for news groups, SMTP for sending e-mail, and POP3 for receiving e-mail.

Now let's look at something a little more interesting to the developer. Figure 1.3 shows the communication protocols employed when a Web client

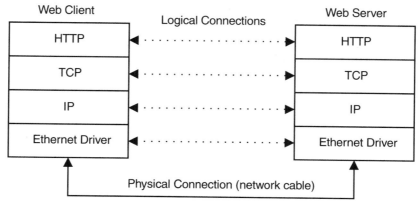

Figure 1.3   Protocols Used for Communication Between a Browser and Web Server

makes a request to a Web server. The *logical connections* convey the idea that when writing software for the application layer (where servlet developers spend most of their time) the developer is not concerned with any other protocol. He has a logical connection from the application layer of his machine to the application layer of the server. The TCP/IP protocol stack takes care of all lower-level layers. Likewise, a developer working on the transport layer need not concern himself with the complexities of the Internet and network interface layers. The logical connection between layers simplifies the development process. For additional information on TCP/IP, see RFC 1180 entitled "A TCP/IP Tutorial" (for information about RFCs and where to find them, see the Internet Standards section later in this chapter).

Brief History of the Internet

The *Internet* is a TCP/IP based, global network connecting millions of computers around the world. In order to get an idea of where the Internet is headed, it may be useful to know where it has been. This section presents a brief history of the Internet.

The precursor to the Internet, known as the ARPANET, was originally developed in the late 1960s by the U.S. Department of Defense (DOD) in conjunction with a number of universities and military contractors. The ARPANET project was intended to produce a fail-safe network capable of functioning even in the case of global nuclear war. With the end of the cold war, the DOD's interest in the ARPANET cooled. However, the private sector was just starting to investigate the vast possibilities of a global network. In 1983, the transition of the ARPANET to the TCP/IP suite of protocols was completed and the Internet was born. Universities and research facilities quickly adopted the Internet as a medium through which to send and receive e-mail and electronically publish findings. The usefulness of this new communications medium caught on quickly and the Internet spread to countries around the world. If you are interested in reading more about the Internet and its origins, see RFC 1462.

Today, the Internet is well on its way to becoming as ubiquitous as the telephone. Virtually every major corporation has staked its claim in cyberspace and many projections show that by the year 2000 a majority of households will have Internet access. People are using the Internet for activities ranging from shopping for cars to purchasing books to playing games. As the phenomenal growth of the Internet continues, those with the knowledge and skills to build Internet applications will be poised to take advantage of the great opportunities that arise.

Internet Addresses

Each computer connected to the Internet is identified by a unique numeric address. The IP protocol requires that this address consist of four bytes (each byte ranging from 0 to 255). For example, the IP address of my Web site is currently *209.68.35.199* (IP addresses are frequently subject to change). To ensure uniqueness, all Internet addresses are assigned by a single organization, the Internet Network Information Center (InterNIC). Although the four byte address standard, known as IPv4, seemed more than sufficient when IP was first developed, the InterNIC is rapidly running out of unique addresses. Fortunately, a new sixteen byte addressing scheme, known as IPv6, is currently being tested.

NOTE: The U.S. Department of Commerce and various other U.S. and international agencies (both public and private) are currently evaluating proposals to alter the manner in which domain names and IP addresses are assigned and managed. According to some of these proposals, a nonprofit international board may be commissioned to administer domain names and IP addresses worldwide.

Though numeric addresses are easy for a computer to work with, they are extremely difficult for humans to remember. For this reason, it is possible to assign an alias, known as a *hostname,* to an IP address. For instance, my Web site is accessible on the Internet by using the IP address of *209.68.35.199* or the hostname *www.sourcestream.com.* Certainly, the latter is much easier to remember.

Let's take a moment to dissect this hostname and look at its parts individually. The first portion of the hostname (*www* in this case) is arbitrary. Its meaning is interpreted by the server. Regardless, *www* is the standard convention for sites that serve HTML pages using the HTTP protocol (*www* stands for World Wide Web). Another common value for this position is *ftp* for file transfer services, such as *ftp.sourcestream.com.* Though terms like *www* and *ftp* are commonly used, the server does not use this data to determine the type of service to provide. The type of service (e.g., HTTP, FTP, Telnet) is determined by the port on which the connection was established (ports are discussed in the next section). Though it is common to designate a service to begin a hostname, any string can occupy this location. For example, *sales.sourcestream.com* or *service.sourcestream.com* is permissible and might direct users to different portions of a Web site (or different Web sites altogether).

Table 1.1   Common Top-Level Domains

Domain	Description
.com	For-profit companies, corporations, partnerships, and so forth (e.g., *www.netscape.com*)
.edu	Educational facilities such as universities and technical colleges (e.g., *www.byu.edu*)
.gov	Nonmilitary government organizations (e.g., *www.ustreas.gov*)
.mil	Military organizations (e.g., *www.navy.mil*)
.net	Network facilities such as ISPs and network integrators (e.g., *www.internic.net*)
.org	Nonprofit organizations (e.g., *www.pbs.org*)

The final string, .com (pronounced "dot com"), is referred to as the *top-level domain*. The top-level domain defines the type of organization (see Table 1.1) within the United States or the country of origin (.ca = Canada, .uk = United Kingdom, etc.) outside of the United States. (For more information on the structure of the domain name system, see RFC 1591.) Lastly, the middle string combined with the top-level domain (*sourcestream.com*) creates a unique *domain name* that allows Internet users around the world to locate a site. In addition to assigning Internet addresses, the InterNIC is also responsible for registering unique domain names.

It is worth noting that, beyond being easier to remember, there is another advantage to using domain names rather than IP addresses. Hostnames are often less likely to change than the underlying IP address. What if, for instance, a commercial Internet Service Provider (ISP) hosted your Web site. Service providers effectively "rent" you a static IP address so that your site can be located via your domain name. However, what if you decided to move to another provider or chose to host your own site? The answer is that nothing would happen as long as Internet users reference your site using your domain name rather than your IP address. Simply update the Domain Name Service (DNS) entry for

NOTE: Similar to the manner in which a domain name resolves to an IP address, the term *localhost* resolves to the "loopback" IP address of *127.0.0.1*, which refers to the local macine. This term is often used in network programming as an alias for the local machine's IP address.

your domain name to point to a new IP address and the transition will be seamless. DNS and the process of converting hostnames into their proper numeric IP addresses are discussed in the "Name Resolution" section later in this chapter.

Ports

Host machines are uniquely identified by IP addresses[4] but the applications running on them are identified by port numbers. A *port* is a logical channel to an application running on a host. Keep in mind that we are referring to logical ports, not physical ports like the serial or parallel port on your computer. Ports provide a means of routing requests to the applications that service them. They ensure that e-mail is not sent to a Web server and that FTP requests are not sent to a mail server.

To illustrate, Web servers typically "listen" for connections on port 80. This port has been reserved for HTTP transactions (the protocol used on the World Wide Web). Though it is possible for an HTTP server to be listening on another port, this is somewhat unusual and would require the port to be explicitly specified by the user. By default, a Web browser will request all HTTP connections from port 80. To specify port 81, for example, the user would have to type `http://www.sourcestream.com:81`. Similarly, an FTP client application would, by default, connect to port 21 (reserved for FTP) or, if designated by the user, another port on which an FTP server was listening.

Port numbers can range from 1 to 65535; however, ports 1 to 1023 are reserved. These reserved ports are referred to as "well-known ports" because the applications that use them are publicly documented by the Internet Assigned Numbers Authority (IANA). Table 1.2 lists several of the well-known ports in use today (also provided in Appendix A).

NOTE: On UNIX systems, ports under 1024 are privileged. Only the super-user can bind to these ports.

It is possible to write a simple Java application, called a port scanner, that will scan all ports on a host and display only the ports on which a server is responding. For example, a port scanner can determine if an FTP server is running on a particular host or if a server is responding on the echo port. See Appendix B for the source code and sample output for a Java port scanner.

---

4. Though an IP address uniquely identifies a host, it is possible (and common) for a host to have more than one IP address.

Table 1.2   Common Well-Known Port Assignments

Name	Port	Description
echo	7	Echo is used to test the connection between hosts. Any data sent to port 7 is echoed back to the sender.
daytime	13	Responds to any connection with the time of day on the server.
ftp	21	Used for transferring files.
telnet	23	Allows for remote login to a host machine.
whois	43	A directory service for looking up names of users on a remote server.
gopher	70	A distributed document retrieval application.
finger	79	Displays information about a user or all users logged into a server.
http	80	Responds to HyperText Transfer Protocol requests. HTTP is the protocol used for communicating on the World Wide Web.
pop3	110	Post Office Protocol 3 allows users to retrieve stored e-mail messages.
nntp	119	Network News Transfer Protocol provides access to thousands of news groups for the exchange of information. Commonly known as "Usenet."
https	443	Secure HTTP protocol. This is the HTTP protocol running on top of the Secure Sockets Layer (SSL) for encrypted HTTP transmissions.

Sockets

A *socket* insulates the programmer from the complexities of network programming by making network communication appear identical to reading or writing to a file or any other standard stream. Network sockets interface Java's standard IO with its network communication facilities. The abstraction of network functionality provided by sockets is similar to the manner in which one layer of the TCP/IP protocol stack insulates another layer from some complexity of network communications. A socket connection is established between any available port on the client and a specified port and IP address of a server. Figure 1.4 illustrates this point, depicting a client establishing a socket connection to port 80 of a Web server. If you wrote a program to interpret the HTTP headers returned from the server and render a view of the HTML, you would have your own Web browser.

Sockets were originally developed for Berkeley UNIX but the simplicity of treating network connections like any other standard input/output routines attracted the attention of many operating systems and programming languages. For instance, a sockets interface called WinSock has been developed for the Windows environment. In addition, Java implements a sockets interface that makes reading and writing to the network no more difficult than reading and

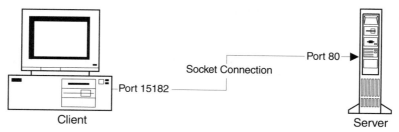

Figure 1.4 Simple Socket Cconnection from Client to Server's HTTP Port

writing a file on the local hard drive. The Java code in Listing 1.1 demonstrates a simple application that uses a socket connection to retrieve the time of day on a specified host. If no host is specified on the command line, the local host is presumed.

Listing 1.1 Opens a socket connection to a host's daytime port to retrieve the time on the server.

```
import java.io.*;
import java.net.*;

/**
 * Get Time
 *
 * Queries a server's daytime port for the time of day.
 *
 * @author Dustin R. Callaway
 * @version 1.0, 01/09/98
 */
public class GetTime
{
  //main is invoked by the JVM at execution
  public static void main(String[] args)
  {
    Socket socket; //socket connection to host
    String host = "localhost"; //default host

    if (args.length > 0)
    {
      //host was passed on command-line, set host value
      host = args[0];
    }

    try
    {
      //open socket connection to daytime port 13
      socket = new Socket(host, 13);
      //get handle to input stream to read the time
      BufferedReader in = new BufferedReader(
```

```
            new InputStreamReader(socket.getInputStream()));
         //read the first line from host
         String time = in.readLine();
         //print time to standard out
         System.out.println("The time on host " + host + " is " +
            time);
      }
      catch (UnknownHostException e) //host not found
      {
         System.out.println("Host is invalid.");
      }
      catch (IOException e) //problem opening socket
      {
         System.out.println("Error opening socket: " + e);
      }
   }
}
```

The output looks like this:

```
C:\>java GetTime www.mit.edu
The time on host www.mit.edu is Wed Jan 7 12:32:17 1998
```

Name Resolution

As discussed earlier, Internet addresses can be referenced by hostname or IP
address. Hostnames are provided to make it easier for us to remember addresses. Unfortunately, the computer does not understand hostnames, only
numeric IP addresses. Therefore, every time an Internet address is requested
using a hostname, the computer must look up the IP address that corresponds
to it. *Name resolution* is the process of mapping a hostname to its corresponding IP address.

One way to translate a hostname to an IP address is to look it up in a simple text file. This text file, usually called *HOSTS* (or something similar), contains hostnames and their corresponding IP addresses. For example, a mapping
to my Web site in a *HOSTS* file would look like this:

```
209.68.35.199  www.sourcestream.com
```

Whenever a hostname is referenced, the computer determines its IP address by
locating the name in the *HOSTS* file and retrieving its IP address.

This method is simple and straightforward but there are several major
drawbacks. First, every site that you reference by name would need to be stored
in this text file (it could get rather large). Second, you would have to copy this
file to every computer on which you use named references. Lastly, you would
be required to maintain and update this file to see that it remains current. There
has to be a better way. Luckily, there is. It is called the Domain Name Service.

The *Domain Name Service* is a distributed database containing all registered hostnames on the Internet and their IP addresses. Using DNS to resolve names to IP addresses is vastly different from using a *HOSTS* file. Rather than looking in a local text file for a hostname's IP address, the computer queries a DNS server for the information. This approach frees the user from maintaining a constantly growing *HOSTS* file and, since any computer can reference a DNS server, all hosts on the network can share the same information.

In addition, a DNS server is normally configured to use a sequence of name servers when resolving a hostname. DNS servers on the Internet are organized in a hierarchical fashion in order to most efficiently process requests. For instance, if your company's local DNS server does not contain a particular hostname, it can query the next higher DNS server for the translation, and so on. If properly registered, the hostname will eventually be found and the IP address returned to the host that requested it. If the hostname cannot be found, an error message indicating that the server does not have a DNS entry will be returned. For additional information on DNS, see RFC 1034 and RFC 1035.

Firewalls

A *firewall* is a piece of network hardware that serves as a secure gateway between an internal network and the Internet. It protects the internal network from unauthorized access or activity. Usually, a firewall is just an ordinary server running specialized software, through which all network traffic between the internal network and the Internet must flow. The firewall examines each packet passing through it and verifies that the packet does not violate any established security policies. To illustrate, a firewall can deny access to all hosts within a specified IP range. It may allow outgoing FTP connections but block all incoming FTP requests. It may not allow external connections to a Web server's administration port. A properly configured firewall allows network administrators to sleep at night.

Protocol Tunneling

Protocol tunneling is the process of encapsulating one protocol within another protocol that operates on the same layer (for TCP/IP, this usually takes place at the transport layer). Tunneling is commonly used to circumvent firewall restrictions. For example, if a firewall allows HTTP connections but blocks all FTP requests, HTTP tunneling can be implemented to encapsulate FTP protocol commands within an HTTP message. In this way, FTP operations can be performed through the unblocked HTTP port.

Proxy Servers

A *proxy server* is a host that makes Internet requests on behalf of other machines on the network. Proxy servers are often used to cache frequently requested files or to monitor Internet use within a corporation. Some companies prefer that each employee not have direct access to the Internet. Rather, these employees can request Internet services from the proxy server. Rules set on the proxy server can either grant or deny these service requests. In addition, proxy servers can cache frequently requested files. Thus, when a user requests a file from a proxy server, the server first looks in its own cache for the file. If found, the server returns the file. Otherwise, the file is requested from the source. In this manner, performance is improved and network traffic is reduced. Lastly, proxy servers provide some degree of security for an internal network. Because the proxy server makes all external requests, external hosts cannot learn the name or IP address of computers on the internal network. Only the proxy server shares this information with the outside world. Firewalls and proxy servers are commonly used in conjunction to provide a comprehensive network security strategy.

Internet Standards

Assembling a global network of compatible protocols is no small task. You may wonder how such an enormous effort was coordinated and how new standards are determined. The whole process centers around documents known as Internet Drafts (IDs) and Requests for Comments (RFCs). These documents are the driving force behind current and proposed Internet standards. They are also the most current and accurate references for information on Internet standards and protocols. Unfortunately, they are often a bit lengthy and esoteric.

There are numerous locations on the Internet where RFCs and IDs can be found. A few locations that are not likely to change are listed here.

- For RFCs:
  http://info.internet.isi.edu/1/in-notes/rfc
  http://www.rfc-editor.org

- For Internet standards:
  http://info.internet.isi.edu/1/in-notes/std

- For IDs:
  http://info.internet.isi.edu/1/in-drafts

Table 1.3   Small Sampling of Important RFCs

RFC	Status	Title	Description
821	Draft Standard	SMTP	Defines the Simple Mail Transfer protocol for sending e-mail
1034, 1035	Standard	Domain Names	Describe the Domain Name System
1462	Informational	FYI on "What is the Internet?"	Describes the Internet and its origins
2045, 2046, 2047, 2048, 2049	Draft Standard	MIME Parts 1–5	Specification for MIME
1866	Proposed Standard	Hypertext Markup Language—2.0	Specification for HTML 2.0
1942	Experimental	HTML Tables	Specification for adding table support to HTML
1945	Informational	Hypertext Transfer Protocol	Specification for HTTP/1.0
2068	Proposed Standard	Hypertext Transfer Protocol—HTTP/1.1	Specification for HTTP/1.1
2200	Standard	Internet Official Protocol Standards	Often updated to give the current status of many protocols

Many RFCs are of particular interest to the servlet developer. Table 1.3 shows several important RFCs of which you should be aware. For more detail on the Internet standardization process, see Appendix C.

Summary

A firm understanding of networking basics is essential to developing robust Internet applications. The information in this chapter provides a good foundation in basic networking concepts that can be applied to servlet development. In Chapter 2, we will focus on fundamental concepts pertaining to the World Wide Web.

Chapter Highlights

- A *network* is a group of computers and other devices connected in a manner that promotes communication between them.

- A *protocol* is a formal set of rules that must be followed in order to communicate.

- *TCP/IP* is a collection of protocols used to communicate across a network.

- The *Internet* is a TCP/IP based, global network connecting millions of computers around the world.

- Each computer connected to the Internet is identified by a unique IP address. In addition, aliases known as hostnames can often be used in place of numeric IP addresses.

- A *port* is a logical channel to an application running on a host.

- A *socket* insulates the programmer from the complexities of network programming by making network communication appear identical to reading or writing to a file or any other standard stream.

- *Name resolution* is the process of mapping a hostname to its corresponding IP address.

- A *firewall* is a piece of network hardware that serves as a secure gateway between an internal network and the Internet.

- *Protocol tunneling* is the process of encapsulating one protocol within another protocol that operates on the same layer (for TCP/IP, this usually takes place at the transport layer).

- A *proxy server* is a host that makes Internet requests in behalf of other machines on the network.

- Internet standards are proposed, documented, and revised in documents called Internet Drafts and Requests for Comments.

CHAPTER 2

Web Basics

Java is an extremely powerful language for developing Web applications that run on the client or the server. However, until you understand the basics behind communicating on the World Wide Web, your network programming projects may be confined to writing animated applets to enhance your Web site. On the other hand, with the proper background, you will be able to build complex sites ranging from order entry to customer tracking to decision support systems. Though these projects may not provoke the same "that's cool!" response, they sure can make a positive impact on your company's bottom line.

This chapter describes the basic concepts behind the World Wide Web. The following topics are covered in this chapter:

- Brief history of the Web
- URLs and URL encoding
- Web browsers and browser/server communication
- Web servers
- Introduction to the Common Gateway Interface (CGI)

If you are already familiar with this material, you may prefer to skim or skip this chapter.

Brief History of the Web

The humble beginnings of the World Wide Web go way back to 1989 (about 100 years ago in "Web time"). During this year, Tim Berners-Lee of the European Laboratory of Particle Physics (CERN) proposed a new network composed of files containing links to related files. These links, called *hypertext*, would allow a reader to find additional information by simply clicking on any hypertext word or phrase within a document. In 1990, the first text-only browsers were developed and implemented at CERN and other research facilities. For the first time, a network of linked documents was available for publishing research worldwide. Though this network proved to be successful, the Web was still very young and required further refinement and standardization. In order to standardize the format of hypertext documents, Tim Berners-Lee drafted the first HTML specification. As more and more browsers began to support this new specification, HTML quickly became the *de facto* standard for publishing documents on the Web.

The growth of the Web was relatively modest until the National Center for Supercomputing Applications (NCSA) developed the first "killer" Web application in 1993. Their new browser, called Mosaic, allowed users to view graphical images on the World Wide Web for the first time. The popularity of this browser increased rapidly as the Web started to grow at a dizzying rate.

In the fall of 1994, Netscape Communications Corporation released the first browser that added unique, nonstandard extensions to the HTML language. These extensions, such as HTML tables, became wildly popular and made Netscape's browser, called Navigator, the most popular on the Internet (at one point, Navigator owned nearly 90 percent of the Web browser market). Netscape's practice of implementing the latest features at a breakneck pace spawned a vicious race between several companies to be the first to reach the market with newer and better browser features. At times, new versions of a browser were released every month or two. The rate at which this new technology advanced was unprecedented in the history of the industry.

Today, the World Wide Web is still the fastest growing sector of the Internet. From its beginnings as a simple method for sharing research, the Web has captured the imagination of Internet users and businesses around the world.

Inside URLs

A *Uniform Resource Identifier* (URI) is a term referring to any specification that identifies an object on the Internet. Today there are two types of URIs— the Uniform Resource Locator and the Uniform Resource Name.

A *Uniform Resource Locator* (URL) is a specification for identifying an object, such as a file, newsgroup, CGI program, or e-mail address, by indicating its exact location on the Internet. URLs are the most common type of URI and are fully supported by today's software.

A *Uniform Resource Name* (URN) is a method for referencing an object without declaring the full path to the object. The idea behind a URN is that rather than specifying a resource by its location, it is referenced by an alias (similar to the way a hostname aliases an IP address). In this manner, even if the resource is moved, it will still be locatable via its URN. In addition, several copies of a resource could be stored on different servers in different parts of the world. When a request is made for a particular URN, the browser could locate the nearest copy of the resource and return it—increasing performance and reducing network traffic. For more information on the syntax of URNs, see RFC 2141. Though URNs sound promising, they are not currently supported by most software. Because of the current lack of support for URNs, this section will focus on the widely implemented URL specification.

The syntax of a URL is dependent on the protocol (referred to as the "scheme" in the RFC) required to access the object. Though the syntax of URLs varies, most URLs assume one of these two forms:

```
protocol://host[:port]/url-path
protocol://username:password@host[:port]/url-path
```

For instance, the standard syntax of an HTTP URL is:

```
http://host[:port]/path/resource_name[#section][?query_string]
```

Here are a few examples of valid HTTP URLs:

http://www.sourcestream.com/index.html
http://www.ietf.org/tao.html#What_Is_IETF
http://www.awl.com
http://www.webcrawler.com:80/cgi-bin/WebQuery?searchText=servlets

Let's further examine the last URL shown above. An HTTP URL consists of a host and an optional port, path, filename, section, and query string. A *query string* is a set of parameters listed as key/value pairs (key = value format) with each pair separated by an ampersand (&) character. In the example URL above, the *http* string specifies that the URL should be accessed using the HTTP protocol. *www.webcrawler.com* is the hostname pointing to the server on which the resource resides and *:80* explicitly indicates that the connection will be on port 80 (this is, however, unnecessary since port 80 is the default for HTTP transactions). The string */cgi-bin/WebQuery* states that there is a CGI application called WebQuery in a directory named *cgi-bin* (CGI is discussed later in this chapter). Finally, the query string *?searchText=servlets* passes a parameter called searchText with a value of servlets. As you might have guessed, this URL queries the WebCrawler Internet search engine for sites related to servlets.

NOTE: Although URLs can be constructed using both upper- and lower-case letters, the URL specification for a hostname does not differentiate based on case. Therefore, *http://WWW.AWL.COM* is the same as *http://www.awl.com*. Though they are not case-sensitive, hostnames are typically written in lower-case letters. In addition, though the hostname is not case-sensitive, the path information that follows may be (depending on the server). For example, though *http://WWW.AWL.COM* and *http://www.awl.com* are the same, *http://www.awl.com/INDEX.HTML* and *http://www.awl.com/index.html* may not be the same (if the server uses case-sensitive resource names).

In contrast to the previous examples, the URL format for FTP is different. The syntax for an FTP URL is as follows:

```
ftp://username:password@host[:port]/path
```

Here are a few examples of FTP URLs:

ftp://anonymous@ftp.netscape.com/
ftp://guest:password@ftp.sourcestream.com/incoming
ftp://ftp.sun.com:21/

As you can see, the syntax of the URL varies greatly depending on the protocol in use. Appendix D shows the URL syntax for many common protocols (for more detail, see RFC 1738).

URLs are commonly used as links within an HTML document, to reference objects from a browser, or in Java network applications. For example, the Java code in Listing 2.1 uses an HTTP URL to retrieve an HTML file and print it to standard out.

Listing 2.1   Downloads an HTML file using the Java URL object.

```
import java.io.*;
import java.net.*;

/**
 * Get URL Data
 *
 * This class downloads data from the specified URL and prints
 * it to standard out.
 *
 * @author Dustin R. Callaway
 * @version 1.0, 01/07/98
 */
public class GetURLData
{
   public static void main(String[] args)
```

```
    {
      URL url=null; //define the URL object
      String nextLine; //string to store the HTML output

      try
      {
        try
        {
          //create the URL object from a valid URL
          url = new URL("http://java.sun.com/index.html");
        }
        catch(MalformedURLException e) //this catch required
        {
          System.err.println("Error: " + e);
        }

        //open an input stream from the URL
        BufferedReader in = new BufferedReader(
          new InputStreamReader(url.openStream()));

        //get data, line by line
        while((nextLine = in.readLine()) != null)
        {
          System.out.println(nextLine); //print to standard out
        }
      }
      catch(Exception e)
      {
        System.err.println("Error: " + e);
      }
    }
  }
```

The first few lines of output from GetURLData look like this:

```
<!DOCTYPE HTML PUBLIC "-//W3C//DTD HTML 3.2//EN">
<HTML>
<HEAD>
<TITLE>Java Home Page</TITLE>
```

Up to this point, every URL we have seen has been fully qualified. That is, all information necessary to find the object was completely specified in the URL.

This type of URL is called an *absolute URL*. An absolute URL designates the protocol, host, path, and name of a resource. When a Web browser references an absolute URL, it stores the protocol, host, and path information in order to support another type of URL. A *relative URL* is not fully qualified, but rather it inherits the protocol, host, and path information from its parent document (the document that links to it). To illustrate, let's look at an example of each type of URL in an HTML document. Listing 2.2 shows a simple HTML document, called *test.html,* with two hyperlinks—one using an absolute path and the other using a relative path.

Listing 2.2   An example of an absolute and relative URL.

```
<HTML>
<HEAD>
<TITLE>Absolute vs. Relative URLs</TITLE>
</HEAD>
<BODY>

<A HREF="http://www.awl.com/index.html">Absolute URL to
AWL</A><BR>

<A HREF="link.html">Relative URL to a document called
link.html</A>

</BODY>
</HTML>
```

Notice how the absolute URL fully specifies the protocol, host, path, and resource name. On the other hand, the relative URL only designates the filename. For the relative URL, the browser will "fill in the blanks" and assume that the protocol, host, and path information is the same as the document that linked to it. Thus, the *link.html* file would need to be in the same directory as the *test.html* file shown in Listing 2.2.

Relative URLs offer two advantages over absolute URLs. The first advantage is that they are much shorter to type. The second and most important advantage is the portability provided by relative URLs. Since a host and path are not specified, an entire directory, or directory tree, of HTML files can be moved to a new directory or server without having to change any of the internal links. For instance, assume that Listing 2.2 is stored at the location *http://www.sourcestream.com/test/.* If only relative URLs are used in the HTML, all files in the *test* directory can be moved to *http://www.awl.com/ examples/* without modification. For additional information on relative URLs, see RFC 1808.

URL Encoding

URLs are comprised of a string of printable characters within the US-ASCII coded character set. Any unsafe or nonprintable characters within a URL must be encoded. *URL encoding* involves replacing all unsafe and nonprintable characters with a percent sign (%) followed by two hexadecimal digits corresponding to the character's ASCII value. Control characters are a good example of nonprintable characters. Unsafe characters are those that may be misinterpreted or altered by network software or hardware. Within URLs, there are many unsafe characters. A good rule of thumb is that any character not described in the following list should be encoded:

- Upper- and lowercase letters
- Numbers
- Underscores
- Periods
- Hyphens

Thus, any character outside of those listed above must be used according to the URL specification or it must be encoded. For instance, within a URL the characters ";", "/", "?", ":", "@", "=", and "&" all have special meaning (see Appendix E). If these characters are used in a manner that is not consistent with the URL specification, they must be encoded. For example, if a filename contains a question mark, the question mark must be encoded or the URL will construe this character as the beginning of the query string. According to the URL specification, a question mark is used to separate the name of a resource from a list of parameters (the query string) being passed to the server.

One special case worth noting is the space character. Because they are so common, spaces can be encoded using a single plus sign (+) rather than the normal encoding scheme (%20). Since the plus sign designates a space, the plus sign itself must be encoded using %2B. See Appendix F for the hexadecimal encoding of many nonprintable and unsafe URL characters.

There are a number of reasons that some characters are considered unsafe and must be encoded in a URL. Spaces are encoded because blank spaces may disappear or be introduced when transcribing the URL from code to print or when modifying it with a text editor. Some systems may use other characters, such as "<", ">", and the quotation mark ("), as delimiters. The URL specification itself uses characters "#", "/", "?", "=", and "&" to delimit sections of the URL. Finally, some unsafe characters can be modified by gateways or other transport agents.

Let's take a look at an example to make sure that we have a good handle on URL encoding. Assume that we would like to reference a resource called *sun's java.html* stored on the server *java.sun.com*. According to the rules, the apostrophe (') and the space are unsafe and must be encoded. The encoded URL would look like this:

http://java.sun.com/sun%27s+java.html

It is as simple as that. The apostrophe is encoded using %27 (see Appendix F) and spaces are encoded with a plus sign. Encoding makes the URL more difficult to read, but it allows the request to safely travel across the Internet without being mangled by network hardware or varying operating systems.

Fortunately for the servlet developer, Java includes a class to help convert resource names and other references into URL safe strings. The URLEncoder class in the java.net package contains a single static method for encoding strings for use in URLs. The method, called encode(), accepts a standard Java string and returns the URL encoded equivalent. Listing 2.3 demonstrates the URLEncoder class by outputting several URL encoded strings.

Listing 2.3   URLEncoder class demonstration.

```java
import java.net.URLEncoder;

/**
 * Encode Demo
 *
 * Demonstrates URL encoding using the URLEncoder class.
 *
 * @author Dustin R. Callaway
 * @version 1.0, 01/09/98
 */
public class EncodeDemo
{
  public static void main(String[] args)
  {
    String encodeText;

    System.out.println("NORMAL STRING\t\t\tURL ENCODED STRING");
    encodeText = "Inside Java Servlets";
    System.out.println(encodeText + "\t\t" + URLEncoder.encode(
      encodeText));
    encodeText = "Java's here to stay!";
    System.out.println(encodeText + "\t" + URLEncoder.encode(
      encodeText));
    encodeText = "Velocity Formula: v = d/t";
    System.out.println(encodeText + "\t" + URLEncoder.encode(
      encodeText));
  }
}
```

The output from Listing 2.3 looks like this:

```
NORMAL STRING                   URL ENCODED STRING
Inside Java Servlets            Inside+Java+Servlets
Java's here to stay!            Java%27s+here+to+stay%21
Velocity Formula: v = d/t       Velocity+Formula%3a+v+%3d+d%2ft
```

Web Browsers

A *Web browser* is a client application that requests, receives, and displays HTML pages. However, current browsers do much more than just render HTML pages. Today's browsers display animated images, play sound and video, cache pages for improved performance, provide secure connections through encryption, and much more. Browsers are the "window to the Web" for Internet users around the world.

Current Web Browsers

Currently, two browsers enjoy the vast majority of the browser market. Netscape Navigator and Microsoft Internet Explorer are the most popular browsers on the Web and both implement many of the latest HTML extensions. This additional functionality is referred to as extensions because many new HTML features supported by these browsers have not been adopted as official Internet standards. Features such as frames, blinking and scrolling text, background sounds, and cookies are just a few of the exciting but nonstandard extensions implemented by these browsers. For the servlet developer, testing your new Web site using both of these browsers as a client is essential. If your site supports both, you can feel confident that over 90 percent of Web users can successfully view your site.

HotJava from Sun is another browser worth mentioning. Written entirely in Java, the HotJava browser provides an excellent "proof of concept" for the power of a Java application. HotJava supports many of the latest HTML extensions including tables, frames, and cookies. Though its popularity languishes in relation to the other two browsers, HotJava is a remarkably interesting and impressive implementation of the Java language.

Browser/Server Communication

To successfully develop, debug, and deploy servlet driven Web sites, it is imperative to understand the process in which a browser communicates with a Web server. Fortunately, the process is simple and not difficult to grasp. The specifics of the language used by browsers and servers to communicate, however, will be covered in Chapter 3. This section will discuss, at a high level, the manner in which a browser sends a request to a server and receives a response.

The first step in the process involves the browser requesting a file from the Web server. A sample request in which the browser requests a file called *index.html* may look something like this:

You type this URL into your browser:

```
http://www.sourcestream.com/index.html
```

Your browser resolves *www.sourcestream.com* to a valid IP address using DNS (as described in Chapter 1) and sends this HTTP request to the host:

```
GET /index.html HTTP/1.0
```

You may remember this command from the first chapter. The browser uses this very basic HTTP request to instruct the server that it wants a file called *index.html*. See Chapter 3 for a detailed discussion about the format of this request. If the file is available and the client has proper authorization, the server will return the requested file. The response might look like Listing 2.4.

Listing 2.4   Sample response from Web server; includes HTTP header and HTML content.

```
HTTP/1.0 200 OK
Server: Netscape-Enterprise/2.01
Content-type: text/html
Content-length: 359

<HTML>
<HEAD>
<TITLE>SourceStream Software</TITLE>
</HEAD>
<BODY BGCOLOR="BLACK">
<CENTER>
<IMG BORDER=0 HEIGHT=78 SRC="images/sourcestream.GIF" WIDTH=462>
<BR>
<BR>
<BR>
<IMG BORDER=0 HEIGHT=250 SRC="images/earth.GIF" WIDTH=443>
<BR>
<BR>
<BR>
<FONT COLOR=WHITE>&copy;1998, SourceStream All Rights
Reserved</FONT>
</CENTER>
</BODY>
</HTML>
```

The server returned the contents of the HTML page requested. But what about the images referenced in the HTML? If you examine the HTML above, you will see that there are two images referenced (the <IMG> tags). After receiving the contents of the requested file, the browser parses the HTML looking for other information that may need to be downloaded. This information could be images, Java applets, background sounds, or any other format that the browser supports. Upon locating an image tag, the browser opens a new connection to the server using the URL provided in the tag and downloads the image data. The image is then displayed in its appropriate location on screen. This process is repeated for all images referenced in the HTML (see Figure 2.1).

You have probably often noticed that when a Web page is downloaded, the text is displayed first, followed by the images. This is due to the fact that the browser does indeed receive the text first (embedded in the HTML), which it displays, and then proceeds to "fill in the blanks" with images, applets, or

Figure 2.1 Simple Transaction Between a Web Browser and Web Server

whatever. Each new image is downloaded using a new connection. For further illustration, see the output from Listing 2.4.

NOTE: For some browsers to render a page properly before the image files are downloaded, all image tags must include height and width information. For example, the following tag includes the necessary information to allow the browser to reserve space on the page for the image.

```
<IMG HEIGHT=90 WIDTH=439 SRC="/images/sourcestream.gif">
```

Without the height and width information, the browser would not know how much space to reserve for each image. Thus, the browser would either have to wait until all images were downloaded before displaying the page or rebuild the page after each new image was received. To avoid the performance penalty this incurs, it is good practice to include the HEIGHT and WIDTH attributes in every image tag.

Web Servers

A *Web server,* also known as an HTTP server, responds to requests from a Web browser by returning HTML, images, applets, or other data. The Web server is also responsible for enforcing security policies, storing frequently requested files in cache, logging requests, and much more. These servers are the workhorses of the Web that sit quietly behind the scenes waiting to fulfill any valid request.

The market for Web servers is much more open than that for browsers. There are many popular servers in use today. A few of the most popular servers include the following:

- Netscape FastTrack Server
- Netscape Enterprise Server

- Microsoft Internet Information Server
- Apache Web Server
- Java Web Server

FastTrack is the "personal edition" Web server from Netscape intended for low-traffic sites with lower functionality requirements. Alternatively, *Netscape Enterprise Server* is a heavy-duty Web server often employed to service many of the most active sites on the Web, including Netscape's own. Netscape Enterprise Server is programmable via NSAPI (Netscape Server Application Programming Interface), WAI (Web Application Interface), and CGI (Common Gateway Interface). In addition, as of version 3.5, Netscape Enterprise Server provides native support for Java servlets. Netscape Enterprise Server runs on Windows NT, Macintosh, and numerous flavors of UNIX.

Microsoft Internet Information Server (IIS) is Microsoft's entry into the Web server market. The biggest drawback to IIS is that it is available only on the Windows NT platform. However, if you are only deploying on NT, this can be an advantage because of its tight integration with NT security. IIS provides several simple scripting options for customizing a Web site as well. Development on IIS can be accomplished using the Internet Database Connector (IDC), Active Server Pages (ASP), ISAPI (Internet Server Application Programming Interface), or CGI.

The *Apache Web Server* is an industrial strength, public domain HTTP server for UNIX and Windows NT. It is based on many of the innovations found in the original NCSA httpd server. Since its inception, the Apache Web Server has evolved to become arguably the fastest, most functional, and most popular HTTP server on the Web. It is also the cheapest. The Apache Web Server is available free of charge for Windows NT and many flavors of UNIX. Apache is programmable via CGI and now supports Java servlets via the Apache JServ servlet engine.

Although fairly new, the Java Web Server certainly deserves some serious attention. Originally code-named *Jeeves,* the *Java Web Server* is an HTTP server implemented in Java. The Java nature of this server allows it to be run on a wide array of platforms. In addition to the standard functionality supported by other HTTP servers, the Java Web Server supports a revolutionary new way of extending the server's functionality with server-side applications. Unlike many CGI, NSAPI, or ISAPI solutions, these server-side applications, called *servlets,* are also cross-platform and cross-server.

This portability is a result of the fact that, like the Java Web Server itself, servlets are written in pure Java. Servlets are introduced in more detail in Chapter 4. It should also be noted that servlet support can be added to current versions of servers from Netscape, Microsoft, and Apache using the *Java*

Figure 2.2   Browser Rendering of Listing 2.4

Servlet Development Kit from Sun Microsystems or third-party applications such as JRun from Live Software or ServletExec from New Atlanta Communications.

Although Web servers can be very complex, the basic service they provide is simple. A Web server listens on a port for a connection and a request from a client. The Web server interprets the request according to the HTTP protocol specification and fulfills the request accordingly. Most often, this simply involves returning an HTML file from the file system or running a CGI application. To demonstrate the basic concepts behind a generic Web server, Appendix G shows a basic Java HTTP server that accepts requests from clients and returns HTML and image files from the local file system.

The output from the HTML shown in Listing 2.4 looks like Figure 2.2 in the browser. With verbose mode enabled, the `HttpServer` application shown in Appendix G can give you a good idea of how the browser requests files and the server responds. After fulfilling the browser's request, the output generated in the `HttpServer` console window looks like the following:

```
C:\>java HttpServer -v

Listening for connections on port 80...

Connection opened. (Sat Jan 10 18:27:12 GMT+00:00 1998)
File /index.html of type text/html returned.
Connection closed.

Connection opened. (Sat Jan 10 18:27:13 GMT+00:00 1998)
File /images/sourcestream.gif of type image/gif returned.
Connection closed.

Connection opened. (Sat Jan 10 18:27:14 GMT+00:00 1998)
File /images/earth.gif of type image/gif returned.
Connection closed.
```

From this output, you can clearly see the browser opening a new connection for each request. Every new image within an HTML file requires the browser to generate a new request.

Common Gateway Interface

The Common Gateway Interface, or CGI, is a standard interface between an HTTP server and an application. CGI enables the Web server to generate dynamic content rather than just return static HTML files. In addition, because CGI can accept and process information submitted by the user, it can provide two-way interaction between the client and the Web server. For example, CGI is commonly used to create dynamic HTML pages from information in a database or to process user input such as validating a credit card when a product is ordered online. Many popular Internet search engines use CGI. These engines receive search criteria from a user, process the input, and return the search results. CGI was the first and continues to be the most popular method of building dynamic Web sites. Typically, CGI scripts are written in Perl, Tcl, C, or a UNIX shell, but almost any language can be used, including Java.

A CGI application works in the following manner. The Web server receives a request that maps to a CGI application, the Web server executes a CGI program that runs in its own process space, the CGI program returns HTML to the Web server, and the Web server returns the HTML to the client. To illustrate, a typical CGI transaction might go like this:

1. The server receives a request for a resource called */cgi-bin/guestbook.cgi*.

2. Either because the file has a *.cgi* extension or because it is located in the */cgi-bin* directory, the server recognizes the file as a CGI request and launches the *guestbook.cgi* program, passing any parameters received from the client.

3. The *guestbook.cgi* program executes, processing any information passed as a parameter, and returns an HTML document to the Web server.

4. The Web server returns the HTML to the client.

To the user, this process is completely transparent. The user simply requested a resource using a URL and received an HTML document in return. Other than the format of the URL, the user would have no way of knowing that the document was created dynamically on the server rather than simply stored in a static file. Using this process, the Web server can vary its response based on user input. Prior to CGI, this kind of two-way interaction on the Web was not possible.

One important note is that all CGI applications run as independent processes. Creating a new process for every CGI request hurts performance and is resource intensive. We will discuss this issue further in Chapter 4, where we learn that servlets take a different approach.

Summary

This chapter provided a basic foundation in several important areas of Web technology. Understanding URLs and the way browsers and servers communicate is essential to servlet development. In Chapter 3, we will discuss advanced Web topics including the HTTP protocol, MIME, and HTML forms.

Chapter Highlights

- The Web got its start in 1989 when Tim Berners-Lee of the European Laboratory of Particle Physics proposed a new network composed of files containing links to related files. Shortly thereafter, the first text-only browsers were developed and the Web was born.

- A *Uniform Resource Locator* is a specification for identifying an object such as a file, newsgroup, CGI program, or e-mail address by indicating its exact location on the Internet (see RFC 1738).

- *URL encoding* is the process of replacing all unsafe and nonprintable characters with a percent sign followed by two hexadecimal digits corresponding to the character's ASCII value.

- A *Web browser* is a client application that requests, transfers, and displays HTML pages.
- A *Web server*, also known as an HTTP server, responds to requests from a Web browser by returning HTML, images, applets, or other data.
- *CGI* is a standard interface between an HTTP server and an application.

CHAPTER 3

Beyond Web Basics

This chapter covers critical topics designed to give you a stronger foundation in Web development. Much of this chapter will serve as a brief tutorial and reference for HTTP, MIME, and HTML forms. Hopefully, this information will save you the frustration of searching through hundreds of pages of RFCs. However, the RFCs referenced in this chapter are the authoritative documents on the subject and contain additional detail. Please refer to the appropriate RFC if you desire more information.

The following topics are covered in this chapter:

- Hypertext Transfer Protocol (HTTP)
- Multipurpose Internet Mail Extensions (MIME)
- HTML forms

Of course, if you are already familiar with these topics, feel free to jump ahead to the next chapter where servlets are introduced.

HTTP

The *Hypertext Transfer Protocol* is a stateless, TCP/IP based protocol used for communicating on the World Wide Web. HTTP defines the precise manner in which Web clients communicate with Web servers. HTTP/1.0 is the most common version in use today. Oddly enough, this protocol is not officially recognized as an Internet standard. It is documented in the informational RFC 1945. Its successor, HTTP/1.1, is currently a proposed Internet standard and many browsers and servers now support this new version (see RFC 2068).

HTTP Basics

The HTTP protocol follows a very simple request/response paradigm. In short, a conversation between a Web browser and Web server goes something like this: the client opens a connection to the server, the client makes a request to the server, the server responds to the request, and the connection is closed (see Figure 3.1). To better illustrate an HTTP conversation between a browser and a server, let's step through the four stages of a simple Web transaction.

1. *The client opens a connection to the server.*   The client opens a TCP connection to the server. Since TCP connections are established down in the transport layer of the protocol stack, there is not a lot of HTTP specific activity in this stage. (Remember that HTTP is an application layer protocol.) By default, the connection on the server is made to port 80 (the well-known HTTP port), unless otherwise specified. The client uses any port that is available.

2. *The client makes a request to the server.*   This is where we get our first look at HTTP syntax. Let's assume that the Web browser makes a very basic request to retrieve an HTML file. The URL entered into the Web browser might look like *http://www.awl.com/index.html*. However, the HTTP request sent by the browser to the server would look something like this:

```
GET /index.html HTTP/1.0
```

This request can be broken into three parts: the request method, the resource name, and the protocol. GET is an HTTP method requesting the server to send a file. HTTP methods are discussed in detail later in the chapter. */index.html* is a relative path to the file being requested. Because a TCP connection to the server was established in stage 1, it is not necessary to fully qualify the file name using *http://www.awl.com/index.html*. It is assumed that the requested resource resides on the server with which the browser is currently connected. HTTP/1.0 is the name and version of the protocol implemented by the client. Finally, the request is terminated by a pair of carriage return/linefeeds.

In addition to the GET command, the browser may send other information about itself to the server. We will take a closer look at what other information a browser may send later in this chapter.

3. *The server responds to the request.*   The server responds with a status code, various header fields, and, if possible, the contents of the requested file. If the file requested in stage 2 is available and the client has proper authorization, the server's response may look something like this:

```
HTTP/1.0 200 OK
Server: Netscape-Enterprise/2.01
```

```
Content-Type: text/html
Content-Length: 87

<HTML>
<HEAD>
<TITLE>HTTP Request Successful</TITLE>
</HEAD>
<BODY>
It Worked!
</BODY>
</HTML>
```

The first line of the response indicates the server's protocol and returns a status code stating that the request was fulfilled successfully. The OK message on this line simply provides a brief, human-readable description of the status code 200. This message, called a *Reason-Phrase,* is only for our benefit and is actually not required since the browser evaluates only the status code number. However, it is recommended that a brief description of the status always be included.

Every HTTP response includes a status code. Possible status codes for HTTP/1.0 are documented in Appendix H. The other lines above the blank line are called *header fields* (though perhaps not technically correct, header fields are often referred to simply as *headers*). The combination of the status code line plus all header fields is known as the *HTTP header.* Header fields convey some information about the server or the requested resource (see Appendix I for a list of header fields).

The header fields shown previously designate the type of Web server that generated the request, the MIME type of document being returned (see the section on MIME later in this chapter), and the length of the document content. The lines below the blank line are the content of the file that was requested. All HTTP responses consist of a status code line followed by a series of header fields followed by an empty line. In many cases, a block of MIME encoded data immediately follows the empty line.

4. *The connection is closed.* The TCP connection may be closed by either the server or the client or both. Usually, it is the server that terminates the connection after the response has been sent. Similarly, a browser will often close

NOTE: There is an HTTP method, known as *persistent connections* or *keep-alive,* whereby a single connection can service multiple requests. In fact, this is the default behavior of all HTTP/1.1 transactions. Similarly, some HTTP/1.0 clients and servers also implement a form of persistence. Persistent connections are discussed in the HTTP/1.1 section a little later in this chapter.

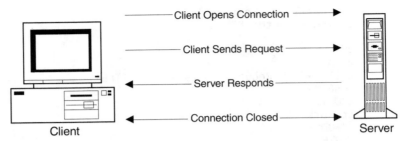

Figure 3.1 Request/Response Nature of HTTP

the connection once the complete response has been received. Regardless, the connection is closed and the HTTP transaction is complete. If the client wishes to make another request, the whole process starts over again (see Figure 3.1).

Connectionless Protocol

HTTP is a connectionless protocol. As you may have guessed, the difference between a connectionless and a connection-oriented protocol is in the way they handle connections. Using a *connectionless* protocol, the client opens a connection with the server, sends a request, receives a response, and closes the connection. Each request requires its own connection. With a *connection-oriented* protocol, the client connects to the server, sends a request, receives a response, and then holds the connection open in order to service future requests.

The connectionless nature of HTTP is both a strength and a weakness. Because it holds a connection open only long enough to service the request, very few server resources are required to service large numbers of users. In fact, many popular Web sites service millions of users in a single day. The drawback to a connectionless protocol is that a connection must be established with every request. Opening a new connection with each request incurs a performance penalty that translates into additional delays for the user.

Alternatively, a connection-oriented protocol such as FTP has a strong performance advantage over a connectionless protocol. This is due to the fact that the overhead required to open a new connection is incurred only once rather than with every request. Unfortunately, each open connection consumes some amount of server resources. These finite resources, such as memory and disk space, limit the number of concurrent users the server can handle. In contrast to a Web site, an FTP site can rarely support more than a few hundred users at a time.

Stateless Protocol

As stated in the definition, HTTP is a stateless protocol. A protocol is said to be *stateless* if it has no memory of prior connections and cannot distinguish one client's request from that of another. In contrast, FTP is a *stateful* protocol, because the connection is not opened and closed with every request. After the initial login, the FTP server maintains the user's credentials throughout the session. On the other hand, due to its stateless nature, there is no inherent method in HTTP for tracking a client's traversal of a Web site. Every connection is a new request from an anonymous client.[1] In Chapter 14, State/Session Management, we will investigate strategies for adding state to HTTP. State allows the server to identify the client and is extremely useful for secure sites where a user must log in or for electronic commerce sites that provide customers with a virtual shopping cart. Additionally, HTTP authentication can also convey client identity to the server (see the Basic Authentication section later in this chapter).

The stateless nature of HTTP is both a strength and a weakness. It is a strength in that its stateless nature keeps the protocol simple and straightforward. It also consumes fewer resources on the server and can support more simultaneous users since there are no client credentials and connections to maintain. The disadvantage is in the overhead required to create a new connection with each request and the inability to track a single user as he traverses a Web site.

HTTP/1.0

HTTP/1.0 is currently the most widely supported version of HTTP. However, this is changing rapidly as Web software evolves to support the new HTTP/1.1 specification. Since HTTP/1.1 simply builds upon the 1.0 foundation, the following information applies equally well to HTTP versions 1.0 and 1.1.

Status Codes

Every HTTP response returned from the server begins with a status code. These codes convey important information if you know what they mean. Table 3.1

---

1. Actually, the server can often distinguish one client from another using the source IP address transmitted along with the request. However, this IP address cannot guarantee a unique identification. For instance, many Internet Service Providers dynamically assign IP addresses to users. Each time a user logs in, he may receive a new IP address. In addition, if a proxy server is being used, requests from many users will be generated from the same IP address.

Table 3.1   HTTP Status Code Category Descriptions

Code Range	Category	Description
1xx	Informational	A provisional status code for use in experimental applications only. HTTP/1.0 does not define any informational status codes, but HTTP/1.1 does.
2xx	Successful	The request was successfully received, understood, and accepted.
3xx	Redirection	The server is requesting the Web client to redirect to another URL. The Web client can automatically redirect only in response to a GET or HEAD request. Redirection of a POST request requires user confirmation. A client should never automatically redirect more than five times.
4xx	Client Error	The request is improperly formatted or cannot be fulfilled. Unless responding to a HEAD request, the server should return information describing the error and whether it is a temporary or permanent condition in the response body. The client must immediately stop sending requests to the server.
5xx	Server Error	A valid request was received but the server cannot fulfill it. Unless responding to a HEAD request, the server should return information describing the error and whether it is a temporary or permanent condition in the response body.

documents the meaning behind different ranges of HTTP/1.0 status codes. For a complete list of HTTP/1.0 status codes and their meanings, see Appendix H.

Due to the large number of response status codes, it is much easier to just remember the ranges instead. Status codes in the 2xx range indicate success, 3xx indicates redirection, 4xx indicates client error, and 5xx indicates server error.

The status code line may be followed by any number of HTTP header fields. These fields convey additional information to the client, such as the time and date of the response, the type and version of server, when the file was last modified, the length of the requested file, and the file type (e.g., plain text, HTML, GIF image, JPEG image). The sample HTTP response below illustrates the status code line followed by several HTTP header fields.

```
HTTP/1.0 200 OK
Date: Sun, 18 Oct 1998 01:10:32 GMT
Server: Apache/1.2.6
Last-Modified: Wed, 14 Oct 1998 05:31:49 GMT
Content-Length: 359
Content-Type: text/html
```

As we saw earlier, every HTTP request begins with a request method (and also may be followed by any number of header fields). A request method indicates the operation the client is asking the server to perform. Now that we have seen what a simple HTTP transaction looks like, let's explore a little deeper and examine the various HTTP/1.0 methods.

The GET Method

GET is the most common HTTP method. It is used to request a resource from the server. Containing no body content, a GET request is comprised of only a method statement and various request header fields. An example GET request follows.

```
GET /login.html HTTP/1.0
User-Agent: Mozilla/4.02 [en] (Win95; I)
Accept: image/gif, image/jpeg, image/pjpeg, */*
```

You can see from the method statement (first line) of this request that the GET method is being employed to request the *login.html* file using the HTTP/1.0 protocol. The User-Agent header field conveys the type of browser that initiated the request. In this case, the browser is the English version of Netscape Navigator 4.02 running on Windows 95 (*Mozilla* was the original code name for Navigator). The Accept header field indicates the file types supported by the client (see the "MIME" section later in this chapter). Even though a GET request does not send any information in the body of the message, data can still be passed as part of the GET statement itself. The following example passes username and password information to the server:

```
GET /login.html?username=dustin&password=servlets HTTP/1.0
User-Agent: Mozilla/4.02 [en] (Win95; I)
Accept: image/gif, image/jpeg, image/pjpeg, */*
```

This GET request is identical to the first example except that it passes two parameters called username and password with values of *dustin* and *servlets*, respectively. This information can be passed to the server by manually appending the query string to the URL or by an HTML form. For example, the above GET request may be generated by the browser in response to a user requesting this URL:

http://www.sourcestream.com/login.html?username=dustin&password=servlets

It is somewhat uncommon, however, for users to create their own query strings and append them to a URL. More often, the above GET request would have been generated by the browser in response to the user clicking the submit button on an HTML form. An example of such a form is shown in Figure 3.2.

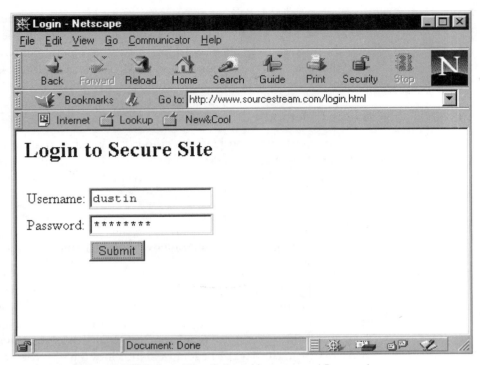

Figure 3.2   A Simple HTML Form That Collects Username and Password

The HTML code used to build this form is presented in the HTML Forms section later in this chapter.

NOTE: The GET method is normally used to request static data. Responses to GET requests are often cached by proxy servers for use in future requests. In contrast, the POST method is usually used to request dynamic data. Therefore, responses to POST requests should not be cached.

A drawback to using a GET method for login transactions is that the information entered by the user is appended to the URL and displayed in plain text by the browser. Therefore, if a user enters login information and clicks *Submit*, the username and password will be visible in the URL on the next page. Another disadvantage is that a limited amount of data can be passed as part of the URL in a GET request. For example, earlier versions of Microsoft Internet Explorer could pass no more than 255 characters in the URL. This is because

HTTP servers traditionally store GET parameters in system environment variables that can be accessed by CGI programs and other out-of-process applications. Unfortunately, the amount of information that can be stored in environment variables is limited and varies between operating systems. Both of these disadvantages are remedied in another HTTP method called POST.

NOTE: If a GET request includes an If-Modified-Since header field, the request becomes a *conditional GET*. This means that the content of the resource requested is only returned if the information has changed since the date specified in the If-Modified-Since header field. This allows the browser to display a cached copy of the page if it has not been modified since it was last downloaded. A conditional GET statement might look like this:

```
GET /login.html HTTP/1.0
If-Modified-Since: Sat, 17 Jan 1998 20:43:07 GMT
User-Agent: Mozilla/4.02 [en] (Win95; I)
Accept: image/gif, image/x-xbitmap, image/jpeg, */*
```

In the conditional GET request shown here, the server will return the *login.html* file only if the page has been modified since January 17, 1998. Otherwise, a status code of "304 Not Modified" will be returned by the server without any message body and the browser should load the page from cache. This technique reduces network traffic and improves performance.

The POST Method

POST is an HTTP method commonly used for passing user input to the server. The POST method differs from GET in that all parameter information is stored in the body of the request rather than in the URL portion of the method statement. This approach has two advantages. First, the information submitted by the user is not visible in the URL. Second, there is no limit to the amount of information that can be passed when it is stored in the body of the request. This is because the name/value pairs passed in a POST request are accessed via the client's input stream rather than the server's environment variables (like GET parameters).

Unlike the GET method, there is no way to issue a POST by altering the URL in the browser. A POST is typically generated by the browser in response to the user clicking the *Submit* button on an HTML form that utilizes the POST method. Such an HTML form might look identical to the one shown in Figure 3.2. An actual POST request looks like the following:

```
POST /login.html HTTP/1.0
User-Agent: Mozilla/4.02 [en] (Win95; I)
Accept: image/gif, image/jpeg, image/pjpeg, */*
Content-Length: 34

username=dustin&password=servlets
```

Notice that the user input is passed in the body of the request rather than in the method statement. This is the primary difference between the GET and POST methods. HTTP/1.0 requires that a valid Content-Length header field accompany all POST requests.

The HEAD Method

The HEAD method is identical to the GET method except that it only returns the HTTP header—the body content is excluded. The HTTP header returned by the server in response to a HEAD request should be identical to the header that would have been returned in response to a GET. This method is very useful for debugging, verifying hypertext links, or checking the status of a file before attempting to retrieve it. For instance, using HEAD makes it possible to check when a file was last modified or to check the length of the file without actually having to download it. If included in the HEAD request, the If-Modified-Since header field is ignored.

Other Methods

There are four additional methods that are implemented either inconsistently or by few HTTP/1.0 implementations. These nonstandard methods include PUT for file uploads, DELETE for deleting resources on the server, LINK for establishing relationships between resources, and UNLINK for breaking relationships between resources. In contrast to HTTP/1.0, PUT and DELETE are standard methods in the HTTP/1.1 specification. These methods will be discussed further in the HTTP/1.1 section later in this chapter.

Basic Authentication

The original HTTP specification (RFC 1945) describes a simple method, or "scheme," to provide client authentication before returning sensitive data. This method, called *basic authentication*, allows the client to authenticate itself by providing a valid username and password. The basic authentication scheme operates as follows:

1. The browser requests a resource called *salaries.html* using the GET request shown below.

```
GET /salaries.html HTTP/1.0
```

2. After receiving the request, the server determines that the requested resource requires authentication. Since the client's request did not include authorization information, the server responds with a "401 Unauthorized" status code as follows:

```
HTTP/1.0 401 Unauthorized
Server: Apache/1.2.6
Date: Mon, 19 Oct 1998 02:29:07 GMT
WWW-Authenticate: Basic realm="SourceStream"
Content-length: 223
Content-type: text/html

<HTML><HEAD><TITLE>Unauthorized</TITLE></HEAD>
<BODY><H1>Unauthorized</H1>
Proper authorization is required for this area. Either your
browser does not perform authorization, or your authorization
has failed.
</BODY></HTML>
```

In addition to the standard header fields, the server adds a field called WWW-Authenticate. This field indicates the authentication scheme employed by the server and the context, or "realm," in which the authentication is valid. This response is called an *authentication challenge.* In the example above, the server is using basic authentication that is valid within the SourceStream realm. The realm value is arbitrary and only useful in comparison to other realms on this server.

3. If the browser performs authorization for basic authentication, it displays a username/password dialog box when the "401 Unauthorized" response is received. Otherwise, if the browser does not support authorization, it displays the HTML portion of the response indicating this fact.

4. After the username and password are entered, the original request is reissued to the server with the addition of an Authorization header field as shown here:

```
GET /salaries.html HTTP/1.0
Authorization: Basic RHVzdGluOnNlcnZsZXRz
```

The Authorization field indicates the authentication scheme employed by the client followed by the username and password represented as a BASE64 encoded string. The Authorization header field above indicates that the client is using the basic authentication scheme. The username/password string "RHVzdGluOnNlcnZsZXRz" is the BASE64 encoding of the username "Dustin" and password "servlets."

5. If the username and password are valid, the server responds with the requested document. If invalid, the server responds with the same "401 Unauthorized" message. If challenged a second time, the browser may either display the username/password dialog box again or display the HTML portion of the server's response.

The basic authentication scheme is not considered to be a secure method of authenticating clients since the username and password are not encrypted before transmission. Basic authentication is most useful in low security environments or in conjunction with a secure connection (e.g., https). However, more secure authentication schemes do exist. For instance, the HTTP/1.1 protocol includes support for the Digest Access Authentication scheme (see RFC 2069) that improves upon many of basic authentication's primary weaknesses.

HTTP/1.1

HTTP/1.1 is the heir apparent to the rapidly aging HTTP/1.0 protocol. Unlike version 1.0, HTTP/1.1 is being developed in conjunction with the IETF and is currently a proposed Internet Standard (see RFC 2068). HTTP/1.1 adds many new and powerful request methods and response status codes. In addition to GET, HEAD, and POST, HTTP/1.1 adds the methods described in Table 3.2.

Persistent connections are another important feature of HTTP/1.1. A *persistent connection,* also called *keep-alive,* allows the client to use the same connection for multiple transactions. Unlike standard HTTP/1.0, a server that implements the HTTP/1.1 specification does not close the connection after each request from an HTTP/1.1 client. The number of requests that a server will accept on a single connection is configurable on the server. Since persistent con-

Table 3.2   Methods HTTP/1.1 Adds to the Standard HTTP/1.0 Request Methods

Method	Description
DELETE	Requests that the server delete the resource specified in the URL.
OPTIONS	Requests information regarding the communication options supported by the server.
PUT	Requests that a new resource be created on the server at the specified URL using the data included in the request. Typically used for file uploads.
TRACE	Returns the request back to the client for debugging purposes, thus allowing the client to see the request received by the server at the end of the calling chain. This information can be useful for testing or diagnostic purposes.

nections are the default for HTTP/1.1 messages, the following header field must be sent in the request if nonpersistence is preferred:

```
Connection: close
```

It should also be noted that some HTTP/1.0 clients and servers implement a type of persistent connections. Since persistent connections are not the default for HTTP/1.0 transactions, they must be explicitly negotiated. An HTTP/1.0 client may indicate to the server that it wishes to use persistent connections by passing the following header field in each request:

```
Connection: Keep-Alive
```

This header field instructs the server that the HTTP/1.0 client wishes to use the current connection for future requests. If the server supports persistent connections, it will respond with the same Connection: Keep-Alive header field in the response and keep the connection active.

NOTE: Because there was no official specification for persistent connections in HTTP/1.0, many previous experimental implementations of persistence are incompatible or faulty. For instance, many HTTP/1.0 proxy servers do not properly handle the Connection header field and erroneously forward it to the next server. Due to this errant handling, an HTTP/1.0 client should never send a Connection: Keep-Alive header field to a proxy server.

HTTP-NG

HTTP-NG (Next Generation) is a protocol currently being developed to address many of the performance problems inherent in the HTTP specification. HTTP-NG proposes the transformation of HTTP into a stateful, connection-oriented protocol. Similar to FTP, HTTP-NG would not open a new connection with each request, but rather use a single shared connection across all requests. Of course, the trade-off would be that each client connection would require additional server resources. As of mid-1999, the HTTP-NG protocol was advancing rapidly but is still a long way off. For more information see the World Wide Web Consortium at *http://www.w3.org*.

SSL and S-HTTP

SSL (Secure Sockets Layer) is a protocol developed by Netscape for establishing secure connections between two hosts. Security is provided through the use of private key encryption for all data sent over the SSL connection. Secure

Sockets is supported by both Netscape and Microsoft browsers. SSL is commonly used on the Web to insure the privacy of confidential information, such as a customer's credit card number. The URL for an HTTP resource that implements SSL begins with *https://* rather than *http://*. SSL includes the following security measures:

- Encrypts data before transmission
- Prevents the unauthorized modification of data during transit
- Can guarantee the client that it is communicating with the correct server
- Can prevent unauthorized clients from accessing the server

S-HTTP (Secure HTTP) is an extension to the HTTP protocol and is used to transmit data securely over the Web. While SSL creates a secure connection between two hosts across which any amount of data can be sent, S-HTTP is used to securely transfer individual messages. S-HTTP is far less popular than SSL and does not enjoy the same support from browsers. Both SSL and S-HTTP have been submitted to the IETF seeking approval as an official Internet standard.

Examining HTTP Header Fields

Considering the importance of headers when debugging HTTP transactions, it is fortunate that there are a number of different ways in which these headers can be viewed by the developer. Examining the header fields returned by a server or sent by a client is one of the primary methods of troubleshooting problems in a Web conversation. This section presents two methods of viewing the HTTP header returned by the server or sent by the browser.

The simplest way to view the HTTP header returned by a server is to use a standard Telnet client. By simply connecting to the HTTP port with a Telnet client, the entire data stream returned by the server, including the header, can be viewed. The steps required to accomplish this are as follows:

1. Start your Telnet client.
2. Establish a connection to the server using the standard HTTP port 80 (or whatever port on which the HTTP server is listening).
3. Send the server a valid HTTP request such as GET /index.html HTTP/1.0 followed by two carriage return/linefeeds (press *ENTER* twice). If you are only interested in the HTTP header returned by the server and not the contents of a resource, send a request like HEAD /index.html HTTP/1.0. Recall that HEAD returns the same header as the GET method but that no content is included with the response.

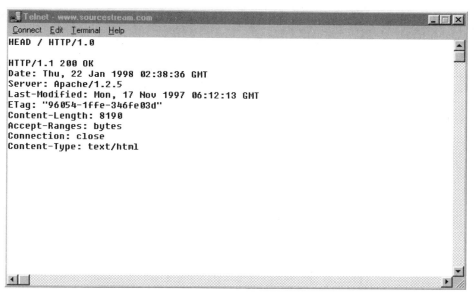

Figure 3.3   Using a Telnet Client to View the HTTP Header

4. The server's HTTP header, followed by the data requested, will be returned and the connection closed by the server. The header displayed in
Figure 3.3 shows that the server is running an Apache Web Server version
1.2.5 implementing the HTTP/1.1 protocol and that the length of the file
requested is 8190 bytes.

NOTE: The HTTP request described in step 3 should be entered rather quickly
because many Web servers have a very short timeout period between the time
the connection is established and the time the request is received. This timeout
ensures that the server is not wasting resources by holding connections open
longer than necessary. It is advisable to copy the request onto the clipboard and
paste it into the Telnet session once a connection has been established.

There is another, less primitive, method for checking a Web server's response header. Included on the accompanying CD-ROM is a program that allows the user to query a server for the HTTP header and data. It can serve as
an excellent diagnostic tool. The program, called *Protocol Explorer,* contains
online documentation accessible via the Help menu. A sample request using
Protocol Explorer is shown in Figure 3.4.

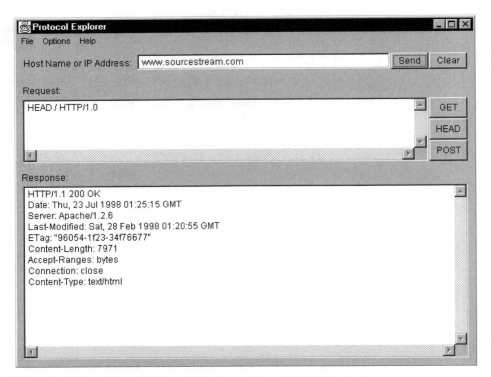

Figure 3.4   Using *Protocol Explorer* to Retrieve a Server's HTTP Header

Examining the HTTP header generated by a browser is almost as simple as viewing the server's header. The process requires a simple server to whom the browser can issue a request. Appendix J documents a Java program called *BrowserRequest* that does nothing more than receive a request from a browser and return the header fields it received. The browser's HTTP header is viewable either in the browser itself or from the console of the *BrowserRequest* program. See Appendix J for complete documentation and source code. Figure 3.5 shows the response when *BrowserRequest* is queried by a Netscape browser.

Lastly, a browser's HTTP header can be viewed with the diagnostics servlet presented in Chapter 17. This servlet is a comprehensive diagnostic tool that shows all browser header fields as well as many additional browser and server properties.

MIME

Multipurpose Internet Mail Extensions, *MIME,* is an extension to the electronic mail format originally defined by RFC 822. Most notably, MIME provides three important Internet services. These services include the following:

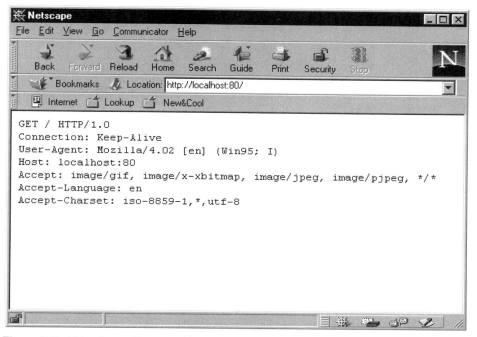

Figure 3.5 Using *BrowserRequest* to View the HTTP Headers from the Browser

- Provides a standard mechanism for encoding binary data into the ASCII format
- Defines a standard for specifying the type of content stored in the body of a message
- Describes a standard method for defining a multipart mail message containing heterogeneous body parts

Let's take a look at how each of these services is of interest to the Web developer.

The original Internet mail system did not provide services to support rich content, such as images or sound. Rather than upgrade the entire Internet mail system to support these new content types, the MIME specification was developed. MIME defines a method for converting binary data into standard ASCII characters for transmission over the Internet. In this manner, MIME-encoded e-mail looks like a standard RFC 822 message to mail transport agents that are not MIME compliant. Only the source and the destination need to understand MIME. All other hosts should simply route the message as if it were a normal RFC 822 mail message. For detailed information on MIME, see RFC 2045–RFC 2049.

MIME specifies two formats for encoding binary data into ASCII characters—BASE64 and Quoted Printable. BASE64 is the most common encoding scheme and is used for encoding pure binary data into standard ASCII. Though MIME was originally developed for e-mail, it is now commonly used by many different Internet technologies and protocols. For example, binary data transferred over the Web, such as downloading a JPEG image on a Web page, uses BASE64 encoding. Quoted Printable encoding is primarily used for documents that are mostly comprised of standard ASCII characters but still contain a small number of non-ASCII characters. This might include a document defining scientific or mathematical formulas. In contrast to BASE64, a Quoted Printable document is largely readable without decoding.

The MIME method for describing a file's contents is used by Web browsers in addition to e-mail clients. For instance, a Web browser uses the MIME specification to determine if a file is an HTML document, a JPEG image, or just plain text. In this way, the client knows how to handle the data it just received. Each MIME type consists of two parts—type and subtype. The *type* is a general description of the information the data contains. It defines whether the data represents text, image, video, or some other type of information. The *subtype* defines the exact kind and format of the data such as whether an image is a JPEG or GIF. The MIME type is communicated from the server to the browser via an HTTP header field called `Content-Type`. The MIME type assumes a *type/subtype* format. For example, the content type of an HTML document is `text/html` and for a GIF image it is `image/gif`. Table 3.3 shows the basic MIME types. See Appendix K for a more comprehensive list of common MIME types.

MIME is also used to define nonstandard or proprietary subtypes. These subtypes are always prefaced by a *x-*. For example, Table 3.3 shows an example audio type of `audio/x-wav`. This type represents a Microsoft WAV sound file. Because the WAV format is proprietary, it begins with *x-*. Since these *x-subtypes* are not industry standards, they may only be readable by a single application (such as FrameMaker or MacPaint) or may be interpreted differently by different programs. See Appendix K for a list of commonly used *x-* subtypes.

Lastly, MIME defines the manner in which boundaries are placed around heterogeneous parts of the same mail message. This specification allows a text e-mail message to contain attachments such as an HTML document or binary image data.

HTML Forms

HTML, or Hypertext Markup Language, is the language used to create hypertext documents on the World Wide Web. HTML describes the semantic value

Table 3.3   Basic MIME Types

Type	Description	Example
application	Binary data that is read or executed by another program	`application/java` `application/zip`
audio	Sound file that can be played by another program	`audio/basic` `audio/x-wav`
image	Picture file that can be displayed by another program	`image/gif` `image/jpeg`
message	Encapsulated mail message	`message/rfc822` `message/news`
multipart	Data consisting of multiple, possibly heterogenous, parts	`multipart/mixed` `multipart/digest`
text	Data consisting of printable text	`text/html` `text/plain`
video	Video file that can be played by another program	`video/mpeg` `video/quicktime`
x-world	Experimental data types	`x-world/x-vrml`

of a document such as the layout of the page or the relative size of fonts. HTML has evolved through a number of specifications including HTML 1.0, HTML 2.0, HTML 3.0, HTML 3.2, and HTML 4.0. However, it is possible that 4.0 could be the last step in the evolution of HTML. Another language called *XML* (Extensible Markup Language) is on the horizon and may possibly replace HTML as the default markup language for Web pages. For the latest HTML specification, see the World Wide Web Consortium home page at *http://www.w3.org.*

Due to the size and scope of a comprehensive introduction to HTML, this book will not attempt to familiarize the reader with the many facets of HTML page design. Rather, we will focus on HTML forms. After all, HTML forms are the most common method of providing user interaction over the Web. They are also the most common method for communicating with servlets. For a complete review of HTML, see RFC 1866 or one of the many good books on the subject.

NOTE: Due to the explosive growth of the Web and the relatively slow Internet standards process, many companies have jumped the gun and implemented experimental features into their products. For instance, both Netscape Navigator and Microsoft Internet Explorer support HTML tables even though tables are currently experimental extensions to HTML (RFC 1942). However, the latest HTML specifications (3.2 and 4.0) include tables, frames, and many other common extensions.

Implementing features before they become standards may not always be bad. After all, if we always waited for an official standard to emerge, the Web would not exist today (HTTP is still not an official Internet standard). Unfortunately, vendors do not always agree on which experimental extensions should be implemented. For example, Netscape Navigator version 3 supports form-based file uploads (RFC 1867), but Microsoft Internet Explorer 3 does not. These HTML support discrepancies among browsers contribute to making cutting edge HTML design a moving target.

Introduced in HTML 2.0, *HTML forms* provide a simple way to prompt a user for input via a formatted HTML page and allow the user to "submit" the information to the server. Forms were the first mechanism to allow true two-way interaction on the Web. See Figure 3.2 for an example of a basic HTML form used to collect username and password information from a user.

The <FORM> Tag

Each HTML form consists of a block of code beginning with the <FORM> tag and ending with the </FORM> tag. Any standard HTML body tags may be included within this block. Though forms cannot be nested, multiple forms can be defined within a single HTML document. The <FORM> tag specifies these three attributes:

- The HTTP method to be used to submit the form
- The action to be performed when the form is submitted
- The type of encoding to be used when submitting the form

The following <FORM> tag will post the data entered within the form to the resource at the relative URL */cgi-bin/login.cgi* using the application/x-www-form-encoded MIME encoding.

```
<FORM METHOD="POST" ACTION="/cgi-bin/login.cgi"
ENCTYPE="application/x-www-form-encoded">
```

NOTE: Although it is good practice to place all values inside of an HTML tag within quotes, most browsers do not require quotes unless there is a space within the value. For example, the <FORM> tag shown above could have been written as:

```
<FORM METHOD=POST ACTION=/cgi-bin/login.cgi
ENCTYPE=application/x-www-form-encoded>
```

However, for consistency, it is good practice to always enclose HTML tag values within quotes (in addition, HTML 4.0 and XML require quotes).

The METHOD Attribute

The METHOD attribute specifies the HTTP method to use when the form is submitted. The two possible methods are GET and POST. As discussed earlier, when a GET method is specified, any form data input by the user is passed to the server as a query string in the URL. If a POST method is used, the user's input is passed within the body of the request. Due to the length constraints of the GET method, in most circumstances it is preferable to use a POST. If no METHOD is defined within the <FORM> tag, the GET method is used by default.

The ACTION Attribute

The ACTION attribute specifies the action that is to be performed when the user submits the form. Usually, the action attribute indicates the URL of the script or servlet that will process the user's input (see the <FORM> tag shown in the previous section). Rather than specifying a URL, it is also possible to indicate an action by name. Currently, the only action supported by most software is the mailto directive. The mailto action is used to e-mail the form data to a specified e-mail address. The <FORM> tag looks like this:

```
<FORM METHOD="POST" ACTION="mailto:callaway@sourcestream.com">
```

Listing 3.1 shows a simple form that performs the mailto action. When the form is submitted, the user's input is URL encoded and e-mailed to the specified recipient. When the e-mail is retrieved, the data appears in the body of the message as a URL encoded string.

Listing 3.1   A simple HTML form utilizing the mailto action.

```
<HTML>
<HEAD><TITLE>Mailing List</TITLE></HEAD>
<BODY>
<FORM METHOD="POST" ACTION="mailto:callaway@sourcestream.com"
ENCTYPE="application/x-www-form-urlencoded">
<P>Name: <INPUT TYPE="TEXT" NAME="name" SIZE="25"></P>
<P>Email Address: <INPUT TYPE="TEXT" NAME="email" SIZE="25"></P>
<P><INPUT TYPE="SUBMIT" VALUE="Submit">
</FORM>
</BODY>
</HTML>
```

A sample of the body of the e-mail message generated by Listing 3.1 follows. Notice how the URL encoded message matches the name of each input element with the value entered by the user (known as a *name/value pair*).

```
name=Dustin+Callaway&email=callaway@sourcestream.com
```

The ENCTYPE Attribute

The ENCTYPE attribute specifies the MIME content type used to encode the form data. The default type, application/x-www-form-encoded, is the same as standard URL encoding. Though other MIME types may be used (such as text/plain or multipart/form-data), x-www-form-encoded is a much safer method because it is designed to prevent characters from being lost or transposed in transit. For more information about why x-www-form-encoded is a safe method, see the "URL Encoding" section in Chapter 2.

The <INPUT> Tag

A form only becomes useful once the appropriate input elements are added to it. Within a form block, input components such as textboxes, radio buttons, and checkboxes can be added to the HTML page using special tags. For example, Listing 3.2 shows the HTML code used to generate the Web page shown in Figure 3.2 (to simplify things, the HTML table tags have been removed).

Listing 3.2   A simple HTML form.

```
<HTML>
<HEAD><TITLE>
Login
</TITLE></HEAD>
<BODY>
<H2>Login to Secure Site</H2>
<FORM METHOD="POST" ACTION="/cgi-bin/login.cgi">

Username: <INPUT TYPE="TEXT" NAME="username" SIZE="25"><BR>
Password: <INPUT TYPE="PASSWORD" NAME="password" SIZE="25"><P>

<INPUT TYPE="SUBMIT" VALUE="Submit">
<INPUT TYPE="RESET" VALUE="Clear">
</FORM>
</BODY>
</HTML>
```

The browser rendering of the HTML code in Listing 3.2 is shown in Figure 3.6. Specifically designed for forms, the <INPUT> tag defines some type of input component. The exact type of component is specified with the TYPE attribute. The elements of the <INPUT> tag are described next.

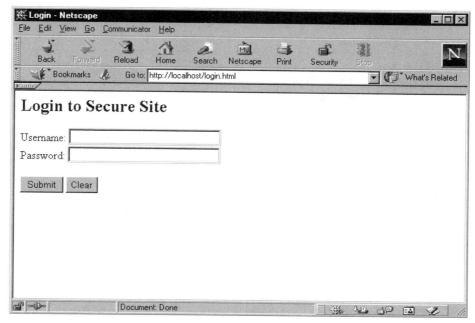

Figure 3.6 Simple HTML Form

The TYPE Attribute

The TYPE attribute defines the exact type of input component represented by the <INPUT> tag. For example, the <INPUT> tag that follows specifies a textbox component that is 25 characters wide.

```
<INPUT TYPE="TEXT" NAME="username" SIZE="25">
```

The valid values for the TYPE attribute are shown in Table 3.4.

Other Attributes

In addition to the TYPE attribute, there are several other important attributes used within the <INPUT> tag. Table 3.5 describes each of these attributes.

The <TEXTAREA> Tag

The <TEXTAREA> tag displays a multiline textbox that is useful for collecting large amounts of text from the client. The syntax for the <TEXTAREA> tag is as follows:

```
<TEXTAREA NAME="name" COLS="x" ROWS="y">Default Text</TEXTAREA>
```

Table 3.4   Possible Values of the <INPUT> Tag's TYPE Attribute

Type	Description
TEXT	Standard textbox. Can be used in conjunction with the SIZE and MAXLENGTH attributes to specify the width of the textbox and the maximum number of characters allowed, respectively. The VALUE attribute specifies the text shown in the textbox when the form is first loaded.
CHECKBOX	Standard checkbox. Used for simple boolean values (*on* or *off*, *true* or *false*). Can be used in conjunction with the CHECKED attribute to specify whether or not it is initially selected. Unselected checkboxes are not included with the name/value pairs when the form is submitted.
RADIO	Standard radio button. Accepts a single value from a group of choices. Can be used in conjunction with the CHECKED attribute to specify whether or not it is initially selected. Unselected radio buttons are not included with the name/value pairs when the form is submitted.
HIDDEN	No field is visible to the user, but its name/value pair is submitted with the other form data. Useful for transmitting state information from page to page (such as a username or session ID).
PASSWORD	Same as the TEXT attribute except that the text is not displayed as the value is entered. This does not affect the value of the field when the form is submitted. Can be used in conjunction with the SIZE and MAXLENGTH attributes to specify the width of the textbox and the maximum number of characters allowed, respectively.
SUBMIT	A button that submits the form. The VALUE attribute specifies the label displayed on the button. If a NAME attribute is specified, the *Submit* button will contribute a name/value pair to the form data when submitted. Otherwise, the *Submit* button does not contribute to the form data.
RESET	A button that resets all form fields to their initial values. The VALUE attribute specifies the label displayed on the button.
IMAGE	An image that, when clicked, submits the form (same as the *Submit* button). Similar to a standard HTML image tag, the SRC attribute specifies the URL of the image. Any VALUE attribute is ignored.
FILE	An experimental type supported by Netscape Navigator and Microsoft Internet Explorer (see RFC 1867) that facilitatesthe selection of a file from the file system by supplying a textbox and a *Browse* button. The ACCEPT attribute specifies file patterns that are accepted by the field and allows the ENCTYPE to be multipart/form-data. This type is used for file uploads.

As you can see, the <TEXTAREA> element allows you to specify not only the number of columns, like the TEXT input type, but also the number of rows. Listing 3.3 shows how HTML displays a typical application of the <TEXTAREA> tag. The HTML example in Listing 3.3 looks like Figure 3.7 in the browser.

Table 3.5 <INPUT> Tag Attributes in Addition to TYPE

Attribute	Description
ALIGN	Used with the IMAGE type for vertical alignment. Alignment values are the same as with the <IMG> tag.
CHECKED	Indicates that a checkbox or radio button is initially selected. This attribute is not set to any value. It is simply either present or not.
MAXLENGTH	Specifies the maximum number of characters that can be entered into a text field. This may be larger than the width specified by the SIZE attribute, in which case the text field will scroll.
NAME	Provides a unique identifier for a field. The NAME attribute is submitted with the form data as part of the name/value pair. Allows the program that processes the data to match fields with their appropriate values.
SIZE	Specifies the visible width, in characters, of a text field.
SRC	Used with the IMAGE type, specifies the URL where the image data is located.
TYPE	Specifies the specific type of input element represented by the <INPUT> tag.

Listing 3.3 A simple HTML form using the <TEXTAREA> tag.

```
<HTML>
<HEAD><TITLE>
Suggestion Box
</TITLE></HEAD>
<BODY>
<H2>Suggestion Box</H2>
<FORM METHOD="POST" ACTION="/cgi-bin/login.cgi">

Please enter your suggestions below:
<BR>
<TEXTAREA NAME="suggestion" COLS="60" ROWS="4"></TEXTAREA>
<BR>

<INPUT TYPE="SUBMIT" VALUE="Submit">
<INPUT TYPE="RESET" VALUE="Clear">
</FORM>
</BODY>
</HTML>
```

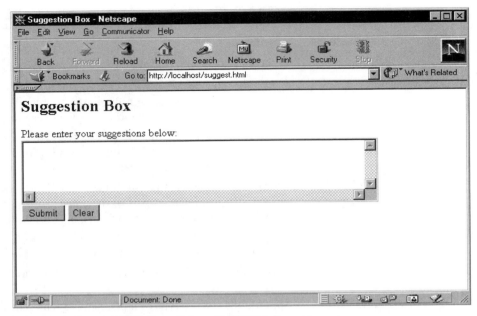

Figure 3.7   Sample HTML Form Using a TEXTAREA Input Element

Summary

This chapter presented an introduction to the HTTP protocol, MIME, and HTML forms. A thorough understanding of these topics will help the reader know how communication takes place on the Web and assist with trouble-shooting when things go wrong. Combined with the appendices referred to in the text, this chapter may serve as a useful reference during your servlet development projects. In the next chapter, you will be introduced to servlets—at last!

Chapter Highlights

- The *Hypertext Transfer Protocol* is a stateless, TCP/IP based protocol used for communicating on the World Wide Web. HTTP defines the precise manner in which Web clients communicate with Web servers.

- The HTTP protocol follows a very simple request/response paradigm.

- HTTP is a connectionless protocol. In a *connectionless* protocol, the client opens a connection with the server, sends a request, receives a response, and closes the connection.

- HTTP is a stateless protocol. A protocol is said to be *stateless* if it has no memory of prior connections and cannot distinguish one client's request from that of another client.
- *SSL* is a protocol developed by Netscape for establishing secure connections between two hosts.
- *MIME* is an extension to the electronic mail format originally defined by RFC 822. It provides a standard mechanism for encoding binary data into ASCII characters, defines a standard for specifying the type of content stored in the body of a message, and describes a standard

PART II

Introduction to Servlets

CHAPTER 4

Why Servlets?

Originally, Web sites were comprised of only static HTML documents stored in the server's file system. There was no way for the client to transmit information to the server in order to customize the information returned or store data in a database. These were the days before Internet search engines, online order processing, and interactive Web-based games. Fortunately, the introduction of CGI breathed life into the static World Wide Web.

In combination with HTML forms, CGI provided a mechanism for true two-way interaction between the client and the server. This new technology paved the way for new ideas like online customer support and electronic commerce. With CGI beginning to show its age in areas of performance and flexibility, new technologies are vying to replace CGI as the standard interface for building dynamic Web sites. With industry momentum growing rapidly, Java servlets are likely to succeed CGI as the most popular Internet development technology.

This chapter provides a high-level introduction to servlets by answering the following basic questions:

- What is a servlet?
- What can servlets do?
- Why are servlets better than CGI?

On completion of this chapter, you should have a good grasp of what a servlet is used for and the advantages of servlets over competing technologies.

What Is a Servlet?

A *servlet* is a server-side software component, written in Java, that dynamically extends the functionality of a server. Similar to the manner in which applets run inside a Java-enabled Web browser on the client, servlets execute on a Java-enabled server. Unlike applets, servlets do not display a graphical interface to the user. A servlet's work is done "behind the scenes" on the server and only the results of the servlet's processing are returned to the client (usually in the form of HTML).

Specifically, servlets are Java classes that conform to a specific interface that can be invoked from the server. Note that the functionality provided by servlets is not restricted to Web servers. Any server that supports the Servlet API may be enhanced through servlets. Common examples include FTP, Telnet, mail, and news servers. The *Servlet API* is a specification developed by Sun that defines the classes and interfaces used to create and execute servlets.

Servlets provide a framework for creating applications that implement the request/response paradigm. For example, when a browser sends a request to the server, the server may forward the request to a servlet. At this point the servlet can process the request (through database access or any other means) and construct an appropriate response (usually in HTML) that is returned to the client.

Servlets have many advantages over competing technologies, including the following:

- Capable of running in-process
- Compiled
- Crash resistant
- Cross-platform
- Cross-server
- Durable
- Dynamically loadable across the network
- Extensible
- Multithreaded
- Protocol independent
- Secure
- Written in Java

Let's briefly discuss each of these points.

Capable of Running In-Process

Servlets are capable of running in the same process space as the server. This capability offers significant performance advantages over many competing technologies. For instance, server-side programming methods like CGI require programs to run as separate processes when servicing client requests. The overhead involved with creating a new process for every request incurs a large performance penalty. Because servlets run in-process, they need only be loaded once (at server start-up or when first invoked). Due to the multithreaded nature of servlets, all client requests can be serviced by separate threads within the server's process space. Context switching between threads is far faster than context switching between processes.

Compiled

Unlike scripting languages, servlets are compiled into Java byte-codes. By virtue of their compilation, Java servlets can execute much more quickly than common scripting languages. Though servlets do not compile to native code, byte-code compilation improves performance through compile-time code optimization. Server-side just-in-time compilers also dramatically improve the performance of the Java virtual machine.

Compilation also offers the advantages of strong error and type checking. Many critical errors are flushed out during compilation. This compilation stage makes servlets more stable and easier to develop and debug than traditional scripting solutions. Lastly, compiled code is more compact and secure than noncompiled options.

Crash Resistant

Though it can't be said that any application is completely crash proof, servlets come much closer to this ideal than native applications. This is primarily due to the fact that servlets are written in Java and executed by a *Java Virtual Machine* (JVM). The JVM does not allow servlets direct access to memory locations, thereby eliminating crashes that result from invalid memory accesses (e.g., errant pointers in C). In addition, before execution, the JVM verifies that compiled Java class files are valid and do not perform illegal operations (e.g., forged pointers, access restriction violations, illegal object casting). Finally, rather than crashing, the JVM will propagate an exception up the calling chain until it is caught (if not caught, the JVM itself will handle the error without crashing). Thus, a poorly written or malicious servlet cannot crash the server.

Cross-Platform

Because servlets are written completely in Java, they enjoy the same cross-platform support as any Java program. This "write once, run anywhere" capability allows servlets to be easily distributed throughout an enterprise without rewriting for each platform. Servlets operate identically without modification whether they are running on UNIX, Windows NT, or any other Java-compliant operating system.

NOTE: Currently, there are some areas in which Java falls short of the "write once, run anywhere" promise. However, since they do not present a graphical interface to the user, servlets provide more consistent cross-platform support than graphics-intensive Java applications. The GUI is a common area wherein some Java programs may require modification in order to run on different platforms.

Cross-Server

Servlets can be run on virtually every popular Web server in use today. More than a dozen major software vendors currently provide native support for servlets within their products, including the IBM Internet Connection Server, O'Reilly WebSite, Lotus Domino Go Web Server, Dynamo Application Server, BEA WebLogic Application Server, Netscape Enterprise Server, and Novell IntranetWare (see *http://java.sun.com/products/servlet/runners.html* for a more complete listing). For those servers that do not currently offer native servlet support, there are many third-party add-ons that allow these servers to load and run servlets. For example, servlet engines like the Java Servlet Development Kit from Sun Microsystems, JRun from Live Software, and ServletExec from New Atlanta Communications add servlet support to many popular Web servers including Microsoft Internet Information Server, Netscape FastTrack and Enterprise Server, and Apache Web Server.

Durable

Servlets are durable objects. *Durable* means that they remain in memory until specifically instructed to be destroyed. In this way, servlets only need to be instantiated a single time in order to service many requests. In addition, a servlet can create other durable objects for use across many requests. For instance, it is common for a servlet to create a single database connection when it is first loaded. This connection can then be shared across all requests.

Dynamically Loadable across the Network

Similar to applets, servlets can by dynamically loaded either locally or from across the network. Dynamic loading ensures that unused servlets do not consume precious server resources. They are only loaded when needed. Fortunately, for performance reasons it is also possible to instruct the server to load a servlet at start-up rather than when it is first invoked.

The ability to load servlets across the network is a great advantage for distributed computing environments. Rather than having to copy each servlet and all modifications to every server, servlets can be dynamically loaded from a remote location on the network. And similar to applets, servlets run in a secure sandbox on the server to ensure security and stability.

Extensible

Since servlets are written in Java, there is a wealth of third-party support for writing and extending them. New development tools, Java class libraries, and database drivers are constantly becoming available and they all can be utilized by servlets.

Multithreaded

Java was designed to be a multithreaded language. Unlike C or C++, threading mechanisms are inherent within the Java language and the thread synchronization syntax is consistent across platforms. Since servlets are written in Java, they support multithreaded functionality. The multithreaded nature of servlets allows client requests to be handled by separate threads within a single process. This approach requires far less overhead and executes much more quickly than the alternative—creating a new process for every request.

Protocol Independent

Though servlets are commonly used to extend HTTP server functionality, they are by no means limited to this protocol. On the contrary, servlets are completely protocol independent. Protocol independence allows a servlet to be specially constructed to support FTP commands, SMTP or POP3 e-mail functionality, Telnet sessions, NNTP newsgroups, or any other protocol (whether standard or created by the servlet developer). The Servlet API does an excellent job of providing strong support for common HTTP functionality without sacrificing the ability to support other protocols.

Secure

Servlets are secure in many different ways. In particular, three important features ensure servlet security. First, because servlets are written in Java, invalid memory access calls and strong typing violations are not possible. A poorly written or malicious servlet cannot bring down the server. Second, servlets use the server's *Security Manager* for the customization and enforcement of specific security policies. For instance, a properly configured Security Manager can restrict network or file access for an untrusted servlet. On the other hand, the Security Manager may grant full rights to a local or digitally signed and trusted servlet. Third, a servlet has access to all information contained in each client request. This information includes HTTP authentication data. When used in conjunction with secure protocols like SSL, servlets can positively verify the identity of every client. These three features combine to make servlets more secure than API server extensions or CGI.

Written in Java

Because servlets are written in Java, they are afforded many advantages provided by the Java language and Java Virtual Machine. A few of these advantages include support for true object-oriented programming (providing extensibility and simplified code maintenance), strong type checking, full multi-threading support, built-in security, optimized code compilation, automatic garbage collection, support for internationalization through Unicode, built-in network support, and "write once, run anywhere" cross-platform and cross-server support. And since Java does not support pointers, difficult-to-find pointer bugs, along with the security risks they present, are eliminated from your code.

NOTE: You may wonder where servlets fit in as far as the standard Java classes are concerned. Beginning with Java 2, the Servlet API has been packaged as a *Java standard extension.* All Java standard extensions are located in the javax package. The servlet packages are javax.servlet and javax.servlet.http. Unlike the core Java packages, standard extensions are not required to be included in every Java environment. The servlet standard extensions are distributed by Sun Microsystems inside of the Java Servlet Development Kit (JSDK).

What Can Servlets Do?

Servlets extend a server's functionality in almost any way imaginable. Similar to CGI, they allow for true two-way interaction between the client and server. The following are just a few of the many possibilities provided by servlets:

- Dynamically build and return an HTML file based on the nature of the client request
- Process user input passed by an HTML form and return an appropriate response
- Facilitate communication between groups of people by publishing information submitted by many clients (e.g., an online bulletin board system)
- Provide user authentication and other security mechanisms
- Interact with server resources such as databases, other applications, and network files to return useful information to the client
- Process input from many clients for interaction among peers for applications such as multiplayer games
- Allow the server to communicate with a client applet via a custom protocol and keep the connection open throughout the conversation
- Automatically attach Web page design elements, such as headers or footers, to all pages returned by the server
- Forward requests from one server to another for load balancing purposes
- Partition a single logical service across servers or between servlets in order to most efficiently process the task
- Virtually any other way you can imagine to enhance or extend a server

Why Are Servlets Better Than CGI?

Servlets offer advantages over CGI in the areas of performance, portability, and security. Each of these advantages will be discussed in turn.

Performance is perhaps the most visible difference between servlets and CGI. Since most servlets run in the same process space as the server and are loaded only once, they are able to respond much more quickly and efficiently to client requests. In contrast, CGI must create a new process to service each new request. The overhead involved with creating a new process incurs a significant performance penalty.

Figure 4.1 illustrates how a Java-enabled server spawns a new thread for each request within its process space and a CGI-based server creates a new process for every request. In addition, the majority of Web sites today are database driven. Since a new process must be created for each request, database-driven pages require a new database connection with every request. Unlike servlets, CGI cannot share a single database connection across multiple requests.

Java-enabled Server

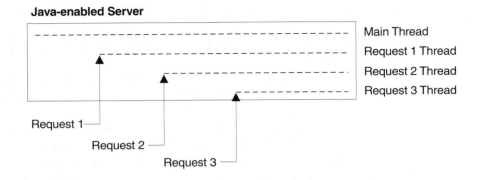

CGI-based Server

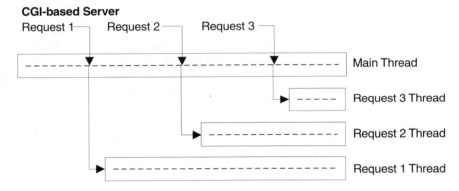

Note: Each solid box represents
a different process space.

Figure 4.1   Difference Between Servlets and CGI Processes

Portability is another strong advantage for servlets. Unlike many CGI applications, servlets can be run on different servers and platforms without modification (similar to Perl scripts). This characteristic can be extremely important when building enterprise-wide distributed applications.

Lastly, servlets are much more secure than CGI. Though CGI scripts can be written in Java, they are often written in more error-prone languages such as C. Since C programs can inadvertently or maliciously access invalid memory locations, CGI programs are less secure. In addition, similar to the manner in which applets run in a browser, untrusted servlets run inside a sandbox on the server. This *sandbox* is a protected memory space wherein a program cannot access outside resources such as file or network services. Of course, these restrictions can be lifted according to the security policies set by the Java Security Manager.

Summary

The purpose of this chapter was to present an initial introduction to servlets: what they are and how they can be used. In the coming chapters, we will abandon the "high-level" descriptions and move into the specifics of servlet implementation. In the next chapter, we will see exactly what a servlet looks like and start writing code—beginning with your first "Hello World" servlet.

Chapter Highlights

- A *servlet* is a server-side software component, written in Java, that dynamically extends the functionality of a server.
- Unlike applets, servlets do not display a graphical interface to the user.
- Servlets offer many advantages over traditional Web development technologies. These advantages include that servlets are capable of running in-process, compiled, cross-platform, cross-server, dynamically loadable across the network, multithreaded, protocol independent, secure, crash resistant, and written in Java.
- Beginning with Java 2, servlets are considered *Java standard extensions*.
- Servlets offer advantages over CGI in the areas of performance, portability, and security.

CHAPTER 5

Servlet Basics

Once you begin writing them, you will quickly notice that servlets handle request/respond operations in an extremely clean, simple, and efficient manner. The Servlet API interface provides an intuitive framework for extending the functionality of Java-enabled servers. Though learning to use servlets can be relatively quick and easy, do not be fooled by their simplicity. Servlets offer significant power and flexibility for building networked applications.

This chapter focuses on the structure and syntax of servlets and the manner in which they are invoked. Specifically, the following topics are covered:

- Basic servlet structure
- Servlet lifecycle
- Dissecting a sample servlet

On completion of this chapter you should understand the structure of a simple servlet and the process by which it is called.

Basic Servlet Structure

Before we take a look at our first functional servlet, let's take a moment to discuss the basic structure of a servlet. As we begin examining servlets, you will quickly notice that they are basic Java applications similar to others you may have written. The only difference is that they extend new classes and implement some unfamiliar methods. Fortunately, servlets are as simple to write as any other Java program. You just have to learn the servlet structure and a new class library.

Practically all servlets that perform some useful function have two things in common. First, they all extend one of two servlet classes—GenericServlet or

HttpServlet.[1] Extending these classes provides a framework for creating a servlet as well as significant default functionality. We will discuss these classes in more detail later in this chapter. Second, all servlets override at least one method wherein custom functionality is implemented. The method that is automatically called by the server in response to a client request is called service(). This method may be overridden to provide custom functionality. However, if the servlet developer chooses not to override the service() method, other methods will be invoked in response to a client request. We will discuss these methods a little later.

In addition to the classes and methods mentioned above, there are two other methods that are implemented by most servlets—init() and destroy(). The init() method is called a single time when the servlet is first loaded. It is similar to a class constructor in that it provides a method wherein initialization code is guaranteed to be run. The destroy() method is executed when the servlet is unloaded. It is used to free any resources held by the servlet.

Based on the brief description of the structure of a servlet given above, let's construct the skeleton of a common servlet. For simplicity, the skeleton servlet that follows does not include parameters passed to the methods or exceptions that are thrown. These details will be presented shortly.

```
public class SkeletonServlet extends HttpServlet
{
  public void init()
  {
    //initialization code goes here
  }

  public void service()
  {
    //meaningful work happens here
  }

  public void destroy()
  {
    //release resources here
  }
}
```

Now that doesn't look too difficult. Of course, the actual implementation of different servlets may vary widely. For example, servlets may or may not implement the init() or destroy() methods. Implementation of these methods is

---

1. Actually, a servlet is not required to extend GenericServlet or HttpServlet. An advanced developer can create a servlet by implementing the Servlet interface and, thus, bypass the need to extend one of these two classes. Extending GenericServlet or HttpServlet is, however, the simplest and most common way to build a servlet.

not mandatory. Likewise, a servlet developer may choose not to override the `service()` method and opt to implement another method that is automatically called by the inherited `service()` method. Similar to `service()`, this method would implement the servlet's unique functionality. The method automatically called by `service()` depends upon the type of HTTP request received (e.g., `doGet()` is called for GET requests and `doPost()` for POST requests). However, regardless of these differences, the basic structure shown above is similar to almost any servlet you might see or write. More details regarding the classes and methods shown above (including the methods' parameters) are presented later in this chapter.

Servlet Lifecycle

Now that you have seen the basic structure of a servlet, let's review the process by which a server invokes a servlet. This process can be broken down into the nine steps described next.

1. The server loads the servlet when it is first requested by a client or, if configured to do so, at server start-up. The servlet may be loaded from either a local or a remote location using the standard Java class loading facility. This step is equivalent to the following Java code:

```
Class c = Class.forName("com.sourcestream.MyServlet");
```

It should be noted that, when referring to servlets, the term *load* often refers to the process of both loading and instantiating the servlet.

2. The server creates one or more instances of the servlet class. Depending on the implementation, the server may create a single instance that services all requests through multiple threads or create a pool of instances from which one is chosen to service each new request. This step is equivalent to the following Java code:

```
Servlet s = (Servlet)c.newInstance();
```

3. The server constructs a `ServletConfig` object that provides initialization information to the servlet.

4. The server calls the servlet's `init()` method, passing the object constructed in step 3 as a parameter. The `init()` method is guaranteed to finish execution prior to the servlet processing the first request. If the server has created multiple servlet instances (step 2), the `init()` method is called one time for each instance.

5. The server constructs a `ServletRequest` or `HttpServletRequest` object from the data included in the client's request. It also constructs a

`ServletResponse` or `HttpServletResponse` object that provides methods for customizing the server's response. The type of object passed in these two parameters depends on whether the servlet extends the `GenericServlet` class or the `HttpServlet` class, respectively.

6. The server calls the servlet's `service()` method (or other, more specific, method like `doGet()` or `doPost()` for HTTP servlets), passing the objects constructed in step 5 as parameters. When concurrent requests arrive, multiple `service()` methods can run in separate threads.

7. The `service()` method processes the client request by evaluating the `ServletRequest` or `HttpServletRequest` object and responds using the `ServletResponse` or `HttpServletResponse` object.

8. If the server receives another request for this servlet, the process begins again at step 5.

9. When instructed to unload the servlet, perhaps by the server administrator or programmatically by the servlet itself, the server calls the servlet's `destroy()` method. The servlet is then eligible for garbage collection.

These nine steps illustrate the entire lifecycle of a servlet. Though the lifecycle described above is consistent across all Java-enabled servers, different servlet engines may implement some servlet functionality in a slightly different way. For instance, the manner in which a request is mapped to a servlet may differ between servers. Regardless, the steps listed above should give you a good understanding of the servlet lifecycle. Figure 5.1 shows the flow of the servlet lifecycle.

NOTE: The terms "server," "Java-enabled server," and "servlet engine" are often used interchangeably throughout the text. Therefore, we'd better define these terms.

A *servlet engine* is the software that actually executes servlets. All servers that support servlets include a servlet engine (either integrated or via an add-on). The term *Java-enabled server* is often used to denote a servlet-enhanced HTTP server (i.e., it includes a servlet engine for running servlets). Finally, the term *server* may be used occasionally with the understanding that it supports servlets via an integrated or add-on servlet engine.

Dissecting a Sample Servlet

By this point you are probably anxious to see what a real servlet looks like. Let's alleviate your anxiety right now. Below is a simple "Hello World" servlet

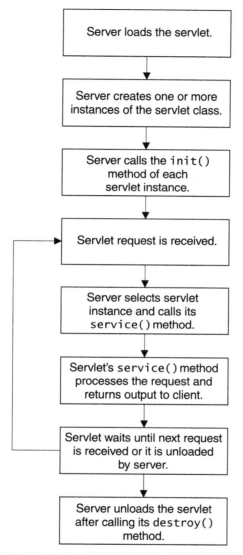

Figure 5.1 The Servlet Lifecycle

that responds to a request from a Web browser. Though servlets can work with any protocol, HTTP servlets that extend the functionality of Web servers are most common and are the primary focus of this book. The servlet shown in Listing 5.1 does nothing more than return the ubiquitous phrase "Hello World" and the number of times it has been requested.

Listing 5.1   A simple "Hello World" servlet.

```java
import javax.servlet.*;
import javax.servlet.http.*;
import java.io.PrintWriter;
import java.io.IOException;

/**
 * Sample Servlet
 *
 * This servlet returns "Hello World" and the number of times
 * the servlet has been requested.
 *
 * @author Dustin R. Callaway
 * @version 1.0, 02/17/98
 */
public class SampleServlet extends HttpServlet
{
  //static makes variable visible to all instances
  static int numRequests = 0; //number of times servlet requested

  public void init(ServletConfig config) throws ServletException
  {
    super.init(config); //pass ServletConfig to parent
    //initialize resources here
  }

  public void service(HttpServletRequest request,
    HttpServletResponse response) throws ServletException,
    IOException
  {
    //set MIME type for HTTP header
    response.setContentType("text/html");

    //get a handle to the output stream
    PrintWriter out = response.getWriter();
    out.println("<HTML>");
    out.println("<HEAD><TITLE>Sample Servlet</TITLE></HEAD>");
    out.println("<BODY>");
    out.println("<H1>Hello World!</H1>");
    numRequests++; //increment hit counter
    out.println("<P>This servlet has been requested " +
      numRequests + " times.");
    out.close(); //always close the output stream
  }

  public String getServletInfo()
  {
    return "Sample Servlet version 1.0";
  }
```

```
public void destroy()
{
   //servlet is being unloaded, free resources here
}
}
```

Let's take a closer look at each part of the Listing 5.1 servlet, starting with the imports:

```
import javax.servlet.*;
import javax.servlet.http.*;
import java.io.PrintWriter;
import java.io.IOException;
```

The entire Servlet API is contained within two packages: `javax.servlet` and `javax.servlet.http`. You will need to include classes from both of these packages in every one of your HTTP servlets. Non-HTTP servlets do not require any classes from the `javax.servlet.http` package.

The simplest way to ensure that you have imported the proper servlet classes is to use the `.*` wildcard as shown in the imports above (this style is used regularly throughout the book). However, in order to provide better code documentation and simplify debugging, it is often a good idea to specifically import each class. In this way, there is no question concerning which classes are being imported or which package contains a particular class. The following import statements document the package in which each class is contained.

```
import javax.servlet.ServletConfig;
import javax.servlet.ServletException;
import javax.servlet.http.HttpServlet;
import javax.servlet.http.HttpServletRequest;
import javax.servlet.http.HttpServletResponse;
import java.io.PrintWriter;
import java.io.IOException;
```

The class declaration is the next important part of this servlet:

```
public class SampleServlet extends HttpServlet
```

Every servlet that you write will either extend the class `GenericServlet` or `HttpServlet` or implement the `Servlet` interface. Although it is possible to write servlets by implementing the `Servlet` interface, this practice is rarely necessary. Almost any servlet that you care to write can be more easily implemented by extending either `GenericServlet` or `HttpServlet`, each of which implements the `Servlet` interface. As you might have guessed, the `HttpServlet` class contains methods specific to the HTTP protocol. The `GenericServlet` class is useful when building non-HTTP servlets such as those that implement FTP, POP3, Telnet, or any custom protocol. In this book we will almost exclusively focus on developing HTTP servlets through extending the Http-Servlet class.

The sample servlet's base class, HttpServlet, provides a number of methods that may be overridden in order to create custom functionality. Four of the most basic methods defined by HttpServlet are used in Listing 5.1—init(), service(), getServletInfo(), and destroy().

```
public void init(ServletConfig config) throws ServletException
```

When the servlet is first loaded, the server executes the init() method once for each instance before handling the first request. After it is instantiated, the servlet stays resident in memory until specifically unloaded by the server. Depending on the server implementation, the server may create a single instance to service all requests or it may create a pool of instances. If all requests are processed by a single servlet instance, the server spawns a new thread for each call to the service() method.[2] The multithreaded nature of servlets allows many service() methods to execute simultaneously. Conversely, if the server creates a pool of instances, it may not spawn a new thread for each call to the service() method. Rather, it may simply select a new instance from the pool of available instances.

Any shared resources created by the init() method are accessible by every invocation of the servlet as long as they are created as static class variables. Shared resources may be declared static (rather than instance variables) in case the server implementation uses multiple instances of a single servlet class. static variables are visible across all class instances.

One caveat to this approach is the possibility that instances of a particular servlet can be distributed across multiple servlet engines. static variables are not visible across servlet engines. To guarantee that a resource is shared between all servlet instances (even across servlet engines), it must be stored in the ServletContext object using its setAttribute() and getAttribute() methods (see Chapter 20 for more information on the ServletContext object). However, since distributing servlet instances across multiple engines is rare, the simpler static variable approach is used in this book.

The init() method is ideal for creating resources that are shared across requests. For instance, it is common to establish database or network connections within the init() method. Once opened, these connections can be shared across all requests and the overhead required to open the connection occurs only once. The parameter passed to the init() method, ServletConfig, is discussed in a later chapter. ServletException is thrown by the init() method

---

2. There is a way to explicitly prevent the server from using a new thread for each request. This is accomplished by implementing the SingleThreadModel interface that will be discussed in Chapter 11.

NOTE: Although most Java server implementations create a single servlet instance that handles all requests (by multithreading the `service()` method), it is possible for a server to create multiple servlet instances. In this case, the `init()` method is called for each instance. Since the `init()` method can be called multiple times, it is possible that shared resources are unnecessarily initialized multiple times (e.g., a database connection could be opened by multiple `init()` methods even though all instances are sharing the same connection). In order to avoid duplicating initialization processing, it is a good idea to first check to see if a resource has already been initialized by the `init()` method of another instance. The sample code below demonstrates this strategy.

```
static Connection dbConnection = null;

public void service(HttpServletRequest request,
  HttpServletResponse response) throws ServletException,
  IOException
{
  if(dbConnection == null )
  {
    //Initialize database connection here..
    dbConnection = getDBConnection();
  }
}
```

and is handled by the parent class (`ServletException` is discussed in a later chapter). Since the server must be able to call the `init()` method when the servlet is first loaded, the method is declared `public`.

```
super.init(config); //pass ServletConfig to parent
//initialize resources here
```

The preceding code is executed inside of the `init()` method. Since the `Servlet` interface defines a method called `getServletConfig()`, you should either save the `ServletConfig` object and implement the `getServletConfig()` method yourself or pass the object to the parent class using `super.init()`. In

NOTE: If an error occurs during initialization that prevents the servlet from properly responding to client requests, `UnavailableException` should be thrown. All errors should be handled in the servlet or thrown to the parent class. The `System.exit()` method should never be called.

this case, we chose to allow the parent class to handle all calls to the getServletConfig() method and simply passed the ServletConfig object up the inheritance chain.

```
public void service(HttpServletRequest request,
    HttpServletResponse response) throws IOException
```

NOTE: Prior to version 2.1, the Java Servlet API defined only one init() method. The definition for this method is shown here:

```
public void init(ServletConfig config) throws ServletException
```

This init() method is still supported and is used throughout this book (primarily for backward compatibility). However, Servlet API 2.1 added a second init() method that can make the developer's job a little easier. The definition for this method looks like this:

```
public void init() throws ServletException
```

This convenience method frees the developer from having to store the ServletConfig object (and implement the getServletConfig() method) or call super.init(config) (to pass the ServletConfig object to the parent class). In fact, this new init() method is actually called by the init(ServletConfig) method (which is called by the servlet engine when the servlet is first loaded). In addition, you'll never even need the ServletConfig parameter since the GenericServlet class now implements the ServletConfig interface. Therefore, you no longer need a ServletConfig object in order to call its getInitParameter() method (or any other ServletConfig method). For example, the code below reads an initialization parameter within the parameterless init() method.

```
public void init() throws ServletException
{
    String rootPath = getInitParameter("Root");
}
```

The server calls the service() method whenever it has a request for the servlet to process. This method accepts two parameters. The first parameter is an object that implements the HttpServletRequest interface. This parameter is an object representation of the client's request. All relevant data in the request (such as HTTP headers) is encapsulated inside of the HttpServletRequest object. This data is accessible via the methods defined by HttpServletRequest.

The second parameter is an object that implements the `HttpServlet-Response` interface. This parameter is an object representation of the server's response to the client. The servlet can customize the response by calling the appropriate `HttpServletResponse` methods. When working with network requests and responses, an `IOException` may occur at any time. This exception should not be caught by the servlet. Rather, it should be thrown by the `service()` method (or `doGet()`, `doPost()`, `doPut()` method). An `IOException` should always be handled by the server.

Since the server must be able to call the `service()` method whenever a servlet request is received, the method is declared `public`. In addition to `service()`, there are other, more specific, methods that are called by the server when a servlet request is received. In fact, when writing HTTP servlets, it is advisable to use the specific HTTP request methods, such as `doGet()`, `doPost()`, or `doPut()`, rather than override the generic `service()` method. These specific methods are discussed in the next chapter. The `service()` method is used in this example to familiarize the reader with its function; however, it is used sparingly in future HTTP servlet examples.

NOTE: The syntax of the `service()` method shown above is accurate only for servlets that extend `HttpServlet`. The syntax of the `service()` method for non-HTTP servlets that extend `GenericServlet` is shown below.

```
public void service(ServletRequest request, ServletResponse
    response)
```

The difference lies in the parameters. A `GenericServlet` receives `ServletRequest` and `ServletResponse` parameters rather than `HttpServlet-Request` and `HttpServletResponse`. `HttpServletRequest` and `HttpServlet-Response` are subinterfaces of `ServletRequest` and `ServletResponse`, respectively.

The following lines are executed inside of the `service()` method.

```
//set MIME type for HTTP header
response.setContentType("text/html");

//get a handle to the output stream
PrintWriter out = response.getWriter();
out.println("<HTML>");
out.println("<HEAD><TITLE>Sample Servlet</TITLE></HEAD>");
out.println("<BODY>");
out.println("<H1>Hello World!</H1>");
numRequests++; //increment hit counter
```

```
out.println("<P>This servlet has been requested " +
   numRequests + " times.");
out.close(); //always close the output stream
```

The first line of code sets the MIME type for the response to text/html using the setContentType() method. This line will add the Content-Type: text/html HTTP header to the response. The content type, or any other HTTP header values, should be set before accessing the output stream using the getWriter() or getOutputStream() method of HttpServletResponse. This is because the HTTP headers may be flushed to the client at any time after the output stream is accessed.

The next line of code gets a handle to the output stream using the getWriter() method. Use getWriter() when you are returning text data to the client. The PrintWriter object returned by getWriter() is specially constructed for outputting text and includes full Unicode support for international languages. For responses consisting of binary data, create a ServletOutputStream object using the getOutputStream() method as follows:

```
ServletOutputStream out = hsrsResponse.getOutputStream();
```

Once the PrintWriter object has been acquired, you can use its print() or println() methods to return information to the client. The println() method is used in the sample servlet because it makes the HTML source easier to read by adding a carriage return/linefeed to the end of each line of output. The sample servlet returns an HTML formatted document.

In addition to sending the phrase "Hello World" to the client, the number of times the servlet has been accessed is also displayed. This is accomplished by incrementing the class variable numRequests each time the service() method is executed. Since numRequests is declared as a static variable at the class level (outside of a method), it is visible to every invocation of SampleServlet and its value persists between requests. Finally, the output stream of the PrintWriter object is closed. Always close the output stream once the response is complete. Normally, the close() method should be invoked within a finally block to ensure that it is always called. For simplicity, no exception handling is included in the sample servlet.

```
public String getServletInfo()
{
   return "Sample Servlet version 1.0";
}
```

The Servlet interface (implemented by GenericServlet) defines a method called getServletInfo() that accepts no parameters and returns a String. The purpose of this method is to provide a simple way for a server to request information about a servlet. It is good practice to always override this method, returning a short description of your servlet.

```
public void destroy()
```

The servlet continues to process requests until explicitly unloaded by the server. The server unloads a servlet after calling its `destroy()` method. The servlet developer should use this method to free resources, such as closing database and socket connections, or to perform any other housekeeping chores that should be completed before the servlet is unloaded. Once the `destroy()` method has been called, the servlet object is eligible for garbage collection. The `destroy()` method in the sample servlet provides no functionality and is intended only to illustrate proper syntax.

This concludes our examination of the sample servlet. You should now have a pretty good idea of what a basic servlet looks like and be familiar with several common methods used in servlet development. Of course, now that you have been exposed to these concepts, more detailed information will be presented in the coming chapters.

Summary

This chapter exposed you to the basic syntax and structure of a servlet. Hopefully, the example presented here demonstrated the fact that though servlets can be very powerful and complex, their basic structure is simple and straightforward. This simplicity facilitates quick learning and application of various servlet features. In addition, you learned the basic steps by which a servlet is created, invoked, and destroyed by the servlet engine.

The next chapter will introduce you to the most common classes and interfaces used to build servlets.

Chapter Highlights

- Nearly all servlets extend one of two servlet classes—`GenericServlet` or `HttpServlet`. Extending these classes provides a framework for creating a servlet as well as significant default functionality.
- The `HttpServlet` class contains methods specific to the HTTP protocol.
- The `GenericServlet` class is useful when building non-HTTP servlets such as those that implement FTP, POP3, Telnet, or any custom protocol.
- Servlets override at least one method wherein custom functionality is implemented. The method that is automatically called by the server in

response to a client request is called `service()`. This method may be overridden to provide custom functionality.

- In addition to the `service()` method, there are two other methods that are implemented by most servlets—`init()` and `destroy()`.

- The `init()` method is called a single time when the servlet is first loaded. It is similar to a class constructor in that it provides a method wherein initialization code is guaranteed to be run.

- The `destroy()` method is executed when the servlet is unloaded. It is used to free any resources held by the servlet.

- The process of creating, invoking, and destroying a servlet is known as the servlet lifecycle.

CHAPTER 6

Servlet API Basics

All of the classes and interfaces required to create and execute servlets are contained within two packages—`javax.servlet` and `javax.servlet.http`. This collection of classes and interfaces is known as the *Java Servlet API* and is part of Sun's Java Servlet Development Kit (JSDK). Though the Servlet API is considered a standard Java extension (as of Java 2), it is not included in the standard Java™ 2 SDK distribution. Therefore, it is necessary to download the JSDK (which includes the Servlet API) and its accompanying documentation separately. This material can be found at *http://java.sun.com/products/servlet*. In addition to the information presented in this book, I recommend reviewing the JSDK documentation provided by Sun Microsystems.

In this chapter, we introduce several of the most commonly used classes and interfaces as well as their most commonly implemented methods, including the following:

- `HttpServlet` class
- `GenericServlet` class
- `ServletRequest` interface
- `HttpServletRequest` interface

NOTE: The classes and interfaces described in this book are based on version 2.1 of the Java Servlet API. Servlet API 2.1 is included in version 2.1 of the JSDK. Therefore, remember that whenever JSDK 2.1 is mentioned, we are referring to version 2.1 of the Servlet API.

- `ServletResponse` interface
- `HttpServletResponse` interface

These classes and interfaces are essential components of the Servlet API. You will certainly use most, if not all, of these components in every one of your servlet projects. The purpose of this chapter is to prepare the reader for the next chapter where we actually build a fully functional servlet. The classes and interfaces presented here are used in the upcoming servlet exercise. Chapter 10 will continue this preview of the Servlet API with additional classes and interfaces used in more advanced servlets (such as those presented in Part III, Advanced Servlet Concepts, and Part IV, Sample Servlets, of this book). The objects and methods described here are based on Servlet API 2.1.

Before we dive into individual classes, methods, and interfaces of the Servlet API, take a moment to examine the class hierarchy diagram in Figure 6.1. This diagram is also in Appendix M.

Now that you've seen the Servlet API from a high level, let's get a little more detailed. The rest of this chapter dissects specific objects within the Servlet API.

NOTE: Although the material presented in this chapter is extremely important, it is also a bit terse and can be rather dry. Therefore, due to the type and volume of information presented here, you may choose to skim portions of this chapter, referring back to it as needed. The important thing is that you familiarize yourself with the interfaces, classes, and methods defined by the Servlet API.

`HttpServlet` Class

`HttpServlet` is an abstract class that resides in the `javax.servlet.http` package. Because it is abstract, it cannot be instantiated. Rather, when building an HTTP servlet, you should extend the `HttpServlet` class and implement at least one of its methods. A functional HTTP servlet must override *at least one* of the

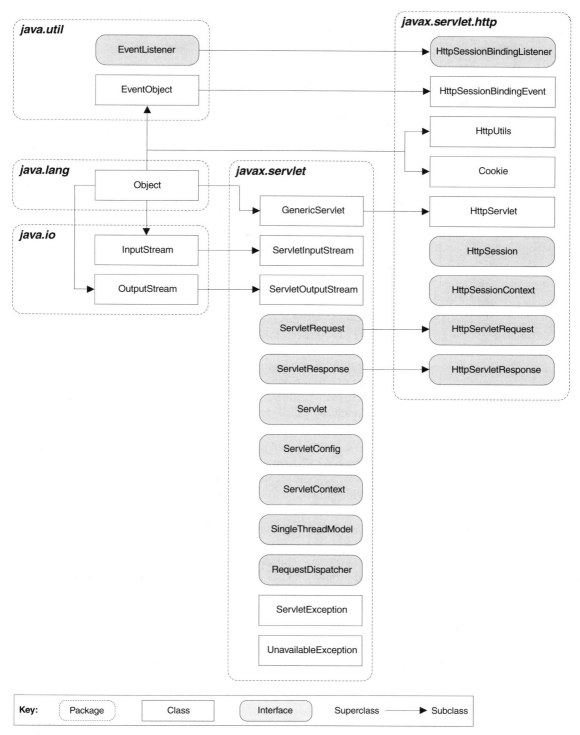

Figure 6.1 Servlet API Class Hierarchy Diagram

methods described in Table 6.1 (typically service(), doGet(), or doPost()). Although HttpServlet does not provide an implementation for most of its methods, it does provide a framework for supporting the HTTP protocol.

In addition, the methods described in Table 6.2, though not required, are commonly implemented. If you examine the JSDK documentation, you may notice that the methods described in Table 6.2 are not shown as methods of the HttpServlet class. HttpServlet inherits these methods from the GenericServlet class, which it extends. Let's take a closer look at each of the methods described in the tables.

Table 6.1   Methods Required to Create a Functional HTTP Servlet

Method	Description
service()	The server calls this method whenever a servlet request is received. For HTTP servlets, this method should usually not be overridden. Rather, one of the methods below should be implemented. If not overridden, the default functionality of the service() method is to call one of the methods below according to the type of HTTP request received. If service() is overridden, these methods are not automatically called (but may be called explicitly by the servlet developer).
doGet()	This method is called in response to an HTTP GET request (including conditional GET requests). Implementing this method automatically provides support for HEAD requests (if the doHead() method is not overridden by the servlet developer). If GET requests are to be supported, this method should be overridden.
doHead()	This method is called in response to an HTTP HEAD request. If doHead() is not overridden by the servlet developer, the default implementation will call the doGet() method in order to generate the appropriate HTTP header fields. A response containing only HTTP header fields is then returned to the client (body content is excluded).
doPost()	This method is called in response to an HTTP POST request. If POST requests are to be supported, this method should be overridden.
doPut()	This method is called in response to an HTTP PUT request. If PUT requests are to be supported, this method should be overridden.
doDelete()	This method is called in response to an HTTP DELETE request. If DELETE requests are to be supported, this method should be overridden.

Table 6.2 Common Servlet Methods

Method	Description
init()	This method is called only once by the server when the servlet is first loaded. It is commonly used to initialize resources to be used by the servlet when requests are received. For example, database or network connections may be established in this method.
destroy()	This method is called by the server immediately before the servlet is unloaded. This method should be overridden by the servlet developer in order to free up any resources being used by the servlet. For example, database or network connections may be closed in this method.
getServletInfo()	It is good practice to implement this method so your servlet can identify itself when queried by the server.

service

```
protected void service(HttpServletRequest request,
    HttpServletResponse response) throws ServletException,
    IOException
```

As mentioned in Table 6.1, the service() method is not normally overridden. This is due to the fact that the HttpServlet class defines methods that are called in response to specific types of HTTP requests (e.g., GET, POST, PUT). Since all of these request methods begin with "do," we will often refer to them as "do" methods (e.g., doGet(), doPost(), doPut(), doDelete()) If the service() method is not overridden, its default implementation is to call the "do" method, passing it to the request and response object that corresponds to the type of request received (e.g., GET, POST, PUT). If the service() method is overridden and "do" methods are implemented, it is up to the servlet developer to evaluate each HTTP request and call the appropriate "do" method. Remember that the servlet engine does not actually call any of the "do" methods. When a servlet request is received, the servlet engine always calls the servlet's service() method which may then call one of the "do" methods.

Although it is possible to implement all of a servlet's functionality within the service() method, the default implementation of this method used in conjunction with the "do" methods makes for cleaner code and provides useful default functionality. For example, the default implementation of the "do" methods returns an HTTP 400 "Bad Request" message to the client. Therefore, the client will automatically receive an error message for any HTTP request type that is not supported (meaning that the corresponding "do" method was not implemented).

> **NOTE:** You may be wondering why Sun chose to return an HTTP 400 "Bad Request" message rather than HTTP 501 "Not Implemented" when a servlet doesn't support a particular HTTP method. The reason is that the "Not Implemented" or "Not Supported" HTTP 501 response indicates a server condition. That is, the server does not support this particular method. However, a server can host multiple servlets, all of which support different HTTP methods. Consequently, stating that the server does not support a specific method is inaccurate. Therefore, HTTP 400 "Bad Request" is returned to indicate a servlet-specific limitation as opposed to a server limitation.

If, for instance, the client attempts to POST to a servlet that does not override the doPost() method, the default implementation of doPost() will discard the request and return an HTTP 400 "Bad Request" message to the client. This functionality is lost when the service() method is overridden unless each of the "do" methods is specifically called by the overriding code. Listing 6.1 shows a typical use of the service() method. Each of the methods shown in Listing 6.1 is discussed later in this chapter.

The service() method throws two exceptions. ServletException indicates a problem with the servlet. The server chooses how to handle this exception when it occurs. An IOException may occur at any time during socket communications. This exception should always be thrown to the server for proper handling.

Listing 6.1   Sample servlet that overrides the service() method.

```
import javax.servlet.http.*;
import javax.servlet.ServletException;
import java.io.PrintWriter;
import java.io.IOException;

public class ServiceServlet extends HttpServlet
{
  public void service(HttpServletRequest request,
    HttpServletResponse response) throws ServletException,
    IOException
  {
    //set MIME type for HTTP header
    response.setContentType("text/plain");

    //get a handle to the output stream
    PrintWriter out = response.getWriter();
```

```
        if (request.getMethod().equals("GET"))
        {
          out.println("Request handled by the service() method");
        }
        else
        {
          response.setStatus(
            HttpServletResponse.SC_BAD_REQUEST);
          out.println("Method Not Supported By This Servlet");
        }

        out.close(); //always close the output stream
    }
}
```

The service() method in Listing 6.1 is executed in response to every type of HTTP request (GET, POST, PUT, DELETE). This servlet sets the Content-Type HTTP header to text/plain and returns a string if the request represents a GET; otherwise it returns HTTP 400 "Bad Request."

doGet

```
protected void doGet(HttpServletRequest request,
    HttpServletResponse response) throws ServletException,
    IOException
```

The doGet() method is called by the default implementation of the service() method in response to an HTTP GET request. This is the most commonly overridden "do" method because GET is the most common HTTP request. If an HTTP GET request is received and the doGet() method (as well as the service() method) is not overridden, the default implementation of this method will return an HTTP 400 "Bad Request" message.

Additionally, implementing the doGet() method provides automatic support for HTTP HEAD requests as long as the doHead() method is not overridden. "Automatic support" means that if the doGet() method is implemented, no other special coding is required to support HEAD requests. This is due to the fact that the default implementation of doHead() automatically calls the doGet() method and allows it to generate the proper HTTP header fields. Any output generated by doGet() other than header fields is discarded. Since all content generated by doGet() is ignored by the doHead() method, you may wish to check if a HEAD request was received and, in that case, bypass sending any body content (to conserve resources since all content is buffered). To illustrate, the following code will ensure that the request is a GET before sending body content to the client (see following Note for more information).

```
StringBuffer output = new StringBuffer("Body content...");
response.setContentLength(output.length());
```

```
if (request.getMethod().equals("GET"))
{
  out.println(output.toString());
}
```

NOTE: Be sure to remember that, even though content is not returned to the client in response to a HEAD request, the Content-Length header should be the same as if the request was a GET. Therefore, if you are setting the Content-Length header (as recommended), you will first need to calculate the length of the content body that would be returned if the request was a GET. A simple way to do this is to build the entire HTML output in a StringBuffer and set the Content-Length based on the length of the StringBuffer as shown here:

```
public void doGet(HttpServletRequest request,
  HttpServletResponse response) throws ServletException,
  IOException
{
  response.setContentType("text/html");

  PrintWriter out = response.getWriter();

  StringBuffer output = new StringBuffer();

  output.append("<HTML>\n");
  output.append("<HEAD><TITLE>Sample</TITLE></HEAD>\n");
  output.append("<BODY>\n");
  output.append("Content-length header included.\n");
  output.append("</BODY>\n");
  output.append("</HTML>");

  //always set all headers before sending output
  response.setContentLength(output.length());

  if (request.getMethod().equals("GET"))
  {
    out.print(output.toString());
  }

  out.close();
}
```

Like all of the "do" methods, the doGet() method is passed an object representation (or encapsulation) of the client's request and the server's response. Reading from the request object and customizing the response object is the primary function of a servlet. Listing 6.2 demonstrates a sample servlet that implements the doGet() method.

Listing 6.2   Sample servlet that implements the doGet() method.

```
import javax.servlet.http.*;
import javax.servlet.ServletException;
import java.io.PrintWriter;
import java.io.IOException;

public class GetServlet extends HttpServlet
{
  protected void doGet(HttpServletRequest request,
    HttpServletResponse response) throws ServletException,
    IOException
  {
    //set MIME type for HTTP header
    response.setContentType("text/plain");

    //get a handle to the output stream
    PrintWriter out = response.getWriter();

    out.println("Request handled by the doGet() method");

    out.close(); //always close the output stream
  }
}
```

The doGet() method in the sample servlet above is called in response to any HTTP GET request. The doGet() method is declared protected because it is not called from outside of the class. Remember that the server actually calls the servlet's service() method whenever a request is received. The default implementation of the service() method calls the doGet() method in response to a GET request. The sample servlet above sets the HTTP Content-Type header to text/plain and returns a message to the client.

doHead

```
protected void doHead(HttpServletRequest request,
  HttpServletResponse response) throws ServletException,
  IOException
```

The doHead() method is called in response to a HEAD request. Recall that a HEAD request is identical to a GET request except that only HTTP headers are returned—the body content is excluded. In other words, the HTTP headers returned by the server in response to a HEAD request are identical to those that would have been returned in response to a GET.

As discussed previously, the default implementation of doHead() simply calls the doGet() method and allows it to generate the proper HTTP header fields. Any body content generated by the doGet() method is discarded and only the header fields are returned to the client. Therefore, the doHead()

method need not be overridden in order to support HTTP HEAD requests (as long as the doGet() method is implemented). Nevertheless, if you choose, you may override this method and generate all HTTP headers yourself. However, since the headers returned by a HEAD request should exactly match those returned by a GET, it is recommended that the doGet() method be used to generate the headers in order to guarantee an exact match. Since implementing the doGet() method automatically supports HEAD requests, the doHead() method is typically not overridden.

doPost

```
protected void doPost(HttpServletRequest request,
    HttpServletResponse response) throws ServletException,
    IOException
```

The doPost() method is called whenever an HTTP POST request is received by the servlet. This method is commonly used to process information collected from an HTML form. The information entered by the user into an HTML form is encapsulated inside of an HttpServletRequest object and passed to the doPost() method (we will discuss the HttpServletRequest object in detail later in this chapter). If a POST request is received and the doPost() method is not implemented, an HTTP 400 "Bad Request" message is returned to the client.

Listing 6.3 uses both the doGet() and doPost() methods to create a functional servlet. The doGet() method is used to create a simple HTML form. When the user clicks the *Submit* button, the form data is posted to the servlet and handled by the doPost() method. In this case, the doPost() method simply constructs an HTML document that displays the data that was submitted and returns it to the client. When building a servlet to collect information from the client, utilizing the doGet() method to create an HTML form and subsequently handling the submission with the doPost() method is very common.

Listing 6.3   Sample servlet that implements the doGet() and doPost() methods.

```
import javax.servlet.http.*;
import javax.servlet.ServletException;
import java.io.PrintWriter;
import java.io.IOException;

public class PostServlet extends HttpServlet
{
  public void doGet(HttpServletRequest request,
    HttpServletResponse response) throws ServletException,
    IOException
  {
```

```
        //set MIME type for HTTP header
        response.setContentType("text/html");

        //get a handle to the output stream
        PrintWriter out = response.getWriter();

        out.println("<HTML><HEAD>");
        out.println("<TITLE>Sample POST Servlet</TITLE>");
        out.println("</HEAD>");
        out.println("<BODY>");
        out.println("<H1>GUEST BOOK</H1>");
        out.println("<P>Please enter your name and e-mail " +
          "address below:</P>");
        out.println("<FORM METHOD=\"POST\" ACTION=" +
          "\"http://localhost:8080/servlet/PostServlet\">");
        out.println("<P>Name: <INPUT TYPE=\"TEXT\" NAME=\"name\" " +
          "SIZE=\"20\"><BR>");
        out.println("E-mail: <INPUT TYPE=\"TEXT\" NAME=\"email\" " +
          "SIZE=\"30\"></P>");
        out.println("<INPUT TYPE=\"SUBMIT\" VALUE=\"Submit\">" +
          "<INPUT TYPE=\"RESET\" VALUE=\"Clear\">");
        out.println("</FORM></BODY></HTML>");

        out.close(); //always close the output stream
    }

    public void doPost(HttpServletRequest request,
      HttpServletResponse response) throws IOException
    {
        //set MIME type for HTTP header
        response.setContentType("text/html");

        //get data from request object
        String name = request.getParameter("name");
        String email = request.getParameter("email");

        //get a handle to the output stream
        PrintWriter out = response.getWriter();

        out.println("<HTML><HEAD>");
        out.println("<TITLE>Sample POST Servlet</TITLE>");
        out.println("</HEAD>");
        out.println("<BODY>");
        out.println("<H1>Thank You</H1>");
        out.println("<P>The following information was submitted:");
        out.println("<P>Name: " + name + "<BR>");
        out.println("E-Mail: " + email + "</P>");
        out.println("</BODY></HTML>");

        out.close(); //always close the output stream
    }
}
```

Listing 6.3 uses a doGet() method to respond to the first GET request issued by the browser. The doGet() method builds an HTTP form and returns it to the client. When the user submits the form, the doPost() method is called to handle the POST request. We can tell that this form generates a POST request by evaluating the <FORM> tag in the HTML document constructed in the doGet() method (FORM METHOD="POST"). Finally, using a method from the HttpServletRequest object discussed later in this chapter, the data input by the user is extracted from the request and added to the HTML document that is returned to the client. Again, at this point don't worry about the HttpServletRequest methods. These will be discussed in detail shortly.

doPut

```
protected void doPut(HttpServletRequest request,
    HttpServletResponse response) throws ServletException,
    IOException
```

The doPut() method is called in response to an HTTP PUT request. PUT requests are used to upload data from the client to the server. If a PUT request is received and the doPut() method is not implemented, an HTTP 400 "Bad Request" message is returned to the client. If doPut() is overridden, all HTTP content headers must be respected, including Content-Base, Content-Encoding, Content-Language, Content-Length, Content-Location, Content-

NOTE: Currently, the doPut() method is not often implemented. This is largely due to the fact that the only specification for HTML form-based file uploads uses the POST method rather than PUT (see RFC 1867). The primary difference between the POST and PUT methods is the manner in which they interpret the URL specified in the request. The POST method interprets the URL as the resource that will process the request's content. Alternatively, the PUT method interprets the URL as the name under which to store the request's contents on the server.

Since a true Internet standard for file uploads does not yet exist, many browser and server vendors have yet to support this functionality. However, it should be noted that Netscape Navigator version 3 and higher and Microsoft Internet Explorer version 4 and higher both support HTML form-based file uploads according to the RFC 1867 specification. As the HTTP 1.1 protocol (which formally defines the PUT method) becomes more prevalent, increasing numbers of browsers and servers will support the PUT method.

Table 6.3   Description of HTTP Content Headers

HTTP Header	Description
Content-Base	Indicates the base URL used to resolve relative URLs within a request (see RFC 1808). The Content-Base field must be an absolute URL. If Content-Base is not present, the base URL is constructed from the Content-Location (if it represents an absolute URL) or, secondly, the URL used to initiate the request.
Content-Encoding	Designates any additional encoding (other than that specified by Content-Type) that has been applied to the entity body, thus conveying the decoding mechanisms that must be employed in order to obtain the media type specified by the Content-Type header. Content-Encoding is commonly used with compressed files.
Content-Language	Indicates the natural language of which the entity body is composed.
Content-Length	Designates the size of the entity body. In response to a HEAD request, this field designates the size of the message body that would have been returned if the request had used GET.
Content-Location	Indicates the current location of the entity requested. Commonly used in conjunction with HTTP 301 "Moved Permanently" or HTTP 302 "Moved Temporarily" messages to specify the new location of the requested resource.
Content-MD5	Provides a type of checksum called a *message integrity check*. See RFC 1864 for more information.
Content-Range	Used if the server returns a partial response to the client's request. This header field designates the total size of the full entity body as well as where this response fits within the entire body.
Content-Type	Designates the MIME type of the entity body. In response to a HEAD request, if returns the MIME type of the entity body that would have been returned if the request had used GET.

MD5, Content-Range, and Content-Type. See Table 6.3 for a description of each of these HTTP content headers (see also RFC 2068). If the overridden method cannot honor all content header fields, it must return an HTTP 501 "Not Implemented" message and discard the request.

doDelete

```
protected void doDelete(HttpServletRequest request,
    HttpServletResponse response) throws ServletException,
    IOException
```

The doDelete() method is called in response to an HTTP DELETE request. The DELETE method allows a client to request that the server delete the resource specified in the request. If a DELETE request is received and the doDelete() method is not implemented, an HTTP 400 "Bad Request" message is returned to the client. It is a good idea to require some type of user authentication as well as store a backup copy of any resource removed from the server in response to a DELETE request. In addition, it is common for the doDelete() method to simply move a resource to an inaccessible location in response to a DELETE request rather than actually delete it permanently. This method is not typically overridden.

doTrace

```
protected void doTrace(HttpServletRequest request,
    HttpServletResponse response) throws ServletException,
    IOException
```

The doTrace() method is called in response to an HTTP TRACE request. A TRACE request is a diagnostic tool that allows the client to see exactly what its request looks like to the server. A TRACE request should contain no body content, only headers. When a TRACE request is received, the server packages the entire request inside the entity body of an HTTP 200 "OK" message with Content-Type of message/http. This message is returned to the client. In this manner, the client can ensure that the proper request is arriving at the server. This type of request is commonly used to diagnose transmission problems involving gateways and routers. The default implementation of the doTrace() method responds according to the HTTP/1.1 TRACE specification. That is, the client's entire request is returned within the entity body of an HTTP 200 "OK" message. There is typically no reason to override this method.

doOptions

```
protected void doOptions(HttpServletRequest request,
    HttpServletResponse response) throws ServletException,
    IOException
```

The doOptions() method is called in response to an HTTP OPTIONS request. An OPTIONS request is sent by the client to query the server for the supported protocol methods. The default implementation of this method automatically returns the HTTP options that are supported by the servlet. For instance, if a servlet implements the doGet() and doPost() methods, the server will return an HTTP ALLOWS header as follows:

```
ALLOWS: GET,HEAD,POST,TRACE,OPTIONS
```

The ALLOWS header informs the client of all HTTP methods that the server supports. It is not necessary to override the doOptions() method unless the servlet supports methods beyond those defined in HTTP/1.1. Thus, this method is rarely implemented.

getLastModified

```
protected long getLastModified(HttpServletRequest request)
```

The purpose of the getLastModified() method is to inform the client when a resource was last updated. This information is useful for caching information on the client. The client can determine if a cached page is out of date before downloading a new copy. This method is called by the server in response to a conditional GET request (to determine if a resource has been modified since the time specified in the request's If-Modified-Since header) or other cache control operations. If the resource has not changed since the time specified in the request's If-Modified-Since header, an HTTP 304 "Not Modified" response will be returned without any message body. At this point, the browser should load the page from cache.

Notice that the getLastModified() method returns a long. This number indicates the time the resource was last modified expressed as the number of milliseconds since midnight January 1, 1970 GMT. The default implementation of this method returns a negative number to convey that the method has not been properly implemented. The servlet developer must override this method to make it useful.

GenericServlet **Class**

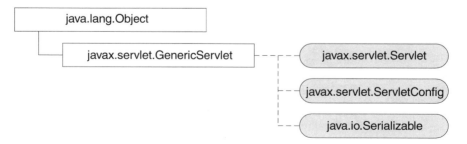

In addition to the methods described above, HttpServlet inherits basic servlet functionality by extending GenericServlet. Some of the commonly used methods inherited from GenericServlet are described here.

getInitParameter

```
public String getInitParameter(String name)
```

The getInitParameter() method returns a string containing the value of the specified initialization parameter. Initialization parameters can be established before a servlet is started. These values are normally read in the servlet's init() method and used to perform some type of initialization. In a later chapter we will discuss how initialization parameters are established on different servers (the process of setting initialization parameters is server dependent). If the specified parameter does not exist, null is returned.

The text that follows demonstrates how initialization parameters are defined using Sun's servlet runner. Servlet runner is a simple servlet engine that ships with the JSDK. It will be discussed in Chapter 8.

```
servlet.phonelist.code=PhoneListServlet
servlet.phonelist.initArgs=maxRows=100,\
    language=English,\
    verbose=true
```

This text is stored in a file called *servlet.properties*. The first line defines an alias, phonelist, for the servlet PhoneListServlet.class. The rest of the lines define initialization parameters that the server passes to the phone list servlet. The back-slashes ("\") serve as line continuation characters. The following code demonstrates how the initialization parameters are read by the servlet.

getInitParameter() is actually a convenience method. It retrieves initialization information from the ServletConfig object that is passed to the init() method. The ServletConfig interface is discussed in detail in Chapter 10. The getInitParameter() method provides a shortcut to the alternative method of getting initialization parameters—retrieving a reference to the ServletConfig object and calling its getInitParameter() method. The sample code that follows demonstrates the use of this method.

```
int maxRows;
String languageMode;
boolean verbose;

public void init(ServletConfig config) throws
    ServletException
{
    super.init(config);
    maxRows = Integer.parseInt(getInitParameter("maxRows"));
    languageMode = getInitParameter("language");
    verbose = getInitParameter("verbose").equals("true");
}
```

getInitParameterNames

```
public Enumeration getInitParameterNames()
```

The getInitParameterNames() method returns the names of all initialization parameters as an Enumeration of String objects. If no initialization parameters have been defined, an empty Enumeration is returned. Like getInitParameter() described in the previous section, this method is supplied in GenericServlet for convenience. It actually gets the parameter names from the ServletConfig object that was passed to the init() method. This method is often used in conjunction with getInitParameter() to retrieve the name and value of all initialization parameters. The sample code here shows how the names and values of the servlet's initialization parameters can be retrieved.

```
public void init(ServletConfig config) throws
  ServletException
{
  String name, value;

  super.init(config);

  Enumeration enum = getInitParameterNames();

  while (enum.hasMoreElements())
  {
    name = (String)enum.nextElement();
    value = (String)getInitParameter("name");
    System.out.println("Name: " + name + ", Value: " +
      value + "\n");
  }
}
```

The init() method shown previously extracts the initialization parameter names and values from the ServletConfig object and prints them to standard out.

getServletConfig

```
public ServletConfig getServletConfig()
```

The getServletConfig() method returns a ServletConfig object that contains servlet start-up configuration information. This information includes any initialization parameters and a ServletContext object. The getInitParameter(), getInitParameterNames(), and getServletContext() convenience methods described earlier are also implemented by the ServletConfig object. The ServletConfig and ServletContext objects are discussed in detail in Chapter 10.

getServletContext

```
public ServletContext getServletContext()
```

The getServletContext() method returns a ServletContext object that contains information regarding the server environment in which the servlet is running. This method is provided in the GenericServlet class for convenience. It actually gets ServletContext from the ServletConfig object that was passed to the servlet's init() method.

log

```
public void log(String msg)
public void log(String message, Throwable t)
```

The log() method writes the specified string along with the name of the servlet class file to the servlet log file. The name and location of this log file are server specific. This method is often used to log events for administrative or debugging purposes. The log() method that includes an exception (i.e., a Throwable object) also prints the stack trace to the log file.

ServletRequest Interface

javax.servlet.ServletRequest

ServletRequest is an interface that resides in the javax.servlet package. This interface is used to convey request information to a servlet. When a request is received, the servlet engine encapsulates vital request information in an object that implements the ServletRequest interface. This object is then passed to the servlet's service() method.

The ServletRequest interface is used by non-HTTP servers. HTTP servers encapsulate requests in objects that implement the HttpServletRequest interface (which extends ServletRequest). Some of the most commonly used methods of the ServletRequest object are described here.

getContentLength

```
public abstract int getContentLength()
```

The getContentLength() method returns an integer representing the total length of the request's data portion, or -1 if unknown. When using the HTTP protocol, this information can be useful when processing POST or PUT operations (file uploads).

Table 6.4 Common MIME Types

MIME Type	Description
text/plain	Plain ASCII text; contains no formatting tags
text/html	HTML formatted document
image/gif	GIF image
image/jpeg	JPEG image

getContentType

```
public abstract String getContentType()
```

The getContentType() method returns the MIME media type of the request's data portion, or null if the request contains only headers (no data). With this information the servlet can properly process or store the data portion of the request. To illustrate, Table 6.4 shows a few of the most common MIME types.

getInputStream

```
public abstract ServletInputStream getInputStream() throws
    IOException
```

The getInputStream() method returns an input stream in the form of a ServletInputStream object. The ServletInputStream class is discussed in Chapter 10. This input stream allows the servlet to read binary data from the body of the request (often used in conjunction with HTTP POST and PUT operations). For reading text information from the request, the getReader() method should be used.

getParameter

```
public abstract String getParameter(String name)
```

The getParameter() method returns the value of the specified parameter or null if the parameter does not exist. Note that this method returns only a single value. If a parameter might contain multiple values, use the getParameter-Values() method. getParameterValues() returns a String array containing all values of a specified parameter. getParameter() is actually a convenience method for when you know that a parameter contains only a single value. In the event that a parameter does contain multiple values, the value returned by getParameter() should be the same as the first value in the array returned by getParameterValues().

The sample code that follows demonstrates how to use getParameter().

```
public void service(HttpServletRequest request,
  HttpServletResponse response) throws ServletException,
  IOException
{
  String name;

  //set MIME type for HTTP header
  response.setContentType("text/plain");

  //get a handle to the output stream
  PrintWriter out = response.getWriter();

  //get the value of the name parameter
  name = request.getParameter("name");

  out.println("Hello, " + name); //send message to client

  out.close(); //always close the output stream
}
```

NOTE: There is an interesting side-note concerning the getParameter() method. This method was actually deprecated in Servlet API 1.1 in favor of the getParameterValues() method. It was deemed by Sun that since a parameter could contain multiple values, multiple values should always be received. However, obtaining a single value from the getParameterValues() method requires a line of code that looks like this:

```
name = request.getParameterValues("name")[0];
```

Not nearly as simple or convenient as the getParameter() alternative. Fortunately, due to strong developer feedback, getParameter() has become the first Java method ever to be removed from deprecation!

getParameterNames

```
public abstract Enumeration getParameterNames()
```

The getParameterNames() method returns the name of each name/value pair passed in the request. The names are returned as an Enumeration of String objects. If no parameters are passed in the request, this method returns an empty

Enumeration. The following sample code demonstrates this method. (Requires java.util.Enumeration to be imported.)

```
public void service(HttpServletRequest request,
  HttpServletResponse response) throws ServletException,
  IOException
{
  int numParams=0;

  //set MIME type for HTTP header
  response.setContentType("text/plain");

  //get a handle to the output stream
  PrintWriter out = response.getWriter();

  Enumeration enum = request.getParameterNames();

  if (!enum.hasMoreElements())
  {
    out.println("No parameters in this request");
  }
  else
  {
    while (enum.hasMoreElements())
    {
      numParams++;
      out.println("Parameter Name " + numParams + ": " +
        enum.nextElement());
    }
  }

  out.close(); //always close the output stream
}
```

If the code was invoked with this URL:

http://localhost:8080/servlet/ParmNameServlet?age=28&name=Dustin

the response would look like this:

```
Parameter Name 1: age
Parameter Name 2: name
```

getParameterValues

```
public abstract String[] getParameterValues(String name)
```

The getParameterValues() method returns the values of the specified parameter. The values are returned as an array of String objects or null if the parameter does not exist. Often, a parameter will have only a single value. In this case, the value of this parameter can be determined using the following code (or using the getParameter() method):

```
Name = request.getParameterValues("name")[0];
```

The following sample code demonstrates how to extract parameter names and values from a request. (Requires java.util.Enumeration to be imported.)

```
public void service(HttpServletRequest request,
  HttpServletResponse response) throws ServletException,
  IOException
{
  int numParams=0, loop=0;
  String name;
  String[] values;

  //set MIME type for HTTP header
  response.setContentType("text/plain");

  //get a handle to the output stream
  PrintWriter out = response.getWriter();

  Enumeration enum = request.getParameterNames();

  if (!enum.hasMoreElements())
  {
    out.println("No parameters in this request");
  }
  else
  {
    while (enum.hasMoreElements())
    {
      numParams++;
      name = (String)enum.nextElement();
      out.println("Parameter Name " + numParams + ": " +
        name);
      values = request.getParameterValues(name);
      loop = 0;
      while (loop < values.length)
      {
        out.println(" Value: " + values[loop]);
        loop++;
      }
    }
  }

  out.close(); //always close the output stream
}
```

If the previous code was invoked using the following URL:

*http://localhost:8080/servlet/ParamServlet?drive=floppy&drive=zip&ram=64
&input=keyboard&input=mouse&computer=pentium*

the output would look like this:

```
Parameter Name1: drive
 Value: floppy
 Value: zip
Parameter Name2: ram
 Value: 64
Parameter Name3: input
 Value: keyboard
 Value: mouse
Parameter Name4: computer
 Value: pentium
```

getProtocol

```
public abstract String getProtocol()
```

The getProtocol() method returns a String describing the protocol used by the servlet. The format of the protocol string looks like this:

```
<protocol>"/"<major version>"."<minor version>
```

This sample code demonstrates the use of the getProtocol() method.

```
public void service(HttpServletRequest request,
  HttpServletResponse response) throws ServletException,
  IOException
{
  //set MIME type for HTTP header
  response.setContentType("text/plain");

  //get a handle to the output stream
  PrintWriter out = response.getWriter();

  out.println(request.getProtocol());

  out.close(); //always close the output stream
}
```

The output from the service() method above looks like this:

```
HTTP/1.1
```

getReader

```
public abstract BufferedReader getReader() throws IOException
```

The getReader() method returns a BufferedReader for the purpose of reading text from the data portion of the request. The BufferedReader class translates character set encodings as required. This method is useful for protocols that include text data along with the protocol headers. For binary data, the `getInputStream()` method should be used.

getRemoteAddr

```
public abstract String getRemoteAddr()
```

The `getRemoteAddr()` method returns the IP address of the client that sent the request. Consider the following code:

```
public void service(HttpServletRequest request,
    HttpServletResponse response) throws ServletException,
    IOException
{
  //set MIME type for HTTP header
  response.setContentType("text/plain");

  //get a handle to the output stream
  PrintWriter out = response.getWriter();

  out.println(request.getRemoteAddr());

  out.close(); //always close the output stream
}
```

If a servlet containing the above `service()` method was invoked from the local machine, the output would look like this:

```
127.0.0.1
```

You may recognize this as the local loopback address (meaning that the computer is communicating with itself).

getRemoteHost

```
public abstract String getRemoteHost()
```

This method returns the client's fully qualified hostname. Consider the following code:

```
public void service(HttpServletRequest request,
    HttpServletResponse response) throws ServletException,
    IOException
{
  //set MIME type for HTTP header
  response.setContentType("text/plain");
```

```
                    //get a handle to the output stream
                    PrintWriter out = response.getWriter();

                    out.println(request.getRemoteHost());

                    out.close(); //always close the output stream
                }
```

If a servlet containing the above service() method was invoked from the local machine, the output would look like this:

```
localhost
```

Local host refers to a service running on the current machine.

getScheme

```
        public abstract String getScheme()
```

The getScheme() method returns the scheme (usually refers to the protocol) used by the request. For example, common schemes include "http," "https," "ftp," and "telnet." The URL requested by the client can be reconstructed by combining the scheme, hostname or IP address, port, request URL, and query string (request URL and query string are discussed in the "HttpServletRequest Interface" section). For more information about schemes, see RFC 1738.

getServerName

```
        public abstract String getServerName()
```

The getServerName() method returns the hostname of the server on which the servlet is running.

getServerPort

```
        public abstract int getServerPort()
```

The getServerPort() method returns an integer representing the port on which the client's request was received (i.e., the port on which the server is listening).

HttpServletRequest Interface

```
javax.servlet.ServletRequest
      javax.servlet.http.HttpServletRequest
```

HttpServletRequest is an interface that resides in the javax.servlet.http package. This interface extends ServletRequest and, therefore, supports all of its methods in addition to those presented below.

HttpServletRequest defines methods that describe an HTTP request. An object that implements the HttpServletRequest interface is passed to the servlet's service() method or any of the "do" methods. The request information encapsulated within this object includes information collected from the HTTP header such as the HTTP method (GET, POST, PUT, etc.), cookies, and authentication information. The name/value pairs passed by an HTML form or in the query string are also accessible via the HttpServletRequest object. The following descriptions and sample code illustrate many of the most common methods of the HttpServletRequest object.

getAuthType

```
public abstract String getAuthType()
```

The getAuthType() method returns a string describing the authentication scheme employed by the client. When a request for a protected resource is received by the server, it will usually respond with an HTTP 401 "Not Authorized" message. If authentication is required, the response will include a header like WWW-Authenticate: Basic in the response. This type of response is known as an *authentication challenge*. Most browsers will display a username and password dialog box when a challenge response is received. This allows the user to enter a name and password and resubmit the request with authentication information.

This new request will contain a header like Authorization: Basic that includes the username and password. If the authentication information is correct, the requested resource will be returned. Otherwise, an HTTP 401 "Not Authorized" message will be sent again. The HTTP headers described here indicate the use of the BASIC authentication scheme. The type of authentication scheme being employed by the client is returned by the getAuthType() method. If no authentication scheme is used, null is returned. See Chapter 3 for more information on HTTP authentication.

getCookies

```
public abstract Cookie[] getCookies()
```

This method returns the cookies from the request in the form of an array of Cookie objects. The Cookie object resides in the javax.servlet.http package. This is an extremely useful method that will be discussed in detail in a later chapter. For now, suffice it to say that a *cookie* is a mechanism whereby a server can send a small amount of data to a client which, in turn, sends this information back to the server with each request.

getDateHeader

```
public abstract long getDateHeader(String name)
```

The getDateHeader() method returns the date as reported in the request. Normally, the request's date field represents the date and time the request was sent. The date is returned as a long integer representing the number of milliseconds since midnight, January 1, 1970 GMT. A Java Date object can be created from the long integer returned by the getDateHeader(). The following sample code illustrates how this is done. The String parameter accepted by this method is the name of the date header sent by the client. It is necessary to know the name of this header beforehand. Usually, it is simply called "Date." A -1 is returned if the request does not contain the specified date header field. The following code requires java.util.Date to be imported.

```
public void service(HttpServletRequest request,
  HttpServletResponse response) throws ServletException,
  IOException
{
  long requestDate=0;
  Date date=null;

  //set MIME type for HTTP header
  response.setContentType("text/plain");

  //get a handle to the output stream
  PrintWriter out = response.getWriter();

  requestDate = request.getDateHeader("Date");
  if (requestDate == -1)
  {
    out.println("Date header not found");
  }
  else
  {
    try
    {
```

```
      date = new Date(requestDate);
    }
    catch (IllegalArgumentException e)
    {
      out.println("Invalid request date");
    }

    out.println("Request Date: " + date.toString());
  }

  out.close(); //always close the output stream
}
```

It may be rare that you need to know the date and time at which a request was sent. However, when it is needed, the getDateHeader() method provides a simple way to access this information.

getHeader

```
    public abstract String getHeader(String name)
```

The getHeader() method returns the value of the specified header or null if it does not exist (header name is not case-sensitive). This is an extremely useful method for retrieving the value of any HTTP header. For instance, there is a handy HTTP header called Referer that designates the page from which the user linked to the currently running servlet. This information can be useful if you require users to follow a specific link to get to a page rather than recall a bookmark or type in the URL manually. The following code demonstrates how the getHeader() method can be used to retrieve the page that jumped the user to our servlet.

```
    public void service(HttpServletRequest request,
      HttpServletResponse response) throws ServletException,
      IOException
    {
      //set MIME type for HTTP header
      response.setContentType("text/plain");

      //get a handle to the output stream
      PrintWriter out = response.getWriter();

      out.println(request.getHeader("Referer"));

      out.close(); //always close the output stream
    }
```

In a more advanced servlet, rather than just displaying the page that referred the user to our servlet, we might check the Referer value to make sure that the user arrived via our home page. In this way, we could prevent other sites from linking to our internal resources and, thus, bypassing our main page (which may contain advertisements or other information). Of course, the Referer header is only one example. Any HTTP header (or even nonstandard, custom headers in the HTTP request) can be retrieved with the getHeader() method.

getHeaderNames

```
public abstract Enumeration getHeaderNames()
```

The getHeaderNames() method returns an Enumeration of all headers in the HTTP request. The following sample code demonstrates how the names of the headers are extracted with getHeaderNames() and the header values are returned using the getHeader() method (requires java.util.Enumeration to be imported).

```
public void service(HttpServletRequest request,
   HttpServletResponse response) throws ServletException,
   IOException
{
   String headerName="";

   //set MIME type for HTTP header
   response.setContentType("text/plain");

   //get a handle to the output stream
   PrintWriter out = response.getWriter();

   Enumeration enum = request.getHeaderNames();

   while (enum.hasMoreElements())
   {
      headerName = (String)enum.nextElement();
      out.println(headerName + ": " +
         request.getHeader(headerName));
   }

   out.close(); //always close the output stream
}
```

Figure 6.2 shows the output from this program as rendered by a browser.

getIntHeader

```
public abstract int getIntHeader(String name)
```

The getIntHeader() method is identical to the getHeader() method except that it returns the value of the specified header as an integer (header name is

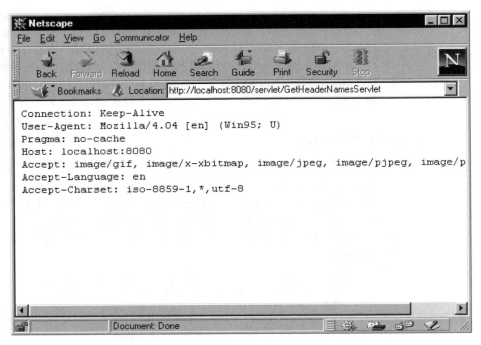

Figure 6.2 Output from the getHeaderNames() Sample Code

not case-sensitive). If the integer header field does not exist, a -1 is returned. If the value of the header field cannot be converted to an integer, a NumberFormatException is thrown.

getMethod

```
public abstract String getMethod()
```

The getMethod() method returns the HTTP method (e.g., GET, POST, PUT) used by the request. Though this method can be very useful, it is often not necessary. Rather, the servlet "do" methods (doGet, doPost, doPut) can be implemented. If the service() method is not overridden, its default functionality checks the method type of each request and calls the appropriate "do" method.

getPathInfo

```
public abstract String getPathInfo()
```

The getPathInfo() method returns any path information following the servlet path but prior to the query string. It returns null if there is no path information following the servlet path. For example, if a servlet called `GetPathServlet` is invoked using this URL:

http://localhost:8080/servlet/GetPathServlet/html/public?id=1234

the value returned by `getPathInfo()` is:

```
/html/public
```

getPathTranslated

```
public abstract String getPathTranslated()
```

The `getPathTranslated()` method returns the real path information (according to the file system or network) relative to the servlet path and prior to the query string. Returns `null` if there is no path information following the servlet path. For example, if a servlet called `GetPathServlet` is invoked using this URL:

http://localhost:8080/servlet/GetPathServlet/html/public?id=1234

the value returned by `getPathTranslated()` looks like this (on Windows):

```
.\html\public
```

getQueryString

```
public abstract String getQueryString()
```

The `getQueryString()` method returns the query string of a URL. For example, if a servlet called `GetQueryServlet` is invoked using this URL:

http://localhost:8080/servlet/GetQueryServlet?name=Dustin&age=28

the value returned by `getQueryString()` is:

```
name=Dustin&age=28
```

getRemoteUser

```
public abstract String getRemoteUser()
```

The `getRemoteUser()` method returns the username submitted by HTTP authentication. For instance, if a resource on the server is protected using basic authentication, the browser is required to send a valid username and password to access the resource. The `getRemoteUser()` method returns the value of the username passed by the browser. Whether or not the username and password are passed on every subsequent request is browser dependent. If no username information exists in a request, `getRemoteUser()` returns `null`.

getRequestURI

```
public abstract String getRequestURI()
```

The getRequestURI() method returns the URI of the request in the form of a URL. The URL, however, only includes path information. The value returned by getRequestURI() should be appended to the value returned by getServerName() and getServerPort() to create the full URL. For example, if a servlet called GetURIServlet is invoked using this URL:

http://localhost:8080/servlet/GetURIServlet/html/public

the value returned by getRequestURI() is:

```
/servlet/GetURIServlet/html/public
```

getServletPath

```
public abstract String getServletPath()
```

The getServletPath() method returns the path to the servlet being invoked. For example, if a servlet called GetPathServlet is invoked using this URL:

http://localhost:8080/servlet/GetPathServlet/html/public

the value returned by getServletPath() is:

```
/servlet/GetPathServlet
```

ServletResponse Interface

> javax.servlet.ServletResponse

ServletResponse is an interface that resides in the javax.servlet package. This interface provides an object representation of the server's response to a client's request. Whenever a servlet is invoked, the servlet engine passes an object that implements the ServletResponse interface to the servlet's service() method. The servlet can then use this object to respond to the client's request. The ServletResponse object provides methods to acquire a handle to the server's output stream and set response headers.

The ServletResponse interface is used by non-HTTP servers. HTTP servers encapsulate responses in objects that implement the HttpServlet-Response interface (which extends ServletResponse). Some of the most commonly used methods of the ServletResponse object are described on the following pages.

getOutputStream

```
public abstract ServletOutputStream getOutputStream() throws
    IOException
```

The getOutputStream() method returns an output stream over which binary data can be transmitted back to the client. Actually, this method returns a specialized type of output stream object called ServletOutputStream. This object is discussed in detail in Chapter 10. This method should be used to transmit binary information to the client. For text responses, the getWriter() method is provided. Listing 6.4 demonstrates the getOutputStream() method as well as the getWriter() method described next.

Listing 6.4 Example of the getOutputStream and getWriter methods.

```java
import javax.servlet.http.*;
import javax.servlet.*;
import java.io.*;
import java.util.Date;

/**
 * Get Output Servlet
 *
 * Returns the requested file. It uses a ServletOutputStream to
 * return binary (image) data and a PrintWriter to return text
 * information.
 *
 * @author Dustin R. Callaway
 * @version 1.0, 04/04/98
 */
public class GetOutputServlet extends HttpServlet
{
  public void service(HttpServletRequest request,
    HttpServletResponse response) throws ServletException,
    IOException
  {
    File fileIn=null;
    FileInputStream streamIn=null;

    try
    {
      //get requested file
      fileIn = new File(request.getPathTranslated());

      //open input stream
      streamIn = new FileInputStream(fileIn);
    }
    catch (FileNotFoundException e)
    {
```

```
      response.setContentType("text/plain");
      PrintWriter textOut = response.getWriter();
      textOut.println("File not found: " +
        request.getPathTranslated());
      textOut.close();
    }
    //create byte array
    byte[] data = new byte[(int) fileIn.length()];

    streamIn.read(data); //read file into byte array
    streamIn.close(); //close file input stream

    if (request.getRequestURI().indexOf(".gif") > 0 ||
      request.getRequestURI().indexOf(".jpg") > 0 ||
      request.getRequestURI().indexOf(".jpeg") > 0) //image
    {
      //get output stream
      ServletOutputStream imageOut = response.getOutputStream();

      if (request.getRequestURI().indexOf(".gif") > 0 ) //gif
      {
        response.setContentType("image/gif");
      }
      else //not gif, so assume jpeg
      {
        response.setContentType("image/jpeg");
      }

      //write binary data to output stream
      imageOut.write(data);

      imageOut.close(); //close output stream
    }
    else //non-image request
    {
      if (request.getRequestURI().indexOf(".htm") > 0) //HTML
      {
        response.setContentType("text/html");
      }
      else //non-HTML file
      {
        response.setContentType("text/plain");
      }

      //get a handle to the output stream
      PrintWriter textOut = response.getWriter();

      //write text data to output stream using PrintWriter
      textOut.println(new String(data));

      textOut.close(); //always close the output stream
    }
  }
}
```

getWriter

```
public abstract PrintWriter getWriter() throws IOException
```

The getWriter() method returns a PrintWriter object for the purpose of returning text information to the client. The PrintWriter object supports
Unicode for providing international language support. Listing 6.4 demonstrates
the getWriter() method. For binary data transmission, the getOutputStream()
method should be used.

setContentLength

```
public abstract void setContentLength(int len)
```

The setContentLength() method sets the value of the Content-Length HTTP
header in the response. The Content-Length header allows the client to determine when all data has been received. Though it is not always mandatory to set
a content length, it is a good practice to include it whenever the content length
is known.

setContentType

```
public abstract void setContentType(String type)
```

The setContentType() method sets the Content-Type HTTP header in the response. This header defines the format of the information returned in the data
portion of the response and allows the client to properly process the information. This method should be called only once. The content type cannot be
changed once it has been set. If the setContentType() method is called a second time with a different MIME type, a java.lang.IllegalStateException is
thrown. See Table 6.4 earlier in this chapter for examples of a few common
MIME types.

HttpServletResponse Interface

HttpServletResponse is an interface that resides in the javax.servlet.http
package. This interface extends ServletResponse and, therefore, supports all of
its methods in addition to those presented here.

HttpServletResponse provides an object representation of the server's response to a client's request. Whenever an HTTP servlet is invoked, the servlet engine passes an object that implements the HttpServletResponse interface to the servlet's service() method. The servlet can then use this object to respond to the client's request. The HttpServletResponse object provides methods to add cookies to the response, set response headers, send redirect instructions, and more. The following descriptions and sample code illustrate many of the most common methods of the HttpServletResponse object.

addCookie

```
public abstract void addCookie(Cookie cookie)
```

The addCookie() method adds a cookie to the HTTP response. The Cookie object resides in the javax.servlet.http package. This is an extremely useful method that will be discussed in detail in Chapter 13. As described previously, a *cookie* is a mechanism whereby a server can send a small amount of data to a client which, in turn, sends this information back to the server with every request.

Cookies are transmitted within the HTTP header. They are very useful for setting user preferences and managing state on the Web. For instance, if a user logs into a protected site, the server may send the client a cookie containing a valid username and password or, more commonly, a unique *session ID* (usually a very large number or sequence of alphanumeric characters). The session ID that is transmitted back to the server inside of every client request allows the server to verify that the request came from the same client that successfully logged into the site. In this manner security can be maintained and a user can be successfully "tracked" throughout a site. More information about cookies and state management on the Web will be provided in later chapters.

containsHeader

```
public abstract boolean containsHeader(String name)
```

The containsHeader() method determines whether a specified header is contained in the response. If the header field exists in the response message, true is returned; otherwise false is returned.

Table 6.5 Common Status Codes Defined in `HttpServletResponse`

Status Code	Description
SC_BAD_GATEWAY	The server received an invalid response from an upstream server while acting as a proxy or gateway.
SC_BAD_REQUEST	The client's request used invalid syntax.
SC_CONFLICT	There was a conflict preventing access to the requested resource.
SC_FORBIDDEN	The request was received and understood but the server refuses to fulfill it.
SC_GATEWAY_TIMEOUT	While serving as a proxy or gateway, the server did not receive a response from an upstream server within the timeout period.
SC_GONE	The resource is no longer available.
SC_HTTP_VERSION_NOT_ SUPPORTED	The HTTP version used by the client is not supported by the server.
SC_INTERNAL_SERVER_ ERROR	An unspecified error occurred on the server that prevented it from servicing the request.

sendError

```
public abstract void sendError(int sc) throws IOException
public abstract void sendError(int sc, String msg) throws
    IOException
```

The `sendError()` methods return an error message to the client according to the specified status code. The `HttpServletResponse` object defines many status codes. These status codes are exposed as `static` constants. Just a few of the many status codes defined by `HttpServletResponse` are listed in Table 6.5.

The first `sendError()` method accepts only an integer that specifies the HTTP status code to return to the client. The second `sendError()` method accepts an integer and a `String`. The integer represents the HTTP status code and the string should be a descriptive message about the error. The status code is part of the HTTP header but the descriptive message is contained in the message content and comprises the body of an HTML page returned to the client. If the status code was previously set by the `setStatus()` method (described shortly), it is reset to the error code specified in the call to `sendError()`. The following sample code illustrates the use of the `sendError()` method.

```
public void service(HttpServletRequest request,
  HttpServletResponse response) throws ServletException,
  IOException
{
  response.sendError(response.SC_GONE,
    "Resource no longer available.");
}
```

The response from the servlet that implements this simple service() method
looks like this:

```
HTTP/1.1 410 Gone
Server: ServletRunner/1.0
Content-Type: text/html
Content-Length: 119
Date: Sun, 05 Apr 1998 21:16:50 GMT

<html><head><title>410 Gone</title></head>
<h1>410 Gone</h1><body>
Resource no longer available.<p>
</body></html>
```

Notice how the string passed to the sendError() method is placed in the body
of the HTML page returned to the client.

sendRedirect

```
public abstract void sendRedirect(String location) throws
    IOException
```

The sendRedirect() method sends a temporary redirect message to the client
according to the specified location. The location parameter must be an absolute
URL; relative URLs are not permitted. On receiving the redirect response,
the browser should immediately request the resource from the new location.
The sample code that follows demonstrates the sendRedirect() method.

```
public void service(HttpServletRequest request,
  HttpServletResponse response) throws ServletException,
  IOException
{
  response.sendRedirect("http://www.sourcestream.com/");
}
```

The servlet that runs the above service() method sends the following HTTP
redirect response to the client.

```
HTTP/1.1 302 Moved Temporarily
Server: ServletRunner/1.0
Content-Type: text/html
Location: http://www.sourcestream.com/
```

```
Content-Length: 161
Date: Tue, 07 Apr 1998 02:26:09 GMT

<head><title>Document moved</title></head>
<body><h1>Document moved</h1>
This document has moved <a
href="http://www.sourcestream.com/">here</a>.<p>
</body>
```

The HTTP status code 302 "Moved Temporarily" instructs the browser to redirect to the URL specified in the Location header. HTTP redirects are discussed in more detail in Chapter 12.

setDateHeader

```
public abstract void setDateHeader(String name, long date)
```

The setDateHeader() method adds a new header to the response. The name parameter sets the name of the header and the date parameter sets the date. The date is specified using the number of milliseconds since the epoch (midnight, January 1, 1970 GMT). The following sample code demonstrates the use of this method.

```
public void service(HttpServletRequest request,
  HttpServletResponse response) throws ServletException,
  IOException
{
  response.setContentType("text/plain");

  response.setDateHeader("MyDate", 1234567890);

  PrintWriter out = response.getWriter();

  out.println("This response includes the MyDate header.");

  out.close();
}
```

The HTTP response sent by the servlet that implements the preceding service() method looks like this:

```
HTTP/1.1 200 OK
Server: ServletRunner/1.0
Content-Type: text/plain
MyDate: Thu, 15 Jan 1970 06:56:07 GMT
Date: Tue, 07 Apr 1998 02:45:44 GMT

This response includes the MyDate header.
```

The new date header, called MyDate, is visible above the server's standard Date header.

NOTE: The Date header field that is automatically included in the HTTP response by the HTTP server cannot be overridden with the setDateHeader() method. For instance, the following line will not change the Date header and will be effectively ignored by the output (it will generate no additional header field).

```
response.setDateHeader("Date", 1234567890);
```

setHeader

```
public abstract void setHeader(String name, String value)
```

The setHeader() method is similar to the setDateHeader() method except that the value of the header is comprised of a String rather than a date. The name parameter sets the name of the header and the value parameter specifies a String value. The following sample code sets the Cache-Control HTTP header to instruct the browser that the response should not be cached.

```
public void service(HttpServletRequest request,
  HttpServletResponse response) throws ServletException,
  IOException
{
  response.setContentType("text/plain");

  response.setHeader("Cache-Control", "no-cache");

  PrintWriter out = response.getWriter();

  out.println("This response should not be cached.");

  out.close();
}
```

The HTTP response produced by the preceding service() method looks like this:

```
HTTP/1.1 200 OK
Server: ServletRunner/1.0
Content-Type: text/plain
Cache-Control: no-cache
Date: Tue, 07 Apr 1998 03:21:09 GMT

This response should not be cached.
```

An HTTP/1.1-compliant browser or proxy server reads the Cache-Control header for instructions on how to cache the page. In this case, the browser or proxy server is instructed not to cache this page but to fetch it again from the server the next time it is requested. HTTP/1.0 uses the Pragma: no-cache header to convey the same "do not cache" instructions. The counterpart to the setHeader() method is the getHeader() method of HttpServletRequest which can be used to read headers passed to the servlet.

NOTE: If a header field is set a second time, the original value is replaced. For example, consider the following two lines of code embedded within a common service() or doGet() method.

```
response.setHeader("MyHeader", "test");
response.setHeader("MyHeader", "test2");
```

The HTTP header returned to the client would look something like this:

```
HTTP/1.0 200 OK
Server: servletrunner/2.0
Content-Type: text/plain
MyHeader: test2
Date: Sat, 31 Oct 1998 20:54:32 GMT
```

Notice that the MyHeader field was initially set to the value of "test." However, by calling the setHeader() method a second time, the initial value was replaced with "test2." When using the setHeader() method, header field values are not cumulative.

setIntHeader

```
public abstract void setIntHeader(String name, int value)
```

The setIntHeader() method is identical to the setHeader() method except that the header value is comprised of an integer rather than a String. The name parameter sets the name of the header and the value parameter sets the integer value of the header. The counterpart to the setIntHeader() method is the getIntHeader() method of HttpServletRequest which can be used to read integer headers passed to the servlet.

setStatus

```
public abstract void setStatus(int sc)
public abstract void setStatus(int sc, String sm)
```

The setStatus() methods are very similar to the sendError() methods. They set the HTTP status code to be included in the response. The first setStatus() method accepts only an integer that specifies the HTTP status code to return to the client. The second setStatus() method accepts an integer and a String. The integer represents the HTTP status code and the String should be a short description of the status code. This description replaces the description that normally accompanies an HTTP status code. For instance, HTTP status code 200 is normally accompanied with the description "OK" and HTTP status code 404 is usually accompanied by the message "Not Found." The status code and description are both part of the HTTP header. This sample code illustrates the use of this method.

```
public void service(HttpServletRequest request,
  HttpServletResponse response) throws ServletException,
  IOException
{
  response.setStatus(200, "Success");

  response.setContentType("text/plain");

  PrintWriter out = response.getWriter();

  out.println("Request serviced successfully.");

  out.close();
}
```

The preceding service() method returns the HTTP response shown here:

```
HTTP/1.1 200 Success
Server: ServletRunner/1.0
Content-Type: text/plain
Date: Tue, 07 Apr 1998 04:04:16 GMT

Request serviced successfully.
```

Notice that the OK that usually accompanies an HTTP status code 200 has been replaced with Success.

Summary

This chapter has introduced you to some of the most commonly used classes and interfaces in the Servlet API. Most likely, you will use many of these objects in every servlet you develop. In the next chapter, we will build a functional servlet from scratch.

Chapter Highlights

- `HttpServlet` class—Most HTTP servlets extend this class. `HttpServlet` defines methods that are called by the server whenever a servlet request is received. `HttpServlet` extends `GenericServlet`.

- `GenericServlet` class—Most non-HTTP servlets extend this class. `GenericServlet` defines the `service()` method that is called by the server whenever a servlet request is received.

- `ServletRequest` interface—For non-HTTP servlets, the information sent in the client request is encapsulated in a `ServletRequest` object. This object is passed to the servlet's `service()` method.

- `HttpServletRequest` interface—For HTTP servlets, the information sent in the client request is encapsulated in an `HttpServletRequest` object. This object is passed to the servlet's `service()` method (which may, in turn, pass it to the `doGet()`, `doPost()`, or `doPut()` method).

- `ServletResponse` interface—For non-HTTP servlets, the methods necessary to customize a response are contained in a `ServletResponse` object. This object is passed to the servlet's `service()` method.

- `HttpServletResponse` interface—For HTTP servlets, the methods necessary to customize a response are contained in an `HttpServlet-Response` object. This object is passed to the servlet's `service()` method (which may, in turn, pass it to the `doGet()`, `doPost()`, or `doPut()` method).

CHAPTER 7

Writing Your First Servlet

In this chapter, we will construct a fully functional Bulletin Board servlet from scratch. This servlet will allow users to view posted comments and append thoughts of their own. For the sake of simplicity, the bulletins will be stored in text files rather than a database. Adding database connectivity is an exercise left to the reader (see Chapter 16 for information about database connectivity). In the following chapters, we will explore how to test and debug your first servlet.

Servlet Requirements

As is critical with any project, we will begin with a brief analysis and design phase. For starters, let's take a look at the requirements for the servlet that we are going to build. The functionality of the Bulletin Board servlet can be described in the following five requirements.

1. The bulletins for each topic should be stored in a separate text file. A simple append operation can be used to add bulletins to the text file. No update, delete, or sorting operation is required. (A second phase of this project might allow the administrator to update, edit, and delete bulletins.)

2. The servlet should retrieve the location of the text files described in requirement 1 from an initialization parameter set on the server. In this way, the location of these files can be easily changed without recompiling the servlet.

3. The servlet must read a list of bulletin board topics from a properties file. In this manner, the administrator can dynamically add and remove topics by altering the properties file and reloading the servlet. (Again, a second

phase of this project might add an administrative screen to allow the topics list to be reloaded without reloading the servlet.)

4. After selecting a topic of interest, the user should be able to view the bulletins relating to that topic or append their own. In addition, a large text area must be provided for typing bulletins that span several lines.

5. Every page must have a link back to the main page. In addition, on returning to the main page, the user's previously selected bulletin board topic should remain selected.

Now that we know the requirements, let's take a look at a few screen shots. A visual mock-up is often the best way to quickly convey an application's functionality.

Main Page

The main page of the Bulletin Board servlet allows the user to select a topic of interest from a drop-down list. Our main page looks like the one shown in Figure 7.1.

The drop-down list is populated with bulletin board topics read from a properties file. The *VIEW BULLETINS* button allows the user to view all bulletins for the selected bulletin board. The *POST BULLETIN* button displays an HTML form that allows users to add their own comments to the selected bulletin board.

Let's take a look at the code that generates this screen. First, the servlet must retrieve the directory where the bulletins are stored from an initialization parameter. This operation is performed in the servlet's `init()` method.

```
//instance variables
String filePath; //stores root path for bulletin files

/**
 * init method is called when servlet is first loaded. It
 * reads from an initialization parameter the directory where
 * the bulletin files are stored.
 */
public void init(ServletConfig config) throws ServletException
{
  super.init(config); //pass ServletConfig to parent

  //get path to support files
  filePath = config.getInitParameter("FilePath");
  if (filePath == null)
  {
    //default directory if no FilePath init parameter exists
    filePath = "/";
  }
}
```

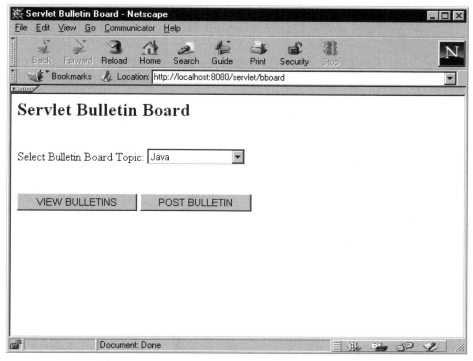

Figure 7.1 Bulletin Board Main Page

The `ServletConfig` object's `getInitParameter()` method is used to retrieve the value of the initialization parameter. Notice how the directory variable, `filePath`, is declared as an instance variable outside of any method. In this way, all requests serviced by this servlet will have access to its value. Since the value of `filePath` is set in the `init()` method and does not change, the use of an instance variable is safe in this case. As we will see Chapter 11, storing volatile information in a class or instance variable is not thread safe and can lead to errors and inconsistent results. Many of these errors are subtle and very difficult to debug.

The first line of the servlet's `init()` method passes the `ServletConfig` object to the parent class. All servlets should implement a `getServletConfig()` method that returns the `ServletConfig` object. Fortunately, the `Generic-Servlet` class (which `HttpServlet` extends) provides an implementation of `getServletConfig()`. Therefore, if you would rather not write a `getServlet-Config()` method yourself, always pass the `ServletConfig` object to the parent and the default implementation provided by `GenericServlet` will be used. The next line retrieves the initialization parameter `FilePath` from the server environment and assigns it to the `filePath` variable. If the `FilePath` initialization parameter was not set, the directory is set to "/" (root) by default.

Now let's take a look at the next piece of functionality required to load the main page. The servlet must read a properties file in order to populate the drop-down list of topics and generate the HTML to render the page. The following code is located in the servlet's doGet() method. Recall that the doGet() method is invoked in response to any HTTP GET request.

```
/**
 * doGet method is called in response to any GET request.
 * Returns an HTML form that allows the user to select a
 * bulletin board topic and choose to view bulletins or post
 * a new one.
 */
public void doGet(HttpServletRequest request,
    HttpServletResponse response) throws IOException
{
    //MIME type to return is HTML
    response.setContentType("text/html");

    //get a handle to the output stream
    PrintWriter out = response.getWriter();

    FileInputStream fileTopics=null;

    try
    {
        //open input stream to topics.properties file
        fileTopics = new FileInputStream(filePath +
            "topics.properties");

        Properties propTopics = new Properties();
        propTopics.load(fileTopics); //load properties object

        //create enumeration from properties object
        Enumeration enumTopics = propTopics.propertyNames();

        //create HTML form to allow user to select a topic
        out.println("<HTML>");
        out.println("<HEAD>");
        out.println("<TITLE>Servlet Bulletin Board</TITLE>");
        out.println("</HEAD>");
        out.println("<BODY>");
        out.println("<H2>Servlet Bulletin Board</H2>");
        out.println("<BR><FORM METHOD=\"POST\">");
        out.println("Select Bulletin Board Topic: ");
        out.println("<SELECT NAME=\"TOPICS\">");

        String topic; //stores description of current topic

        //iterate through all topics in topics.properties file
        while (enumTopics.hasMoreElements())
        {
```

```
        //set topic variable to current topic in enumeration
        topic = (String)enumTopics.nextElement();

        //add each topic from properties file to drop-down list
        if (propTopics.getProperty(topic).equals(
          request.getParameter("curTopic")))
        {
          //if user has selected a topic, keep it selected
          out.println("<OPTION SELECTED>" +
            propTopics.getProperty(topic) + "</OPTION>");
        }
        else
        {
          //not the selected topic, just add to drop-down list
          out.println("<OPTION>" +
            propTopics.getProperty(topic) + "</OPTION>");
        }
      }

      out.println("</SELECT><BR><BR><BR>");
      out.println("<INPUT TYPE=\"SUBMIT\" NAME=\"VIEW\" "+
        "VALUE=\"VIEW BULLETINS\"> ");
      out.println("<INPUT TYPE=\"SUBMIT\" NAME=\"POST\" "+
        "VALUE=\"POST BULLETIN\">");
      out.println("</FORM>");
      out.println("</BODY></HTML>");
    }
    catch (Exception e)
    {
      //send stack trace back to client
      sendErrorToClient(out, e);
    }
    finally
    {
      try
      {
        //close file input stream
        fileTopics.close();
      }
      catch (Exception e) {}
      try
      {
        //close output stream
        out.close();
      }
      catch (Exception e) {}
    }
  }
```

We will now dissect the doGet() method shown previously and evaluate its parts.

```
//MIME type to return is HTML
response.setContentType("text/html");

//get a handle to the output stream
PrintWriter out = response.getWriter();

FileInputStream fileTopics=null;
```

This code is fairly straightforward. We begin the method by setting the content type of our response to HTML. The code then proceeds to get a handle to the output stream. Since we will be returning only ASCII text, a `PrintWriter` object is used. Lastly, a `FileInputStream` variable is declared.

The `FileInputStream` variable is declared outside of the `try/catch` block because it is closed in the `finally` block. If it had been declared inside of the `try/catch`, it would have been out of scope within the `finally` block, resulting in a compile error.

```
try
{
  //open input stream to topics.properties file
  fileTopics = new FileInputStream(filePath +
    "topics.properties");

  Properties propTopics = new Properties();
  propTopics.load(fileTopics); //load properties object

  //create enumeration from properties object
  Enumeration enumTopics = propTopics.propertyNames();
```

The preceding code represents the beginning of our `try` block. The first line following the `try` statement creates a `FileInputStream` to the *topics.properties* file located in the `filePath` directory (`filePath` is read from an initialization parameter). Before running the servlet, be sure to create this file and place it in the `filePath` directory. The contents of the *topics.properties* file used in this example are:

```
Topic1=World Wide Web
Topic2=Internet
Topic3=Java
```

Next, a new `Properties` object is instantiated and, using the `FileInput-Stream` we just created, is loaded with the bulletin board topics. Finally, an `Enumeration` of the property names (or keys) is created. These property names, in conjunction with the `Properties` object's `getProperty()` method, are used to extract the bulletin board topics from the properties file.

```
//create HTML form to allow user to select a topic
out.println("<HTML>");
out.println("<HEAD>");
```

```
out.println("<TITLE>Servlet Bulletin Board</TITLE>");
out.println("</HEAD>");
out.println("<BODY>");
out.println("<H2>Servlet Bulletin Board</H2>");
out.println("<BR><FORM METHOD=\"POST\">");
```

These lines of code begin sending HTML to the client. Notice that an HTML form is created in order to send the user's selection back to the server.

```
out.println("<SELECT NAME=\"TOPICS\">");

String topic; //stores description of current topic

//iterate through all topics in topics.properties file
while (enumTopics.hasMoreElements())
{
  //set topic variable to current topic in enumeration
  topic = (String)enumTopics.nextElement();

  //add each topic from properties file to drop-down list
  if (propTopics.getProperty(topic).equals(
    request.getParameter("curTopic")))
  {
    //if user has selected a topic, keep it selected
    out.println("<OPTION SELECTED>" +
      propTopics.getProperty(topic) + "</OPTION>");
  }
  else
  {
    //not the selected topic, just add to drop-down list
    out.println("<OPTION>" +
      propTopics.getProperty(topic) + "</OPTION>");
  }
}

out.println("</SELECT><BR><BR><BR>");
```

The preceding code creates and populates the drop-down list of bulletin board topics. The bulletin board topic selected by the user on the main page is retrieved using the `getParameter()` method of the `HttpServletRequest` object. Since we know that the `curTopic` parameter consists of a single value, it is safe to use the `getParameter()` method rather than `getParameterValues()`.

When returning to the main page, the `if/else` statement in the preceding code is used to maintain the user's topic selection. As we will see shortly, this is accomplished by passing the currently selected topic from page to page and finally passing it back to the main page in the query string of the *Return to Main Page* hyperlink.

```
    out.println("<INPUT TYPE=\"SUBMIT\" NAME=\"VIEW\" " +
      "VALUE=\"VIEW BULLETINS\"> ");
    out.println("<INPUT TYPE=\"SUBMIT\" NAME=\"POST\" " +
      "VALUE=\"POST BULLETIN\">");
    out.println("</FORM>");
    out.println("</BODY></HTML>");
  }
```

The preceding lines complete the HTML document that is returned to the client. Two SUBMIT buttons are added to the HTML form to allow the user to select whether to view or add bulletins. When either of these buttons are clicked, the form values are transmitted to the server as name/value pairs. These name/value pairs allow the servlet to determine which bulletin board topic was selected by the user and which SUBMIT button was pressed. It is possible to determine the button that was pressed by checking the named parameters passed to the server using the getParameter() method. For example, if the *VIEW BULLETINS* button is pressed, a parameter named VIEW will be passed to the server. On the other hand, if the *POST BULLETIN* button is pressed, a parameter called POST is passed to the server.

```
    catch (Exception e)
    {
      //send stack trace back to client
      sendErrorToClient(out, e);
    }
    finally
    {
      try
      {
        //close file input stream
        fileTopics.close();
      }
      catch (Exception e) {}
      try
      {
        //close output stream
        out.close();
      }
      catch (Exception e) {}
    }
  }
```

The preceding code completes the doGet() method by catching all exceptions and closing the FileInputStream and PrintWriter streams. If an exception is thrown, the sendErrorToClient() method is called, which returns a simple error message to the client. A second phase of the Bulletin Board servlet project might add more robust exception handling.

NOTE: Closing the client output stream (e.g., a `PrintWriter` or `Servlet-OutputStream` object) does not necessarily close the underlying socket connection. However, the server may choose to close the connection to the client when the output stream is closed by the servlet.

View Bulletins Page

The View Bulletins page displays bulletins for the selected topic. This page is displayed in response to the user clicking the *VIEW BULLETINS* button on the main page. Our View Bulletins page is shown in Figure 7.2.

The View Bulletins screen displays all the bulletins for the selected topic in oldest-to-newest order. A link is also provided to return the user to the main page. Later we will see that a query string is appended to the *Return to Main*

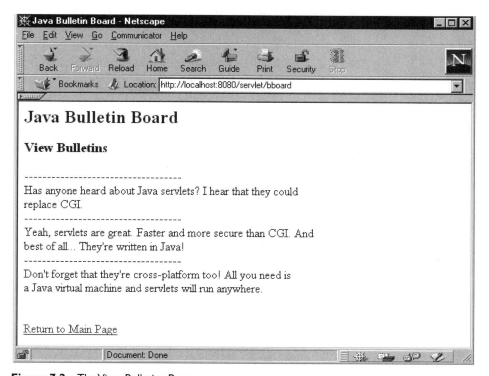

Figure 7.2 The View Bulletins Page

Page link, indicating the currently selected bulletin board topic. In this way, the current topic will remain selected when the main page is displayed.

The code that implements the functionality of the View Bulletins screen is split between the doPost() method and the viewBulletins() method. Remember that the doPost() method is called in response to an HTTP POST request. In this case, the doPost() method is called when the user clicks the *VIEW BULLETINS* button on the main page. However, this is not the only action that invokes the doPost() method. The doPost() method is also called when the user clicks the *POST BULLETIN* button on the main page and the *STORE BULLETIN* button on the Post Bulletin page (which we'll talk about shortly). Let's start by examining the following doPost() method.

```java
/**
 * doPost method is called in response to any POST request.
 * This method determines if it was called in response to the
 * user selecting to view bulletins, post a bulletin, or
 * save a bulletin and responds accordingly.
 */
public void doPost(HttpServletRequest request,
  HttpServletResponse response)
{
  String currentTopic=""; //user's currently selected topic

  PrintWriter out=null;

  //get bulletin board topic selected from drop-down list
  currentTopic = request.getParameter("TOPICS");
  //get the name of file containing bulletins for this topic
  String file = filePath + currentTopic + ".txt";
  //get path to servlet for use in hyperlinks
  String servletPath = request.getServletPath();

  response.setContentType("text/html"); //html output

  try
  {
    out = response.getWriter(); //get handle to output stream

    out.println("<HTML>");
    out.println("<HEAD><TITLE>" + currentTopic +
      " Bulletin Board</TITLE></HEAD>");
    out.println("<BODY>");

    //View Bulletins
    if (request.getParameter("VIEW") != null)
    {
      showBulletins(out, currentTopic, file);
    }
    //Post a bulletin
    else if (request.getParameter("POST") != null)
```

```
        {
          //allows user to enter bulletin and submit it
          postBulletin(out, currentTopic);
        }
        //Save bulletin
        else
        {
          //saves the bulletin to file
          saveBulletin(out, currentTopic, file, request);
        }

        //create hyperlink to return to main page
        out.println("<BR><BR><A HREF=\"" + servletPath +
          "?curTopic=" + java.net.URLEncoder.encode(currentTopic)+
          "\">Return to Main Page</A>");

        out.println("</BODY></HTML>");
      }
      catch (Exception e)
      {
        //send stack trace back to client
        sendErrorToClient(out, e);
      }
    }
```

We will now dissect the doPost() method and evaluate its parts.

```
      String currentTopic=""; //user's currently selected topic

      PrintWriter out=null;

      //get bulletin board topic selected from drop-down list
      currentTopic = request.getParameter("TOPICS");
      //get the name of file containing bulletins for this topic
      String file = filePath + currentTopic + ".txt";
      //get path to servlet for use in hyperlinks
      String servletPath = request.getServletPath();

      response.setContentType("text/html"); //html output
```

Initially, a String variable, currentTopic, is declared in order to store the user's currently selected bulletin board topic. This value is passed to the View Bulletins page from the main page via an HTML form variable called TOPICS. The value of the currently selected topic is assigned to currentTopic using the getParameter() method of the HttpServletRequest object. A PrintWriter variable is declared to store a handle to the output stream back to the client.

Next, a String variable, file, is declared and assigned the value of the full path and filename of the text file that stores the bulletins for the currently selected topic. The getServletPath() method is then used to store the full path of the servlet's directory in a String variable called servletPath. As we will see a little later, this variable is used to provide a hyperlink back to the main page. Lastly, the setContentType() method of the HttpServletResponse object is used to indicate that the response returned to the client will be in HTML format.

```
try
{
   out = response.getWriter(); //get handle to output stream

   out.println("<HTML>");
   out.println("<HEAD><TITLE>" + currentTopic +
     " Bulletin Board</TITLE></HEAD>");
   out.println("<BODY>");
```

This code marks the beginning of the try block. The getWriter() method of the HttpServletResponse object is used to assign the output stream to the PrintWriter variable out that was declared earlier. This output stream is used to transmit HTML back to the client.

```
//View Bulletins
if (request.getParameter("VIEW") != null)
{
   showBulletins(out, currentTopic, file);
}
//Post a bulletin
else if (request.getParameter("POST") != null)
{
   //allows user to enter bulletin and submit it
   postBulletin(out, currentTopic);
}
//Save bulletin
else
{
   //saves the bulletin to file
   saveBulletin(out, currentTopic, file, request);
}
```

The if/else block is used to determine which action prompted the doPost() method to be called. By discovering which SUBMIT button's name/value pair was passed to the servlet, it can be determined which button was clicked. For example, if the *VIEW BULLETINS* button on the main page is clicked by the user, a parameter named VIEW will be passed to the servlet (see the HTML form generated for the main page).

On the other hand, if the user clicks the *POST BULLETIN* button on the main page, a parameter named POST will be passed to the servlet. The showBulletins(), postBulletin(), or saveBulletin() method will be called in response to the user clicking the *VIEW BULLETINS, POST BULLETIN,* or *STORE BULLETIN* button, respectively.

```
      //create hyperlink to return to main page
      out.println("<BR><BR><A HREF=\"" + servletPath +
        "?curTopic=" + java.net.URLEncoder.encode(currentTopic)+
        "\">Return to Main Page</A>");

      out.println("</BODY></HTML>");
    }
    catch (Exception e)
    {
      //send stack trace back to client
      sendErrorToClient(out, e);
    }
  }
```

The first line of the preceding code constructs the hyperlink that allows the user to return to the main page. Notice that a query string named curTopic is passed in the URL. This query string allows the main page to "remember" which topic was selected for the current user. The next line of code closes the HTML document. Finally, the catch block catches all exceptions and calls the sendErrorToClient() method to return an error message to the client.

The showBulletins() method reads bulletins from disk and returns them to the client. If a text file does not exist for the selected bulletin board topic, the user is notified that that topic currently contains no bulletins. To complete our review of the View Bulletins page, let's look at the following code, which comprises the showBulletins() method.

```
/**
 * showBulletins method reads bulletins from disk and sends
 * them to the client. If file does not exist, client is
 * informed that the selected topic contains no bulletins.
 *
 * @param out Client output stream
 * @param currentTopic User's currently selected topic
 * @param file File containing bulletins for selected topic
 */
private void showBulletins(PrintWriter out,
  String currentTopic, String file)
{
  FileReader fr=null;
  BufferedReader br=null;

  try
  {
    File fileTopic = new File(file); //get handle to file
    if (fileTopic.exists()) //file exists, display it
    {
      fr = new FileReader(file);
      br = new BufferedReader(fr); //get file input stream
```

```
        out.println("<H2>" + currentTopic +
          " Bulletin Board</H2>");
        out.println("<H3>View Bulletins</H3>");

        String line = br.readLine();
        //iterate through each line of bulletin board file
        while (line != null)
        {
          //send bulletins to client
          out.println(line + "<BR>\n");
          line = br.readLine();
        }
      }
      else //file doesn't exist, display no bulletins message
      {
        out.println("This topic currently contains no " +
          "bulletins.");
      }
    }
    catch (Exception e)
    {
      //send stack trace back to client
      sendErrorToClient(out, e);
    }
    finally
    {
      try
      {
        br.close(); //close buffered reader
      }
      catch (Exception e) {}
      try
      {
        fr.close(); //close file reader
      }
      catch (Exception e) {}
    }
  }
```

We will now break the showBulletins() method into pieces and examine
its parts, starting with the definition for the showBulletins() method.

```
  private void showBulletins(PrintWriter out,
    String currentTopic, String file)
  {
    FileReader fr=null;
    BufferedReader br=null;
```

This method accepts a PrintWriter object and two String parameters.
The PrintWriter object, out, gives the method a handle to the output stream.
The String parameter, currentTopic, indicates which bulletin board topic
was selected by the user and allows the method to display the bulletins that

correspond to the selected topic. The second `String` parameter, `file`, indicates the full file system path to the text file that stores the bulletins for the currently selected topic. Finally, the first two lines of code simply declare a `FileReader` and a `BufferedReader` variable that will be used to read the bulletins from disk.

```
try
{
  File fileTopic = new File(file); //get handle to file
  if (fileTopic.exists()) //file exists, display it
  {
    fr = new FileReader(file);
    br = new BufferedReader(fr); //get file input stream

    out.println("<H2>" + currentTopic +
      " Bulletin Board</H2>");
    out.println("<H3>View Bulletins</H3>");

    String line = br.readLine();
    //iterate through each line of bulletin board file
    while (line != null)
    {
      //send bulletins to client
      out.println(line + "<BR>\n");
      line = br.readLine();
    }
  }
  else //file doesn't exist, display no bulletins message
  {
    out.println("This topic currently contains no " +
      "bulletins.");
  }
}
```

The preceding code comprises the entire `try` block of the `showBulletins()` method. Initially, a `File` object is created. This object points to the text file that stores the bulletins for the currently selected topic. The `if` statement uses the `File` object's `exists()` method to check for the existence of the file. If the file does not exist, a message conveying that no bulletins currently exist for the selected topic is returned to the client. Otherwise, a `BufferedReader` is chained to a `FileReader` object in order to read the file from disk. The `BufferedReader` provides a simple `readLine()` method for reading one line at a time from a file. The remaining lines of code generate the HTML required to render the View Bulletins page. A `while` loop is used to read all lines of text from the file.

```
catch (Exception e)
{
  //send stack trace back to client
  sendErrorToClient(out, e);
}
```

```
        finally
        {
          try
          {
            br.close(); //close buffered reader
          }
          catch (Exception e) {}
          try
          {
            fr.close(); //close file reader
          }
          catch (Exception e) {}
        }
      }
```

The catch and finally blocks complete the showBulletins() method. All exceptions are caught in this method. In the event an exception is thrown, the sendErrorToClient() method is called to return an error message to the client. The finally block is critical in order to close the open input streams, FileReader and BufferedReader, even in the case of an exception. A finally block should always be used to release open resources.

This concludes the code necessary to implement the View Bulletins functionality. Keep in mind that the doPost() method presented above is also used by the Post Bulletin and Save Bulletin pages.

Post Bulletin Page

The Post Bulletin page displays an HTML form that allows the user to type a new bulletin into an HTML <TEXTAREA> field. This page is displayed in response to the user clicking the *POST BULLETIN* button on the main page. The Post Bulletin page is shown in Figure 7.3.

In addition to providing the user with the means to enter a new bulletin, the Post Bulletin page provides a link back to the main page. Similar to the View Bulletins page, the link to the main page contains a query string indicating the user's currently selected bulletin board topic.

The first portion of code used by the Post Bulletin page is found in the doPost() method. When the *POST BULLETIN* button on the main page is clicked, the browser submits an HTTP POST request to the server which, in turn, calls the doPost() method. As we saw under the "View Bulletins Page" section, the button that was pressed by the user can be determined by checking for the existence of each button's name/value pair. The following if/then block from the doPost() method demonstrates how this is accomplished.

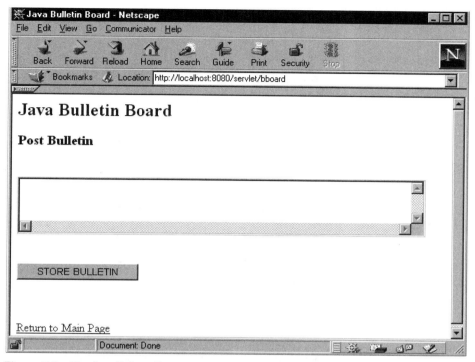

Figure 7.3 The Post Bulletin Page

```
//View Bulletins
if (request.getParameter("VIEW") != null)
{
  showBulletins(out, currentTopic, file);
}
//Post a bulletin
else if (request.getParameter("POST") != null)
{
  //allows user to enter bulletin and submit it
  postBulletin(out, currentTopic);
}
//Save bulletin
else
{
  //saves the bulletin to file
  saveBulletin(out, currentTopic, file, request);
}
```

As we can see from the preceding code, the postBulletin() method is called when the *POST BULLETIN* button is clicked. Let's now examine the postBulletin() method.

```
/**
 * postBulletin method generates the HTML form that allows
 * the user to enter a new bulletin.
 *
 * @param out Client output stream
 * @param currentTopic User's currently selected topic
 */
private void postBulletin(PrintWriter out,
    String currentTopic)
{
    //create HTML form to allow user to enter new bulletin
    out.println("<H2>" + currentTopic + " Bulletin Board</H2>");
    out.println("<H3>Post Bulletin</H3><BR>");
    out.println("<FORM METHOD=\"POST\">");
    out.println("<P><TEXTAREA NAME=\"BULLETIN\" " +
        "COLS=\"65\" ROWS=\"3\"></TEXTAREA>");
    out.println("<BR><BR><BR><INPUT TYPE=\"SUBMIT\" " +
        "NAME=\"STORE\" VALUE=\"STORE BULLETIN\"><BR>");
    //include current topic in hidden field
    out.println("<INPUT TYPE=\"""HIDDEN\" " +
        "NAME=\"TOPICS\" VALUE=\"" + currentTopic + "\">");
    out.println("</FORM>");
}
```

The `postBulletin()` method serves the simple purpose of generating the HTML form that allows a user to enter a new bulletin. Notice that a hidden field is created to store the name of the currently selected bulletin board topic. By passing this topic from screen to screen, the main page is able to maintain the user's selected topic. In addition, passing the selected bulletin board topic in this POST request allows the `saveBulletin()` method to determine the topic to which the user's bulletin should be appended.

Save Bulletin Page

The Save Bulletin page displays a confirmation message to users stating that their bulletin has been saved successfully. It also provides a link back to the main page. This page is displayed in response to the user clicking the *STORE BULLETIN* button on the Post Bulletin page. Our Save Bulletin page looks like Figure 7.4.

As in the View Bulletins and Post Bulletin pages, the first method called in response to clicking the *STORE BULLETIN* button is the `doPost()` method. Again, the following `if/then` block determines which button was pressed and calls the appropriate method.

```
//View Bulletins
if (request.getParameter("VIEW") != null)
```

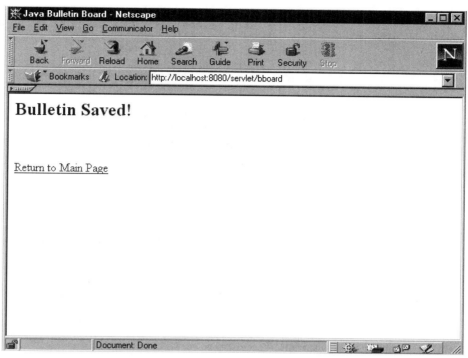

Figure 7.4 The Save Bulletin Page

```
{
    showBulletins(out, currentTopic, file);
}
//Post a bulletin
else if (request.getParameter("POST") != null)
{
    //allows user to enter bulletin and submit it
    postBulletin(out, currentTopic);
}
//Save bulletin
else
{
    //saves the bulletin to file
    saveBulletin(out, currentTopic, file, request);
}
```

The preceding code shows that in the event that neither the *VIEW BUL-LETINS* button nor the *POST BULLETIN* button was pressed, the *STORE BULLETIN* button is assumed. This can be safely assumed because our application contains only three SUBMIT buttons. Therefore, the doPost() method calls the saveBulletin() method in response to the user clicking the *STORE BULLETIN* button. Let's examine this method.

```
/**
 * saveBulletin method saves the bulletin to disk.
 *
 * @param out Client output stream
 * @param currentTopic User's currently selected topic
 * @param file File containing bulletins for selected topic
 * @param request HttpServletRequest object
 */
private void saveBulletin(PrintWriter out,
   String currentTopic, String file,
   HttpServletRequest request)
{
   FileWriter fw=null;
   PrintWriter pw=null;

   try
   {
     fw = new FileWriter(file, true);
     pw = new PrintWriter(fw); //get output stream to file
     //print separator
     pw.println("---------------------------------");
     //print user's bulletin to file
     pw.println(request.getParameter("BULLETIN"));

     out.println("<H2>Bulletin Saved!</H2>");
   }
   catch (Exception e)
   {
     //send stack trace back to client
     sendErrorToClient(out, e);
   }
   finally
   {
     try
     {
       pw.flush(); //flush output stream to file
       pw.close(); //close print writer
     }
     catch (Exception e) {}
     try
     {
       fw.close(); //close file writer
     }
     catch (Exception e) {}
   }
}
```

The purpose of the saveBulletin() method is to write the user's bulletin to disk. Let's break this method into three pieces and examine each individually.

```
private void saveBulletin(PrintWriter out,
   String currentTopic, String file,
   HttpServletRequest request)
```

```
{
  FileWriter fw=null;
  PrintWriter pw=null;
```

From the method definition we can see that saveBulletin() accepts four parameters—a PrintWriter object, two String objects, and an Http-ServletRequest object.

Similar to the previous methods we have explored, the PrintWriter object provides an output stream to the client and the first String parameter, currentTopic, indicates the currently selected bulletin board topic. The second String parameter, file, was declared in the doPost() method and represents the full path and filename of the currently selected topic. Lastly, the HttpServletRequest parameter, request, is the object representation of the client's HTTP request. The getParameter() method of the HttpServletRequest is used in this method to retrieve the user's bulletin from the HTML form data. Next, a FileWriter and PrintWriter object is declared. Both are assigned values within the try block and closed in the finally block.

```
try
{
  fw = new FileWriter(file, true);
  pw = new PrintWriter(fw); //get output stream to file
  //print separator
  pw.println("-----------------------------------");
  //print user's bulletin to file
  pw.println(request.getParameter("BULLETIN"));

  out.println("<H2>Bulletin Saved!</H2>");
}
```

The code here represents the entire try block of the saveBulletin() method. The first line opens a FileWriter output stream to the file specified by the file parameter. The true parameter indicates that data written to the file should be appended to the end. A PrintWriter object is then chained to the FileWriter object. The PrintWriter object is used because it implements a simple println() method. Next, a line of hyphens (to provide separation between bulletins) and the user's bulletin is written to the file. Finally, a confirmation message is returned to the client.

```
catch (Exception e)
{
  //send stack trace back to client
  sendErrorToClient(out, e);
}
finally
{
  try
```

```
      {
        pw.flush(); //flush output stream to file
        pw.close(); //close print writer
      }
      catch (Exception e) {}
      try
      {
        fw.close(); //close file writer
      }
      catch (Exception e) {}
    }
  }
```

The end of the saveBulletin() method consists of the catch and finally blocks. As we have seen before, all exceptions are caught by the catch block in which the sendErrorToClient() method is called. The finally block is used to close the FileWriter and PrintWriter output streams.

The sendErrorToClient() method that follows returns the stack trace the client and prints it to standard out. Returning the stack trace to the client is useful during debugging but should be replaced with a less cryptic error message in a production environment. The sendErrorToClient() method converts the stack trace generated by the error to a String and includes it in an HTML document that is returned to the client. The stack trace is also printed to standard out.

```
/**
 * Return stack trace to client. Useful for debugging.
 *
 * @param out Client output stream
 * @param e Exception
 */
private void sendErrorToClient(PrintWriter out, Exception e)
{
  //send stack trace back to client and to standard out
  StringWriter stringError = new StringWriter();
  PrintWriter printError = new PrintWriter(stringError);
  e.printStackTrace(printError);
  String stackTrace = stringError.toString();

  //send error message to client
  out.println("<HTML><TITLE>Error</TITLE><BODY>");
  out.println("<H1>Servlet Error</H1><H4>Error</H4>" + e +
    "<H4>Stack Trace</H4>" + stackTrace + "</BODY></HTML>");

  //print stack trace to standard out
  System.out.println("Servlet Error: " + stackTrace);
}
```

Complete Bulletin Board Servlet

Now that we have learned the purpose behind each line of code in the Bulletin Board servlet, take this opportunity to examine the entire servlet code shown in Listing 7.1. You should be familiar with every object and method used in the Bulletin Board servlet. If necessary, turn back a few pages to review.

Listing 7.1   The complete Bulletin Board servlet source code.

```java
import javax.servlet.*;
import javax.servlet.http.*;
import java.io.*;
import java.util.*;

/**
 * The BulletinBoard servlet allows the user to view posted
 * bulletins as well as add their own bulletins to be viewed by
 * others.
 *
 * @author Dustin R. Callaway
 * @version 1.0, 04/29/98
 */
public class BulletinBoard extends HttpServlet
{
  //instance variables
  String filePath; //stores root path for bulletin files

  /**
   * init method is called when servlet is first loaded. It
   * reads from an initialization parameter the directory where
   * the bulletin files are stored.
   */
  public void init(ServletConfig config) throws ServletException
  {
    super.init(config); //pass ServletConfig to parent

    //get path to support files
    filePath = config.getInitParameter("FilePath");
    if (filePath == null)
    {
      //default directory if no FilePath init parameter exists
      filePath = "/";
    }
  }


  /**
   * doGet method is called in response to any GET request.
   * Returns an HTML form that allows the user to select a
   * bulletin board topic and choose to view bulletins or post
   * a new one.
   */
```

```
public void doGet(HttpServletRequest request,
  HttpServletResponse response) throws IOException
{
  //MIME type to return is HTML
  response.setContentType("text/html");

  //get a handle to the output stream
  PrintWriter out = response.getWriter();

  FileInputStream fileTopics=null;

  try
  {
    //open input stream to topics.properties file
    fileTopics = new FileInputStream(filePath +
      "topics.properties");

    Properties propTopics = new Properties();
    propTopics.load(fileTopics); //load properties object

    //create enumeration from properties object
    Enumeration enumTopics = propTopics.propertyNames();

    //create HTML form to allow user to select a topic
    out.println("<HTML>");
    out.println("<HEAD>");
    out.println("<TITLE>Servlet Bulletin Board</TITLE>");
    out.println("</HEAD>");
    out.println("<BODY>");
    out.println("<H2>Servlet Bulletin Board</H2>");
    out.println("<BR><FORM METHOD=\"POST\">");
    out.println("Select Bulletin Board Topic: ");
    out.println("<SELECT NAME=\"TOPICS\">");

    String topic; //stores description of current topic

    //iterate through all topics in topics.properties file
    while (enumTopics.hasMoreElements())
    {
      //set topic variable to current topic in enumeration
      topic = (String)enumTopics.nextElement();

      //add each topic from properties file to drop-down list
      if (propTopics.getProperty(topic).equals(
        request.getParameter("curTopic")))
      {
        //if user has selected a topic, keep it selected
        out.println("<OPTION SELECTED>" +
          propTopics.getProperty(topic) + "</OPTION>");
      }
      else
      {
        //not the selected topic, just add to drop-down list
```

```java
          out.println("<OPTION>" +
            propTopics.getProperty(topic) + "</OPTION>");
        }
      }

      out.println("</SELECT><BR><BR><BR>");
      out.println("<INPUT TYPE=\"SUBMIT\" NAME=\"VIEW\" " +
        "VALUE=\"VIEW BULLETINS\"> ");
      out.println("<INPUT TYPE=\"SUBMIT\" NAME=\"POST\" " +
        "VALUE=\"POST BULLETIN\">");
      out.println("</FORM>");
      out.println("</BODY></HTML>");
    }
    catch (Exception e)
    {
      //send stack trace back to client
      sendErrorToClient(out, e);
    }
    finally
    {
      try
      {
        //close file input stream
        fileTopics.close();
      }
      catch (Exception e) {}
      try
      {
        //close output stream
        out.close();
      }
      catch (Exception e) {}
    }
  }


  /**
   * doPost method is called in response to any POST request.
   * This method determines if it was called in response to the
   * user selecting to view bulletins, post a bulletin, or
   * save a bulletin and responds accordingly.
   */
  public void doPost(HttpServletRequest request,
    HttpServletResponse response)
  {
    String currentTopic=""; //user's currently selected topic

    PrintWriter out=null;

    //get bulletin board topic selected from drop-down list
    currentTopic = request.getParameter("TOPICS");
    //get the name of file containing bulletins for this topic
    String file = filePath + currentTopic + ".txt";
```

```java
            //get path to servlet for use in hyperlinks
            String servletPath = request.getServletPath();

            response.setContentType("text/html"); //html output

            try
            {
              out = response.getWriter(); //get handle to output stream

              out.println("<HTML>");
              out.println("<HEAD><TITLE>" + currentTopic +
                " Bulletin Board</TITLE></HEAD>");
              out.println("<BODY>");

              //View Bulletins
              if (request.getParameter("VIEW") != null)
              {
                showBulletins(out, currentTopic, file);
              }
              //Post a bulletin
              else if (request.getParameter("POST") != null)
              {
                //allows user to enter bulletin and submit it
                postBulletin(out, currentTopic);
              }
              //Save bulletin
              else
              {
                //saves the bulletin to file
                saveBulletin(out, currentTopic, file, request);
              }

              //create hyperlink to return to main page
              out.println("<BR><BR><A HREF=\"" + servletPath +
                "?curTopic=" + java.net.URLEncoder.encode(currentTopic)+
                "\">Return to Main Page</A>");

              out.println("</BODY></HTML>");
            }
            catch (Exception e)
            {
              //send stack trace back to client
              sendErrorToClient(out, e);
            }
          }


          /**
           * showBulletins method reads bulletins from disk and sends
           * them to the client. If file does not exist, client is
           * informed that the selected topic contains no bulletins.
           *
```

```
   * @param out Client output stream
   * @param currentTopic User's currently selected topic
   * @param file File containing bulletins for selected topic
   */
  private void showBulletins(PrintWriter out,
    String currentTopic, String file)
  {
    FileReader fr=null;
    BufferedReader br=null;

    try
    {
      File fileTopic = new File(file); //get handle to file
      if (fileTopic.exists()) //file exists, display it
      {
        fr = new FileReader(file);
        br = new BufferedReader(fr); //get file input stream

        out.println("<H2>" + currentTopic +
          " Bulletin Board</H2>");
        out.println("<H3>View Bulletins</H3>");

        String line = br.readLine();
        //iterate through each line of bulletin board file
        while (line != null)
        {
          //send bulletins to client
          out.println(line + "<BR>\n");
          line = br.readLine();
        }
      }
      else //file doesn't exist, display no bulletins message
      {
        out.println("This topic currently contains no " +
          "bulletins.");
      }
    }
    catch (Exception e)
    {
      //send stack trace back to client
      sendErrorToClient(out, e);
    }
    finally
    {
      try
      {
        br.close(); //close buffered reader
      }
      catch (Exception e) {}
      try
      {
        fr.close(); //close file reader
      }
```

```
      catch (Exception e) {}
    }
}


/**
 * postBulletin method generates the HTML form that allows
 * the user to enter a new bulletin.
 *
 * @param out Client output stream
 * @param currentTopic User's currently selected topic
 */
private void postBulletin(PrintWriter out,
  String currentTopic)
{
  //create HTML form to allow user to enter new bulletin
  out.println("<H2>" + currentTopic + " Bulletin Board</H2>");
  out.println("<H3>Post Bulletin</H3><BR>");
  out.println("<FORM METHOD=\"POST\">");
  out.println("<P><TEXTAREA NAME=\"BULLETIN\" " +
    "COLS=\"65\" ROWS=\"3\"></TEXTAREA>");
  out.println("<BR><BR><BR><INPUT TYPE=\"SUBMIT\" " +
    "NAME=\"STORE\" VALUE=\"STORE BULLETIN\"><BR>");
  //include current topic in hidden field
  out.println("<INPUT TYPE=\"HIDDEN\" " +
    "NAME=\"TOPICS\" VALUE=\"" + currentTopic + "\">");
  out.println("</FORM>");
}


/**
 * saveBulletin method saves the bulletin to disk.
 *
 * @param out Client output stream
 * @param currentTopic User's currently selected topic
 * @param file File containing bulletins for selected topic
 * @param request HttpServletRequest object
 */
private void saveBulletin(PrintWriter out,
  String currentTopic, String file,
  HttpServletRequest request)
{
  FileWriter fw=null;
  PrintWriter pw=null;

  try
  {
    fw = new FileWriter(file, true);
    pw = new PrintWriter(fw); //get output stream to file
    //print separator
    pw.println("----------------------------------");
    //print user's bulletin to file
```

```
            pw.println(request.getParameter("BULLETIN"));

            out.println("<H2>Bulletin Saved!</H2>");
        }
        catch (Exception e)
        {
            //send stack trace back to client
            sendErrorToClient(out, e);
        }
        finally
        {
            try
            {
                pw.flush(); //flush output stream to file
                pw.close(); //close print writer
            }
            catch (Exception e) {}
            try
            {
                fw.close(); //close file writer
            }
            catch (Exception e) {}
        }
    }

    /**
     * Return stack trace to client. Useful for debugging.
     *
     * @param out Client output stream
     * @param e Exception
     */
    private void sendErrorToClient(PrintWriter out, Exception e)
    {
        //send stack trace back to client and to standard out
        StringWriter stringError = new StringWriter();
        PrintWriter printError = new PrintWriter(stringError);
        e.printStackTrace(printError);
        String stackTrace = stringError.toString();

        //send error message to client
        out.println("<HTML><TITLE>Error</TITLE><BODY>");
        out.println("<H1>Servlet Error</H1><H4>Error</H4>" + e +
            "<H4>Stack Trace</H4>" + stackTrace + "</BODY></HTML>");

        //print stack trace to standard out
        System.out.println("Servlet Error: " + stackTrace);
    }
}
```

That's it. If you have followed along on your own, you have now written your first fully functional servlet. So what now? The next chapter will teach you how to run your servlet.

Summary

This chapter presented a full, although slightly simplified, servlet development process. We started by defining the requirements for the project at hand. Next, we designed the interface (HTML screens) and implemented functionality using the Servlet API object library. Of course, the servlet development process can differ greatly depending on the scope and complexity of the project. For instance, a more complex project may require extensive data modeling and object-oriented analysis/design before the first line of code is written. Fortunately, it is easy to alter the servlet development process presented here to conform to practically any development methodology. In Chapter 9, we will examine several options for testing and debugging servlets.

Chapter Highlights

- This chapter demonstrated a fully functional Bulletin Board servlet that allows users to view posted comments and append thoughts of their own.
- The development process began with a brief analysis and design phase that flushed out the servlet requirements. These requirements included support for multiple topics and the ability to easily view and create bulletins.
- A visual mock-up was created to convey the required functionality, and code was added to make the screens functional.

CHAPTER 8

Running Servlets

This chapter examines several options for running servlets. Fortunately, due to the cross-server and cross-platform nature of servlets, there is a wide array of options when it comes to running servlets. Although several methods are presented, keep in mind that this chapter discusses only a few of the many options available for running servlets. This chapter covers the following products:

- JSDK Servlet Runner
- Java™ Web Server
- JRun™
- ServletExec™

JSDK Servlet Runner

There are many ways in which to run a servlet. Some Web servers, such as Sun's Java Web Server and Netscape Enterprise Server, natively support servlets. Other popular HTTP servers, such as Microsoft Internet Information Server and Apache Web Server, support servlets through third-party add-ons like JRun from Live Software or ServletExec from New Atlanta Communications. Sun's Java Servlet Development Kit (JSDK) also adds servlet support to these servers but is provided only as a reference implementation and is not recommended

NOTE: A servlet engine for the Apache Web Server, known as *JServ,* is currently under development. As of this writing, JServ is in a beta stage. More information about JServ is available at *http://java.apache.org.* In addition, servlet support can be added to the Apache Web Server using either the JRun or ServletExec servlet engines presented later in this chapter.

for production environments. However, despite the many options available to the servlet developer, the simplest way to run a servlet is to use the JSDK Servlet Runner utility. This section tells us more about Sun's Servlet Runner.

Launching Servlet Runner

Servlet Runner is an executable that resides in the JSDK's */bin* directory and is launched from the command line. This utility contains no GUI interface. Servlet Runner can be launched by simply executing the *servletrunner* program as demonstrated here:

```
C:\JSDK2.0\bin>servletrunner

servletrunner starting with settings:
  port = 8080
  backlog = 50
  max handlers = 100
  timeout = 5000
  servlet dir = .\examples
  document dir = .\examples
  servlet propfile = .\examples\servlet.properties
```

In this case, Servlet Runner will start using the default settings. However, all the settings shown above can be altered using command-line arguments documented in Table 8.1. Also, please note that as of publication time, JSDK 2.1 has not yet been released. Therefore, the material presented here is subject to change in regard to this new version (in particular, names and locations of files may change).

NOTE: It should be noted that the *servletrunner* executable does very little work. In fact, the program's primary function is to simply accept command-line arguments and pass them to the main() method of the sun.servlet.http.HttpServer class. It is this HttpServer class that actually performs the work of running servlets. The sun.servlet package is included in the JSDK. In the next chapter, we demonstrate how to use the HttpServer class to debug servlets within a Java IDE.

Servlet Aliases and Initialization Parameters

Servlet aliases and initialization parameters are defined in a text file called *servlet.properties*. By default, Servlet Runner looks for this file in the servlets directory (specified by the -d switch). However, its location can be changed using the -s command-line switch. Let's examine the *servlet.properties* file for the Bulletin Board servlet. The contents of this file are as follows:

```
servlet.bboard.code=BulletinBoard
servlet.bboard.initArgs=FilePath=c:\jsdk2.0\servlets\
```

Table 8.1   Servlet Runner Command-Line Switches

Switch	Argument	Default Value
-p	Designates the port on which Servlet Runner will be listening for client connections	8080
-b	Number of backlog connections that will be accepted	50
-m	Maximum number of connection handlers	100
-t	Connection timeout value in milliseconds	5000
-d	Directory where servlets are located	`<current_directory>/examples`
-r	Document root directory	`<current_directory>/examples`
-s	Location of *servlet.properties* file	`<servlet_directory>/examples/` `    servlet.properties`
-v	Produce verbose output	off

The first line of this file defines an alias called *bboard* for the `BulletinBoard.class` servlet. Notice that when declaring an alias, the `.class` extension of the Java class file is not included. The next line of the *servlet.properties* file sets an initialization parameter that will be passed to the `init()` method of the Bulletin Board servlet. All initialization parameters assume the following form:

```
<Parameter_Name>=<Parameter_Value>
```

In this case, the parameter name is `FilePath` and the parameter value is `c:\jsdk2.0\servlets\`. Multiple initialization parameters can be defined as illustrated here:

```
servlet.phonelist.code=PhoneListServlet
servlet.phonelist.initArgs=maxRows=100,\
   language=English,\
   encrypted=true
```

Again, the first line defines an alias, `phonelist`, for the servlet `PhoneListServlet.class`. The rest of the lines define initialization parameters that the server passes to the `phonelist` servlet. The back-slashes ("\") serve as line continuation characters. Placing each initialization parameter on a separate line is not required but it does improve readability.

Invoking Servlets

With Servlet Runner, servlets are invoked using the following URL format:

```
/servlet/<servlet_name>[/<path_info>][?<query_string>]
```

The information displayed in brackets is optional. The `<servlet_name>` portion of the URL represents the servlet alias or servlet class name. It is possible to invoke a servlet by using either the alias defined in the *servlet.properties* file or the name of the servlet's class file. For example, the Bulletin Board servlet can be invoked using either of the following URLs:

http://localhost:8080/servlet/bboard
http://localhost:8080/servlet/BulletinBoard

The `<path_info>` part of the URL allows additional path information to be specified. This information can be extracted using the `getPathInfo()` method of the `HttpServletRequest` object. The `getPathInfo()` method returns any path information following the servlet path but prior to the query string. For example, if a servlet called `GetPathServlet` is invoked using this URL:

http://localhost:8080/servlet/GetPathServlet/html/public

the value returned by `getPathInfo()` is:

```
/html/public
```

Finally, the `<query_string>` portion of the URL allows additional information to be passed in a name/value pair format. As demonstrated in the Bulletin Board servlet in the previous chapter, the `getParameterNames()` and `getParameterValues()` methods of the `HttpServletRequest` object can be used to retrieve the names and values, respectively, from the query string (you can use `getParameter()` if only one value is returned). This URL demonstrates how name/value pairs can be passed to a servlet:

http://localhost:8080/servlet/phonelist?name=Gordon+Augat&dept=IT

Servlet Runner Tips

Here are just a few tips that may be useful when using Servlet Runner to test and debug servlets.

1. Use Servlet Runner's console window extensively. Placing `System.out.println()` statements throughout your servlet will aid the debugging process by printing variable values and location flags to the console window. In addition, it is often very useful to print the stack trace to

standard out (for viewing in the console window). See Appendix L for instructions on converting the output of the `Exception` object's `printStackTrace()` method to a `String`.

2. Servlet Runner must be restarted whenever a servlet is changed. Unlike more advanced servlet engines, Servlet Runner cannot detect changes to a servlet and dynamically reload it. Therefore, it is necessary to stop Servlet Runner (on Windows, use *CTRL-C*) and restart it whenever you recompile your servlet.

3. Because you will be constantly stopping and restarting Servlet Runner during the debugging process, write a simple batch or script file to launch Servlet Runner and set the appropriate command-line switches. Over the course of a project, this simple suggestion can save you a lot of time.

Java Web Server

Sun's Java Web Server (JWS) was the first commercial HTTP server to support servlets and should receive strong consideration when selecting a Java-enabled Web server. This section will briefly present how to register and invoke servlets using JWS. The main purpose of this chapter is to familiarize the reader with the Java Web Server. For more detailed information, see the documentation that accompanies this product. The example presented here uses Java Web Server version 1.1.

First, download and install the Java Web Server. A free trial version is available on Sun's Web site at:

http://www.sun.com/software/jwebserver/index.html

Once installed, start the Java Web Server by executing the *httpd* executable in the */bin* directory under the JWS root directory (i.e., the directory where you installed JWS).

```
C:\JavaWebServer1.1\bin\httpd
```

By default, the Java Web Server listens on port 8080 (this is, of course, configurable). Test the server by issuing a request to *http://localhost:8080*. If the server is running properly, you should see the JWS welcome screen.

NOTE: The examples throughout this chapter assume that the user is using the machine on which the server is running. Hence, `localhost` is used in most URLs. However, keep in mind that these services can be accessed from any machine on the network by specifying an IP address (or resolvable hostname) in place of `localhost` in the URL.

Once the Java Web Server is responding to requests, it is ready to host servlets. The simplest way to host a servlet on JWS is to simply place the servlet in the */servlets* directory under the JWS root directory. Now your servlet can be referenced using the following syntax:

```
/servlet/<servlet_name>[/<path_info>][?<query_string>]
```

For example, the following URL will invoke the `BulletinBoard.class` servlet:

http://localhost:8080/servlet/BulletinBoard

Although it is possible to reference a servlet by simply placing it in the */servlets* directory, registering the servlet with the server offers considerable advantages. For instance, once registered, the server can be configured to automatically load the servlet at startup. Additionally, a servlet alias can be

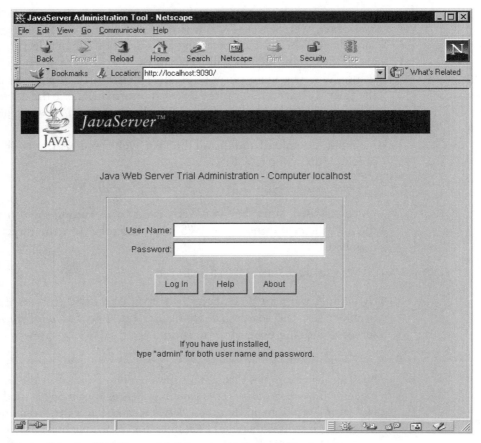

Figure 8.1   Java Web Server Administration Utility Login Screen

created to map any URL to the servlet. For example, you could map the URL *http://localhost:8080/index.html* to your servlet.

To configure the Java Web Server (including servlet registration), use the handy administration utility provided with the server. By default, this applet-based utility can be accessed on port 9090 (this is configurable). Launch the administration tool by requesting the URL *http://localhost:9090* from your browser (requires a Java 1.1-compliant browser), as shown in Figure 8.1. The default username and password is "admin." After login, the JWS admin utility gives you a choice of services to configure.

The screen shown in Figure 8.2 allows any of the JWS services to be stopped, started, or configured. Notice that a secure Web service and proxy service are also included with JWS. To configure the Java Web Server to run your servlet, select *Web Service* and click *Manage*.

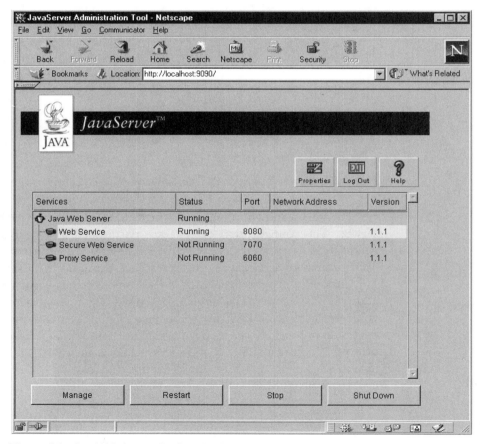

Figure 8.2 Java Web Server Configurable Services

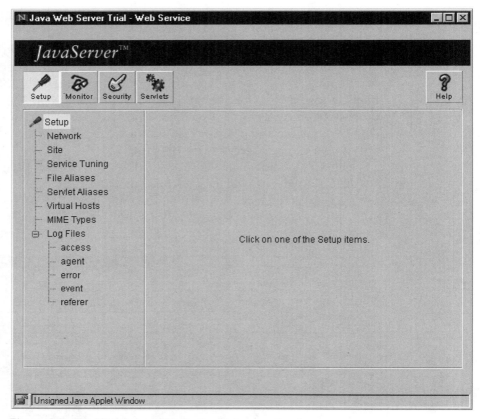

Figure 8.3 Java Web Server Web Services Administration Screen

The screen shown in Figure 8.3 provides options to manage the JWS Web service. The configuration options are partitioned into four screens—Setup, Monitor, Security, and Servlets. Table 8.2 describes the purpose of each screen. To register your servlet with the server, click the *Servlets* button.

Click *Add* in the left column of the Servlets screen shown in Figure 8.4 to add your new servlet. The *Servlet Name* field contains a logical name by which your servlet will be known by the Java Web Server. By convention, logical names do not include spaces or punctuation. The *Servlet Class* field is the name of your servlet class file. If the servlet class is in a package (other than the default package), this field must include full package information such as com.sourcestream.BulletinBoard.[1] The */servlets* directory under the JWS root

---

1 Actually, all Java classes are considered to be in a package. If no package is explicitly stated in the Java class file, then it is a placed in the default, unnamed package. This class file can be referenced without package information as long as it resides in a CLASSPATH root directory.

Table 8.2   JWS Web Services Administration Screens

Screen Name	Description
Setup	Configuration of various Web server settings including server tuning, file and servlet aliases, virtual hosts, MIME types, and logging.
Monitor	Fine-tuned configuration of logging, statistics, and resource usage.
Security	Configuration of users, groups, access control lists (ACL), and certificates.
Servlets	Allows user to add and edit servlets. Configuration settings include loading servlets at start-up and/or remotely and setting initialization parameters.

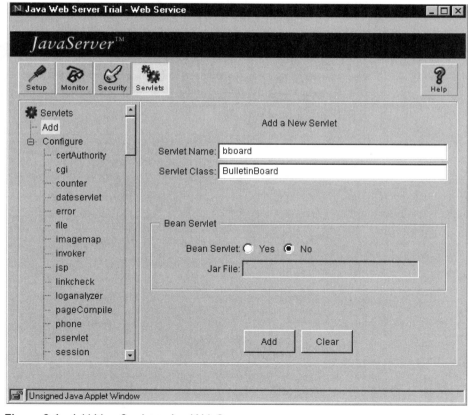

Figure 8.4   Add New Servlet to Java Web Server

directory is a convenient place to store your servlets. This is where the Java Web Server sample servlets reside. Finally, the *Bean Servlet* section declares whether or not the servlet is a JavaBean. A Bean Servlet is used for servlets that require serialization. *Serialization* allows the servlet's exact state to be stored persistently (e.g., in a file) so that it may be re-instantiated to the same state in the future.

Notice in Figure 8.5 that the new servlet has been added (*bboard* in the left column). The next screen allows you to configure your servlet and set initialization parameters. Table 8.3 describes each of the servlet configuration options.

Now that the servlet has been registered, let's create an alias that will simplify requesting the servlet from a client. To create an alias, return to the Setup screen and click *Servlet Aliases*. A list of aliases along with the servlets they invoke is shown in the right panel. The *Alias* column represents the exact URL path that will be mapped to the servlet. The first forward slash ("/") in the alias

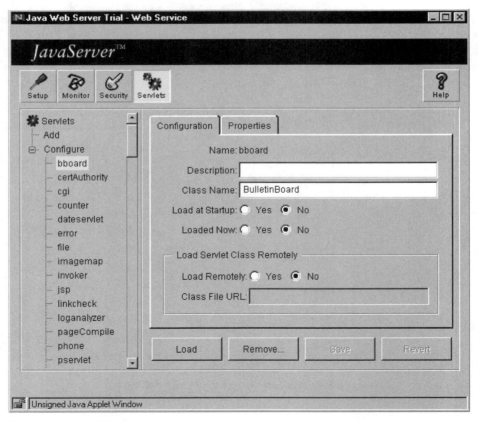

Figure 8.5   Java Web Server Servlet Configuration Screen

Table 8.3 Servlet Configuration Options

Field Name	Description
Description	Brief text description of servlet.
Class Name	Name of servlet class file.
Load at Startup	Instructs the server to automatically load the servlet at server start-up. Without preloading, the first user to invoke the servlet incurs the performance penalty associated with the server having to load the servlet before processing the request.
Loaded Now	Indicates if the servlet is currently loaded. Can be used to manually load and unload servlets.
Load Remotely	Indicates whether the servlet should be loaded from a remote location.
Class File URL	The URL from which to load the servlet (if loaded remotely).
Properties Tab	Allows the user to specify initialization parameters.

represents the Web server root. The *Servlet Invoked* column indicates which servlet will be called when a client requests the resource specified in the *Alias* column. For example, Figure 8.6 shows that */bulletins.html* is an alias for the *bboard* servlet. Therefore, any client request to the URL *http://localhost:8080/bulletins.html* will be routed to the *bboard* servlet. Furthermore, notice that wildcards can be used. For instance, in Figure 8.6 all requests having the extension .jsp are mapped to the *jsp* servlet. A servlet may have any number of aliases.

Servlet aliasing is an extremely useful feature provided by the Java Web Server. In addition, the Java Web Server also supports advanced servlet functionality like servlet chaining and server-side includes. These topics are discussed in Chapter 15.

JRun

JRun is a leading third-party servlet engine from Live Software, Inc., that adds servlet support to numerous Web servers running on various platforms. For example, JRun is available for Windows, Macintosh, NetWare and UNIX platforms and supports the following Web servers:

- Netscape FastTrack and Enterprise Server
- Apache Web Server
- Microsoft Internet Information Server and Personal Web Server

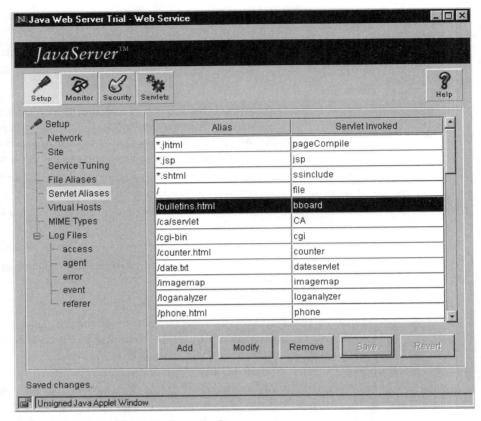

Figure 8.6   Servlet Aliases Configuration Screen

- O'Reilly WebSite Pro
- StarNine's WebSTAR for Macintosh

Best of all, the basic version of JRun is absolutely free! It is available on the CD accompanying this book or can be downloaded from:

   http://www.livesoftware.com

In addition to supporting the Web servers listed above, JRun also includes its own Web server. JRun Web Server is a simple HTTP server useful for testing servlets when a more functional Web server is not available.

Now let's learn how to run servlets using JRun and one of the supported Web servers. The example presented here uses JRun version 2.2. First, install JRun and connect it to your native Web server. The server connection can be completed during installation by answering "Yes" to the *Installation* dialog box that asks "Would you like to install a connector for your native Web server?" If you answer "No" here, you can always add a connector later. For simplicity, select "Yes" and follow the instructions for connecting to your Web server. If you have difficulty connecting to your Web server, check the support area at *http://www.livesoftware.com.*

Once you have JRun installed and connected to your Web server, test your servlet support by invoking the following sample servlet that ships with JRun:

> *http://localhost/servlet/DateServlet*

If the date is returned by this request, JRun is installed properly and serving servlets (it is assumed that the Web server is listening on port 80). Of course, you can also test your servlet using the simple Web server that is included with

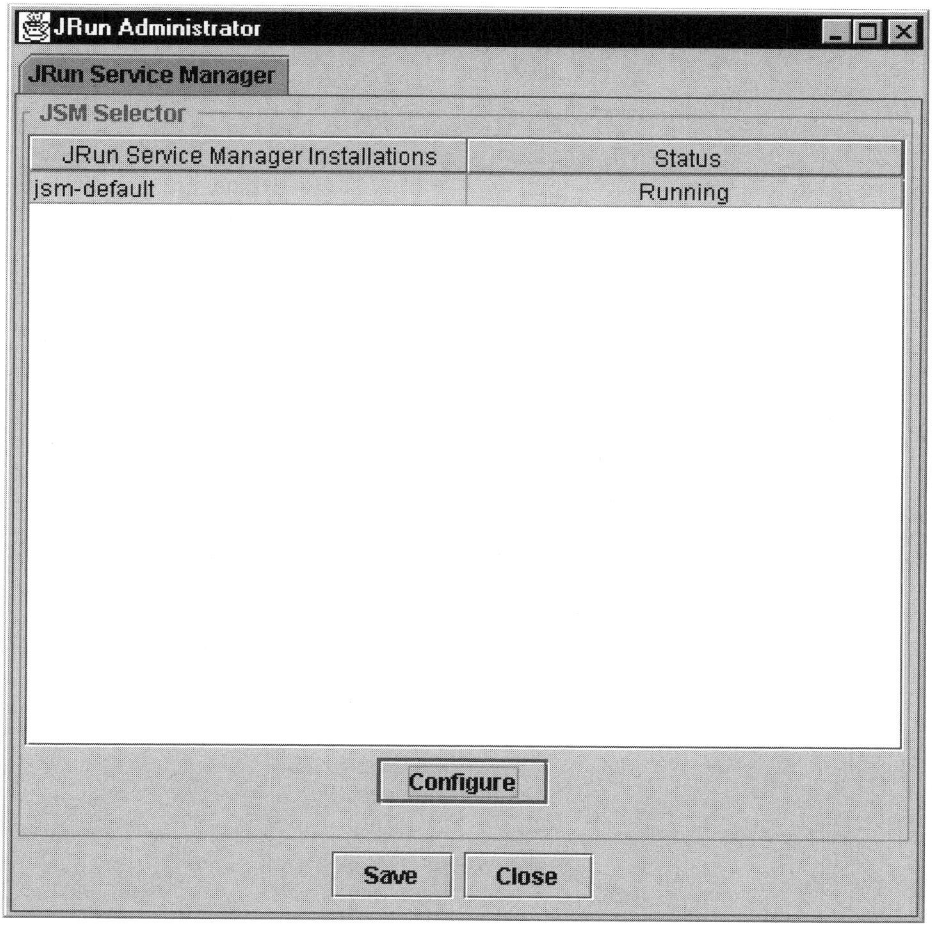

Figure 8.7 *JRun Admin* Utility

the product. By default, JRun Web Server listens on port 8000. You can test it by requesting the following URL:

http://localhost:8000/servlet/DateServlet

Now let's see how to register your servlet and map a URL to it using the JRun administration utility. A JRun folder on your desktop should contain an icon called *JRun Admin*. Run the *JRun Admin* program. The first form in this application (see Figure 8.7 on previous page) allows you to select a JRun service manager. The *jsm-default* service manager is automatically installed. Select this service manager and click *Configure*.

The next screen (Figure 8.8) contains three tabs—*Services*, *General*, and *Licenses*. *Services* shows you which JRun services are currently active and

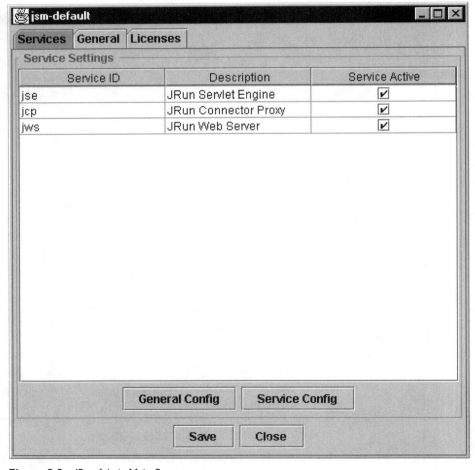

Figure 8.8 *JRun Admin* Main Screen

allows you to activate or deactivate any service. When using a native Web server, we are primarily interested in the *JRun Servlet Engine* service. The *General* tab includes configuration information such as the JRun root directory and various JVM settings. Finally, the *Licenses* section manages software licenses. To register your servlet, select the *JRun Servlet Engine* service and click the *Service Config* button.

The JRun Servlet Engine configuration screen (Figure 8.9) allows the user to configure the servlet engine in a host of ways. In this exercise, we will examine how to add a new servlet and map a URL to it. To add a servlet, select the *Aliases* tab (see Figure 8.10). You may quickly notice a difference in terminology between the Java Web Server and JRun.

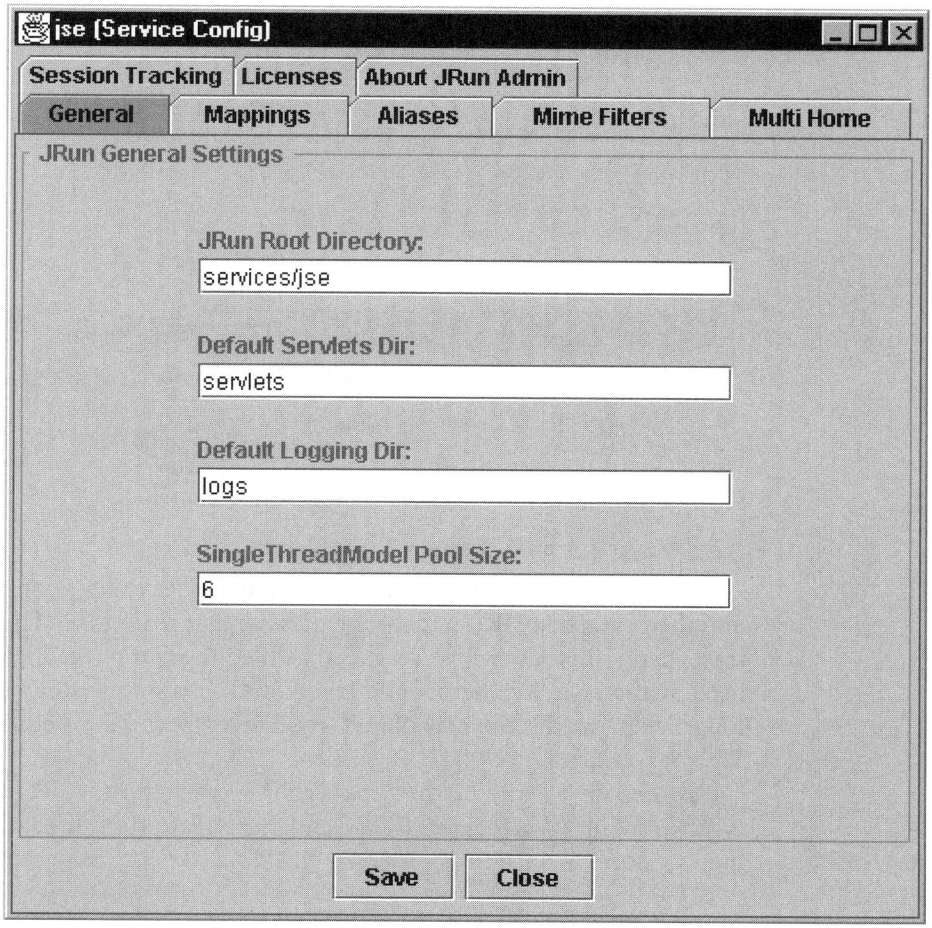

Figure 8.9 JRun Servlet Engine Configuration Screen

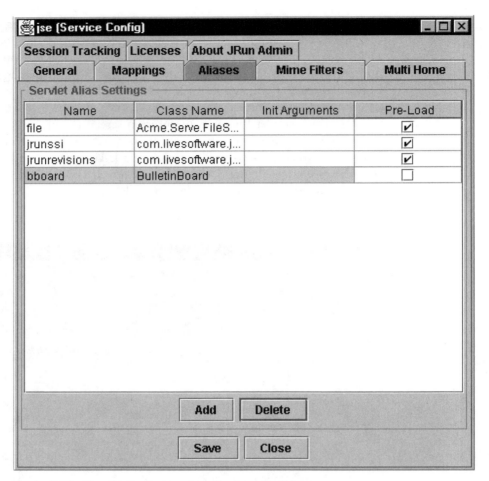

Figure 8.10   JRun Servlet Engine *Aliases* Configuration Tab

With the Java Web Server, we added a servlet using a logical servlet name and then created a URL path as an alias for that servlet (see Figure 8.6). In contrast, JRun's definition of a servlet alias is equivalent to the logical servlet name used by the Java Web Server (see Figure 8.4). It is simply a name that represents a particular servlet class file. Similarly, a JRun *mapping* is equivalent to a Java Web Server alias.

Before we go any further, copy your servlet into the default JRun servlets directory. This directory is located under the JRun root directory at the following location:

/JRun/2.2/jsm-default/services/jse/servlets

Now let's create a servlet alias and map a URL to it. Click the *Add* button to add a servlet alias. In our example, we created an alias for the `Bulletin-Board.class` servlet using the alias *bboard* (see Figure 8.10). If the servlet class is in a package, this field must include full package information such as `com.sourcestream.BulletinBoard`.

Once the servlet alias has been created, we're ready to map any number of URLs to it. Select the *Mappings* tab to view a list of current mappings (see Figure 8.11). The *Virtual Path/Extension* column represents the URL path that will be mapped to the servlet specified by the *Servlet Invoked* column. For instance, all requests for resources under the *jws/* directory are mapped to the *file* servlet. Likewise, all requested resources having the `.jrun` extension are mapped to the *invoker* servlet.

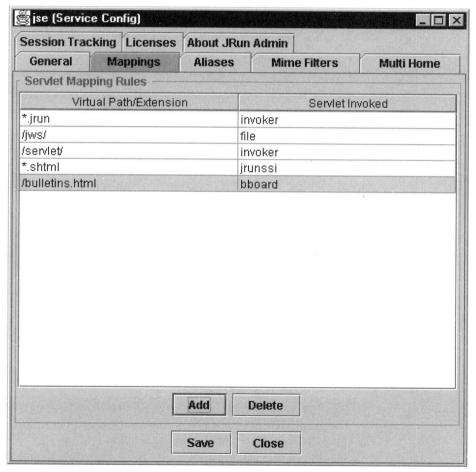

Figure 8.11 JRun Servlet Engine *Mappings* Configuration Screen

To add a servlet mapping, click the *Add* button. As you can see in Figure 8.11, we mapped */bulletins.html* to the `BulletinBoard` servlet. Therefore, the `BulletinBoard` servlet can be requested at the following URL (assuming the Web server is listening on port 80):

http://localhost/bulletins.html

JRun offers many features beyond what has been presented here. To learn more about this product, try installing it from the accompanying CD and experiment on your own. Full documentation is also included on the CD-ROM.

ServletExec

ServletExec, from New Atlanta Communications, LLC, is another leading third-party servlet engine capable of adding servlet support to multiple platforms and Web servers. ServletExec is available for the Windows, Macintosh, and UNIX platforms and supports the following Web servers:

- Netscape FastTrack and Enterprise Server
- Microsoft Internet Information Server and Personal Web Server
- Apache Web Server
- Macintosh W*API compatible Web servers

We will now demonstrate how to add servlet support to your Web server using ServletExec version 2.0. Unlike JRun, ServletExec uses a different installation program for each Web server that it supports. To install ServletExec, find the installation file that supports your Web server and execute it. Follow the prompts to complete the installation. These files can be found on the accompanying CD or can be downloaded from *http://www.newatlanta.com*.

Once ServletExec has been installed, stop and restart the Web server so that any configuration changes take effect. To test that your Web server is now serving servlets, issue a request to the following URL (assuming that the Web server is listening on port 80):

http://localhost/servlet/DateServlet

If ServletExec is running properly, the date and time should be returned.

Now that our Web server supports basic servlet calls, let's see how we can register a new servlet with ServletExec and map a URL to it. To begin with, start the *ServletExec Admin* utility by requesting the following URL:

http://localhost/servlet/admin

The *ServletExec Admin* utility allows the user to configure various settings for the servlet engine. These settings include adding and configuring servlets and mapping URLs. In contrast to the Java Web Server and JRun administration tools, ServletExec uses an HTML-based utility rather than a Java applet or application.

Before creating an alias, copy your servlet into the ServletExec default servlets directory. You can find the location of this directory by clicking on the *Virtual Servers* option in the left frame of the *ServletExec Admin* utility (see Figure 8.12).

The *Servlets Directory* field contains the default location for ServletExec sample servlets (see Figure 8.13). This screen also allows any number of additional servlets directories to be added. So, before we register your servlet, copy it to the directory specified by the *Servlets Directory* field in Figure 8.13. To continue, click the back arrow in your browser and click the *Configure* option in the left frame of the main *ServletExec Admin* screen (see Figure 8.12).

Figure 8.12   *ServletExec Admin Utility*

Figure 8.13   *ServletExec Admin* Virtual Server Configuration Screen

To add your servlet, simply fill out the blank record at the top of the Configure Servlets screen and click the *Submit* button. In Figure 8.14, our sample servlet BulletinBoard has been assigned a logical name of *bboard*. By convention, servlet names do not contain any spaces or punctuation. If the servlet class is in a package, the *Servlet Class* field must include full package information such as com.sourcestream.BulletinBoard. Table 8.4 describes each of the fields on the servlet configuration screen.

Now that your servlet has been registered with ServletExec, click the back arrow on your browser twice and select the *Aliases* option on the main Admin screen (see Figure 8.12). The Servlet Aliases screen allows you to map any number of URLs to a specific servlet (see Figure 8.15).

ServletExec uses terminology similar to the Java Web Server. The *Alias* column represents URL paths that map to a specific servlet. The *Servlet Name(s)*

Figure 8.14 *ServletExec Admin* Servlet Configuration Screen

column is the logical servlet name assigned to the servlet on the Configure
Servlets screen. Notice that wildcards can be used to pass all requests for a resource having a specific extension to a particular servlet. For example, all requests for a resource with a `.jsp` extension are passed to the *JSPServlet* servlet
(see Figure 8.15). To add a new servlet alias, complete the blank row at the top
of the screen. Enter a URL mapping in the *Alias* column and a valid servlet
name (according to the Configure Servlets screen) in the *Servlet Name(s)* (as
shown in Figure 8.15) column. In Figure 8.15 we mapped the servlet alias */bul-
letins.html* to the *bboard* servlet name. After clicking the *Submit* button, the
Bulletin Board servlet can be requested at the following URL (assuming the
Web server is listening on port 80):

http://localhost/bulletins.html

Table 8.4 Servlet Configuration Fields

Field Name	Description
Servlet Name	Logical name of servlet.
Servlet Class	Name of servlet class file. Must contain full package information.
Code Base	Contains the directory, `.jar` file, or `.zip` file containing the class files for remotely loaded servlets. For example: *http://www.sourcestream.com/servlets/*
Initialization Arguments	Comma-delimited list of name/value pairs passed to the servlet as initialization parameters. For example: `param1=value1, param2=value2`
Init Load Order	Indicates whether the servlet should be automatically loaded at server start-up and the order in which it should be loaded.
Loaded	Indicates whether the servlet is currently loaded. Can be used to manually load and unload servlets.

Figure 8.15 *ServletExec Admin* Servlet Aliases Configuration Screen

That's it! Install ServletExec, add a new servlet, map a URL to it, and the servlet can be invoked from any Web browser. Of course, we have only seen a small portion of the full functionality offered by ServletExec. To learn more, install ServletExec from the accompanying CD and experiment on your own. Full documentation for this product is also included on the CD-ROM.

Summary

This chapter presented a number of options for running servlets. Just from the small sampling examined here, we can see that servlets are capable of running on multiple platforms hosted by a variety of Web servers. It is this universal support for servlets that makes them so powerful and popular. In the next chapter, we will learn how to debug your servlet using your favorite Java development tool.

Chapter Highlights

- There are many ways in which to run a servlet. Some Web servers, such as Sun's Java Web Server and Netscape Enterprise Server, natively support servlets. Other popular HTTP servers, such as Microsoft Internet Information Server and Apache Web Server, support servlets through third-party add-ons such as JRun from Live Software or ServletExec from New Atlanta Communications.

- The simplest way to run a servlet is with the Servlet Runner utility that ships with the JSDK. Servlet Runner is an executable that resides in JSDK's */bin* directory and is launched from the command line.

- Servlet aliases and initialization parameters are defined in a text file called *servlet.properties*.

- Sun's Java Web Server was the first commercial HTTP server to support servlets.

- The simplest way to host a servlet on JWS is to just place the servlet in the */servlets* directory under the JWS root directory.

- Although it is possible to reference a servlet by simply placing it in the */servlets* directory, registering the servlet with the server allows the server to automatically load it at start-up and map any URL to the servlet.

- JRun, a leading third-party servlet engine from Live Software, adds servlet support to numerous Web servers running on various platforms. The standard version of JRun is available free of charge.
- ServletExec, from New Atlanta Communications, is another leading third-party servlet engine capable of adding servlet support to multiple platforms and Web servers.

CHAPTER 9

Debugging Servlets

In this chapter, we will demonstrate how to debug servlets using the Java development tool of your choice. In addition, we will also examine servlet debugging with two popular Java development environments—Visual Café from Symantec and Borland JBuilder from Inprise. Specifically, this chapter will cover the following topics:

- Servlet debugging with the `ServletDebug` Class
- Servlet debugging with Visual Café
- Servlet debugging with JBuilder

The first section, "`ServletDebug` Class," uses a basic shareware Java development tool called JPadPro to demonstrate that servlet debugging features can be added to almost any development environment. The remaining two sections demonstrate, step by step, how to debug servlets with two of the most popular Java development environments.

ServletDebug Class

There are a number of methods available for debugging servlets. For example, a few commercial products add servlet debugging functionality to any Java development environment (e.g., ServletDebugger from Live Software). These products are usually in the form of a class library that can be referenced from within a Java IDE (Integrated Development Environment). In addition, some popular Java development tools, such as JBuilder from Inprise, include servlet debugging facilities.

In this section, we will examine a generic debugging method by stepping through the execution of the Bulletin Board servlet presented in Chapter 7. For starters, let's take a look at a simple Java class that can be used to add servlet debugging functionality to most Java development tools (see Listing 9.1). This class invokes the basic HttpServer class that is included with the JSDK. This is the same class that is called by the *ServletRunner* utility (also included in the JSDK).

Listing 9.1   ServletDebug source code.

```
/**
 * ServletDebug starts the sun.servlet.http.HttpServer class
 * listening for servlet requests.
 *
 * @author Dustin R. Callaway
 * @version 1.0, 10/05/98
 */
public class ServletDebug
{
  /**
   * main method reads the command-line arguments, if any, and
   * passes them to the main method of the
   * sun.servlet.http.HttpServer class which runs the servlets.
   * Two command-line arguments are supported. Use as follows:
   *
   * -p 8000 -d /myservlets
   *
   * The -p switch indicates the port on which HttpServer will
   * listen for servlet requests. The -d switch represents the
   * directory where servlets are stored.
   */
  public static void main(String[] args)
  {
    String port = "8080"; //default port
    String servletsDir = "/servlets"; //default directory
    int i=0;

    while (i < args.length-1)//iterate through command-line args
    {
      if (args[i].equals("-p")) //port switch
      {
        port = args[++i]; //set port value
      }
      else if (args[i].equals("-d")) //directory switch
      {
        servletsDir = args[++i]; //set directory value
      }
      else //ignore illegal command-line argument
      {
        i++;
      }
    }

    //create String array arguments list for HttpServer
```

```
        String[] serverArgs = new String[4];
        serverArgs[0] = "-p";
        serverArgs[1] = port;
        serverArgs[2] = "-d";
        serverArgs[3] = servletsDir;
        sun.servlet.http.HttpServer.main(serverArgs); //start server
    }
}
```

NOTE: If you're really in a hurry, you can significantly shorten the
ServletDebug class shown above. In fact, by dropping support for command-line
arguments, the ServletDebug program can be reduced to these few lines:

```
public class ServletDebugLite
{
   public static void main(String[] args)
   {
      String[] serverArgs = {"-p", "8080", "-d", "/servlets"};
      sun.servlet.http.HttpServer.main(serverArgs);
   }
}
```

Since ServletDebugLite does not support command-line arguments, it must be
recompiled whenever you wish to change the port or servlets directory. In the
code above, 8080 indicates the port and /servlets represents the location of the
servlet class files. If desired, simply alter these values and recompile.

To demonstrate servlet debugging using the ServletDebug class, we will use
a popular shareware Java IDE called JPadPro. We will use JPadPro to demonstrate that this debugging technique works with most generic Java development
tools. If you use one of the Windows operating systems, you may wish to
download a trial version of JPadPro from:

http://www.modelworks.com

If you prefer, you may use a different Java development environment to complete this exercise. Of course, you will need to adapt the JPadPro examples presented here to work with your development tool. The example presented here
uses JPadPro version 3.6.

Let's now examine, step-by-step, a typical servlet debugging process. To
begin with, make sure that Sun's JDK (or Java SDK) and JSDK (Java Servlet
Development Kit) are already installed. Next, create a directory called */servlets*
directly off the root of your file system and copy the ServletDebug.java and

BulletinBoard.java files from the CD into it. Now launch your Java IDE. For
JPadPro, you will need to tell it where to find the JDK as well as add the Servlet
API packages to the CLASSPATH. To specify the JDK location, click the *Select
JDK Directory* option under the *JDK* menu. To add the Servlet API pack-
ages, click the *Edit Standard Classpaths* option under the *JDK* directory (see
Figure 9.1). The Servlet API packages are located under the JSDK directory
at */lib/jsdk.jar* (see Figure 9.2).

Now that the environment has been configured, open the ServletDebug.java
and BulletinBoard.java files (use the *Open* option under the *File* menu). If
not already selected, select the ServletDebug.java file using the *Window* menu
(all open files are listed at the bottom of the *Window* menu). Compile
ServletDebug.java by clicking the *Compile ServletDebug.java* option under
the *JDK* menu (or by simply pressing the *F6* key). Now select the Bulletin-
Board.java file from the *Window* menu and compile it. Make sure that the files
compiled without error and that both class files are located in the */servlets*
directory.

Next, run the ServletDebug class in debug mode by clicking the *Debug
Application* option under the *JDK* menu (see Figure 9.1). A *Debug Java
Application* dialog box will appear. Select the ServletDebug.class file from the
/servlets directory and click *OK* (see Figure 9.3). The ServletDebug class will

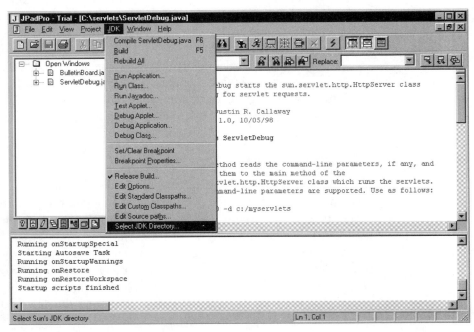

Figure 9.1   JPadPro JDK and CLASSPATH Settings

begin running. However, since we are in debug mode, JPadPro will automatically pause execution on the first line of the main() method (this behavior is specific to JPadPro). Click the *Continue* option under the *Debug* menu to continue the execution. ServletDebug will start the sun.servlet.http.HttpServer running and listening for servlet requests. In the output panel at the bottom of the screen (click *Output Panel* under the *View* menu if not visible), you should see the parameters being used by the HttpServer class (see Figure 9.4).

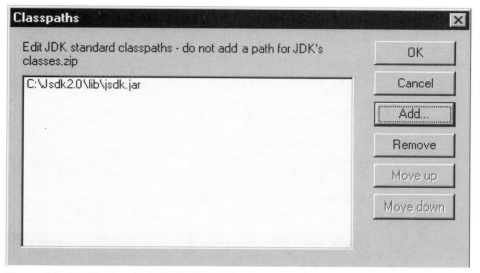

Figure 9.2 JPadPro Standard *CLASSPATHs* Dialog Box

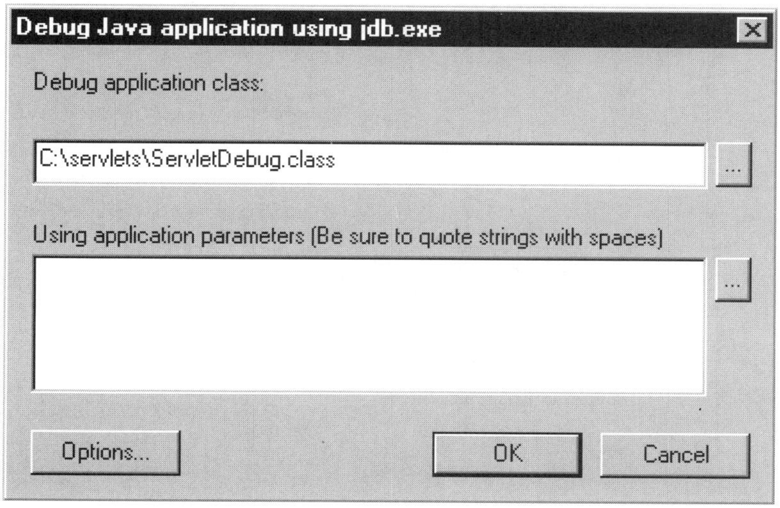

Figure 9.3 JPadPro's *Debug Java Application* Dialog Box

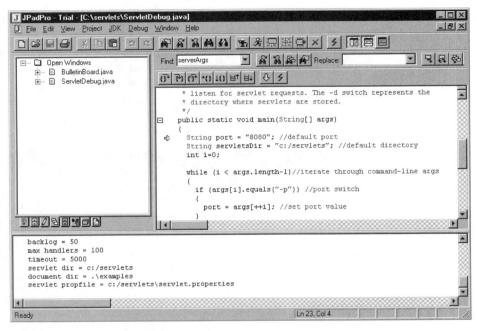

Figure 9.4   ServletDebug Class Running in Debug Mode

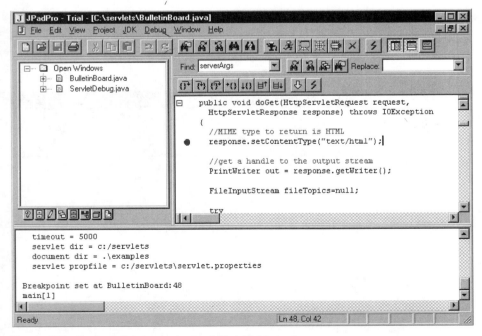

Figure 9.5   Setting a Breakpoint in the doGet() Method

Now we're ready to add a breakpoint to our servlet and step through the code. Make sure that the `BulletinBoard.java` file is selected and scroll down to the `doGet()` method. Place your cursor anywhere on the first line of code in the `doGet()` method and click the *Set/Clear Breakpoint* option under the *JDK* menu to add a breakpoint. The breakpoint line is marked with a red octagon (see Figure 9.5). Make sure to set breakpoints only on valid lines. You cannot set a breakpoint on a comment line or variable declaration.

Once the breakpoint is set, we can invoke the servlet and step through the code. To invoke the servlet, use the following URL (if the `-p` command-line argument was used when running `ServletDebug`, use the specified port):

http://localhost:8080/servlet/BulletinBoard

When the browser requests the above URL, it will appear to "hang" as the activity icon (e.g., the Netscape "N" or Internet Explorer "e" icons) continues to move. At this point, switch back to the JPadPro environment. Notice that execution has halted at your breakpoint (see Figure 9.6). The small yellow arrow indicates the current line of execution.

You may now use the step options under the *Debug* menu (e.g., *Step*, *StepIn*, *StepOut*) or the icons on the debug toolbar to step through your code. Click the *Continue* option under the *Debug* menu at any time to continue execution and return the servlet output to the client.

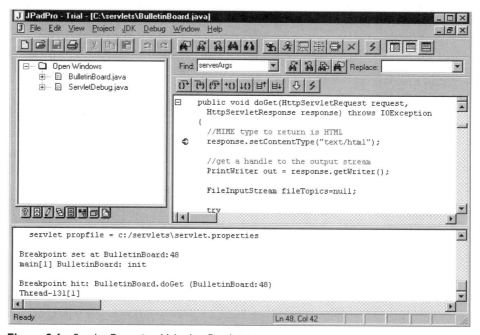

Figure 9.6 Servlet Execution Halted at Breakpoint

Visual Café

The previous section introduced a simple way to debug servlets using a generic Java IDE. Fortunately, this technique can be used with many tools ranging from basic shareware to shrink-wrapped enterprise Java development environments. Let's now examine servlet debugging with a popular commercial Java development tool—Symantec Visual Café. The example presented here uses Visual Café version 2.5.

To debug servlets with Visual Café, we will again be using the Servlet-Debug class (see Listing 9.1). And again, we will evaluate each step in the servlet debugging process. To begin, make sure that the JSDK (Java Servlet Development Kit) is already installed (JSDK 2.0 or later recommended). Next, launch Visual Café and add the Servlet API packages to your CLASSPATH. The Servlet API packages are located under the JSDK directory at */lib/jsdk.jar*. To add this file to your CLASSPATH, click the *Options* item under the *Project* menu and select the *Directories* tab. Click the *New* toolbar icon to add a new item to the CLASSPATH (hover over each toolbar icon and a tooltip will indicate its purpose). Type in the full path to the *jsdk.jar* file and click *OK* (see Figure 9.7).

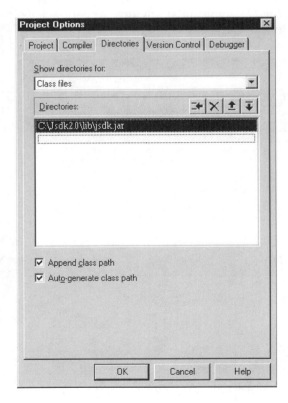

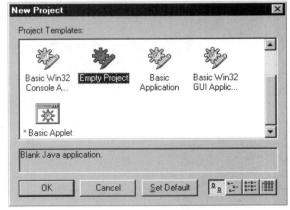

Figure 9.8   Visual Café *New Project* Dialog Box

Figure 9.7
Adding CLASSPATH
Information in
Visual Café

Create a directory called */servlets* directly off the root of your file system and copy the `ServletDebug.java` and `BulletinBoard.java` files from the CD into it. Now, if not already running, launch Visual Café. Close the current project by clicking the *Close Project* option under the *File* menu. Next, create a new project using the *New Project* option under the *File* menu. Select the *Empty Project* icon in the *New Project* dialog box and click *OK* (see Figure 9.8). Add the `ServletDebug.java` and `BulletinBoard.java` files to the project by clicking the *Files into Project* option under the *Insert* menu (see Figure 9.9).

Now that the proper CLASSPATH settings have been made and the servlet files have been added to the project, it's time to debug the `BulletinBoard` servlet. To start the debug process, select the `ServletDebug` object in the project window (upper left pane in Figure 9.10) and click the *Run in Debugger* option

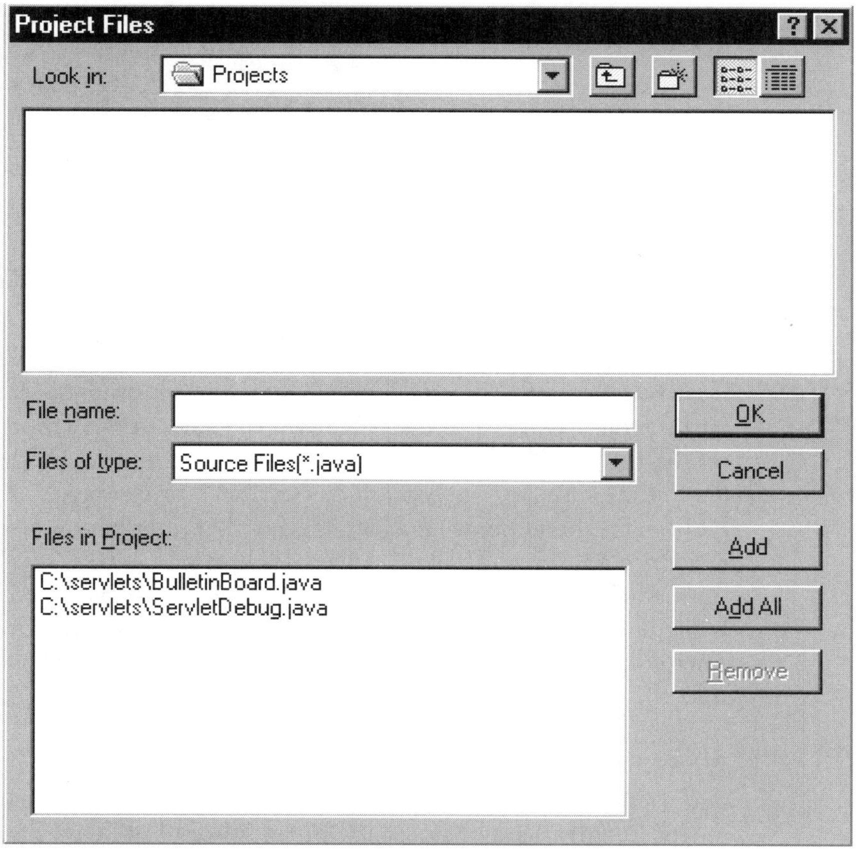

Figure 9.9 Adding Files to a Visual Café Project

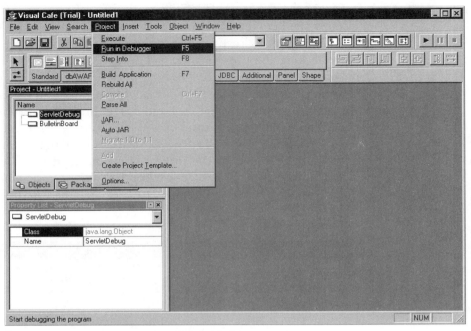

Figure 9.10   Running a Project in Debug Mode

under the *Project* menu (see Figure 9.10). Running the ServletDebug file will automatically compile all files in the project.

Now that the project is running, let's add a breakpoint to the Bulletin Board servlet. To add a breakpoint, double-click on the BulletinBoard object in the project window and scroll down to its doGet() method. Place the cursor on the first line of code in the doGet() method and set a breakpoint by clicking the *Set Breakpoint* option under the *Source* menu or by pressing the *F9* key. The breakpoint line is marked with a red diamond (see Figure 9.11).

Once the breakpoint has been set, we can invoke the servlet and step through the code. According to the ServletDebug class (see Listing 9.1), 8080 is the default port on which the server will be responding to servlet requests. Therefore, the Bulletin Board servlet can be requested with the following URL:

   http://localhost:8080/servlet/BulletinBoard

When the browser requests the above URL, it will appear to "hang" as the activity icon (the Netscape "N" or Internet Explorer "e" icons) continues to move. At this point, switch back to the Visual Café environment. Notice that execution has halted at your breakpoint (see Figure 9.12). A solid red line highlights the current line of execution.

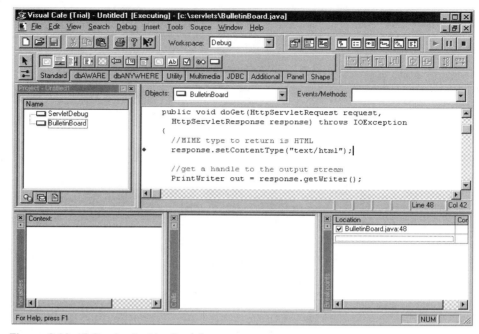

Figure 9.11   A Breakpoint Has Been Set

You may now use the step options under the *Debug* menu (e.g., *Step Into*, *Step Over*, *Step Out*, etc.) to step through your code (see Figure 9.12 on the next page). Click the *Continue to End* option under the *Debug* menu to continue execution and return the servlet output to the client. Additionally, the three lower windows offer essential debug information such as variable values, call stack position, and breakpoints.

JBuilder

In this section we will demonstrate servlet debugging using Borland JBuilder from Inprise Corporation. JBuilder is a leading servlet development tool and, in my opinion, one of the strongest Java IDEs available. Let's take a look at

NOTE: The servlet debugging facility demonstrated in this section is available only in JBuilder version 2.01 and later. JBuilder 2.0 does not include this functionality. For JBuilder releases prior to 2.01, please use the generic debugging technique described earlier in this chapter (use the `ServletDebug` class).

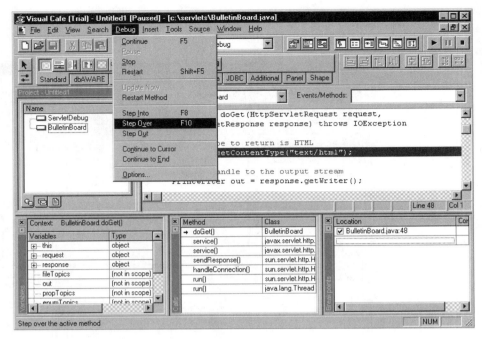

Figure 9.12 Execution Halts at Breakpoint

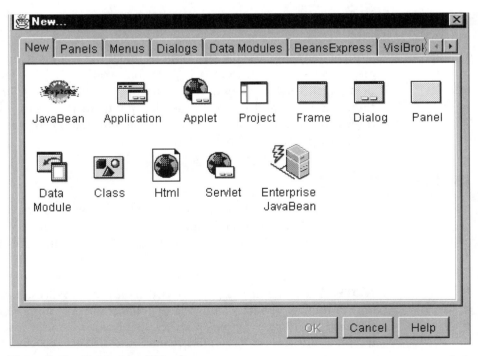

Figure 9.13 JBuilder *New* Dialog Box

how we can debug servlets using JBuilder's built-in functionality. The example presented here uses JBuilder version 2.01.

If you own JBuilder and would like to follow along, launch JBuilder now. Next, close the current project by selecting the *Close All* option from the *File* menu. Select *New* from the *File* menu. The *New* dialog box allows you to choose which type of Java object to create. Select *Servlet* and click *OK* (see Figure 9.13).

Next, we must create a project in which to store our servlet. In JBuilder, all Java files must reside within a project. Because a project is not currently open, JBuilder will automatically prompt you to create a new project. To do so, enter the path and filename of your new project in the *File* field. Complete any other fields that you prefer and click *Finish* (see Figure 9.14). For this example, we will use the default project name *untitled1*.

Once the project has been created, the *Servlet Wizard* dialog box will appear. Notice that JBuilder will automatically create the servlet skeleton for you based upon your selections (see Figure 9.15). For instance, the selection in Figure 9.15 will automatically generate a `doGet()` and `doPost()` method. Make sure that the servlet resides in your project's package (which it does by default).

Once you have completed the Servlet Wizard, click *Finish* and JBuilder will add the necessary files to your project. These files include the servlet, an HTML page for invoking the servlet, and a class called `ServletServer` that will execute your servlet when it is time to run and debug (`ServletServer` performs the same function as the `ServletDebug` class presented earlier).

Figure 9.14 JBuilder *Project Wizard* Dialog Box

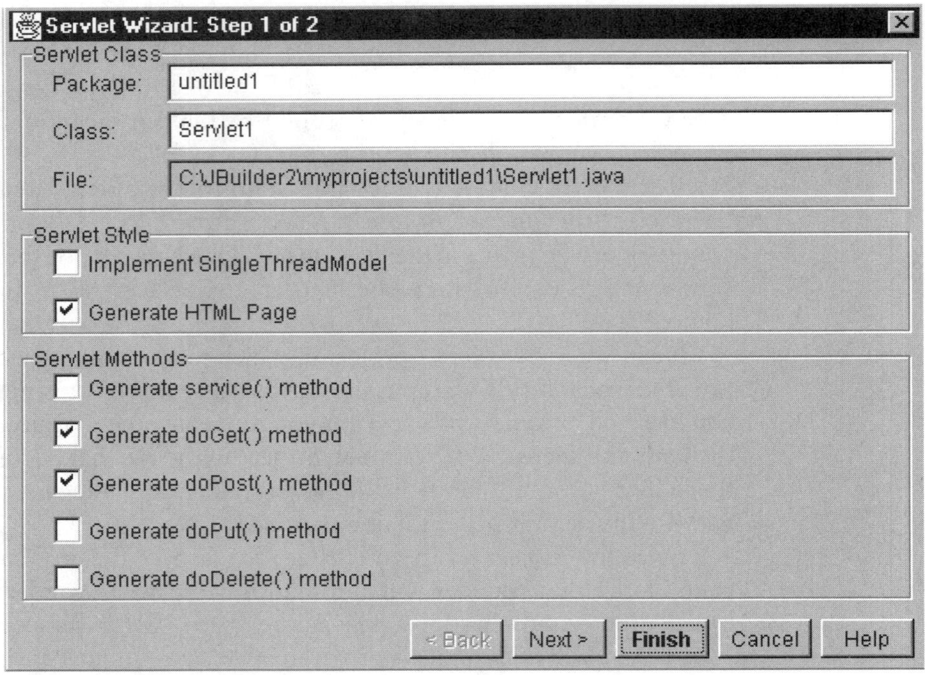

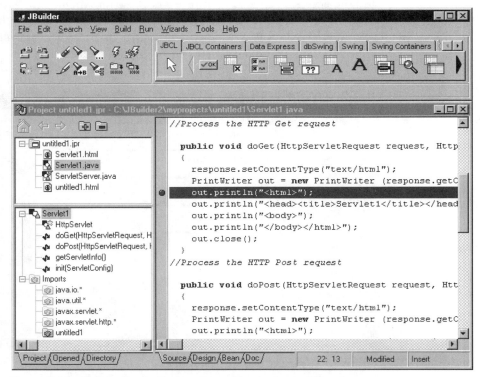

Figure 9.15 JBuilder *Servlet Wizard* Dialog Box

Figure 9.16 JBuilder Servlet Project Created by the Servlet Wizard

Now that the servlet project has been created, let's try some debugging by adding a breakpoint to the doGet() method. Press the *F5* key to toggle a breakpoint in the doGet() method. The breakpoint line is highlighted in red and marked by a red circle in the margin (see Figure 9.16). In addition to the *F5* key, you may also add a breakpoint via the *Run* menu (see Figure 9.17). Now let's run the servlet and step through the code.

To run the servlet, select the ServletServer.java file in the project window (top left frame) and click the *Debug "ServletServer"* option under the *Run* menu (see Figure 9.17). This will run the servlet in debug mode, halting execution at any breakpoints. Once the servlet is running in debug mode, it will simply wait for a request. To continue the debug process, you must invoke the servlet from a Web browser. By default, the ServletServer listens on port 8080. This setting is configurable in the ServletServer.java file. To invoke the sample servlet shown above, issue a request to the following URL:

http://localhost:8080/servlet/untitled1.Servlet1

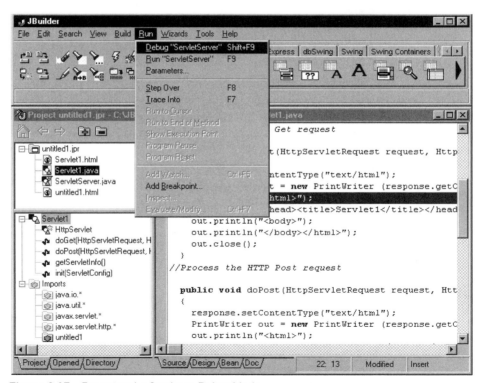

Figure 9.17 Executing the Servlet in Debug Mode

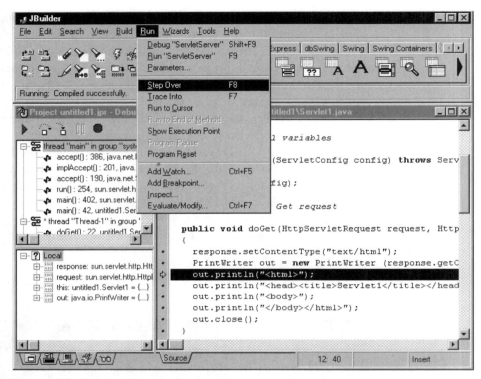

Figure 9.18   Stepping Through a Servlet

From this URL you can see that our servlet is named `Servlet1` and it resides in the `untitled1` package. This URL will invoke the servlet and begin executing the servlet code. The servlet will run until it reaches the breakpoint within the `doGet()` method, at which point execution will pause and the JBuilder environment will automatically move to the foreground (see Figure 9.18). At this point, the developer may follow the execution by stepping into or over each line. Variable values may be inspected throughout the entire debug process. With features like the Servlet Wizard and built-in servlet debugging facilities, JBuilder is a very attractive tool for servlet development.

Summary

From this brief introduction to servlet debugging with a Java IDE, you may realize the enormous power and convenience of an integrated debugger when testing and debugging servlets. Though simple servlets can be debugged by sending messages to standard out or writing them to a log file, for more complex servlets, a fully functional debugger is a tremendous asset. In the next chapter, we will dig a little deeper into the Servlet API.

Chapter Highlights

- There are a number of methods available for debugging servlets. For example, a few commercial products add servlet debugging functionality to any Java development environment (e.g., a servlet debugger from Live Software).

- This chapter presented a simple Java class, called `ServletDebug`, that can be used to add servlet debugging functionality to most Java development tools. This class invokes the basic `HttpServer` class that is included with the JSDK. This is the same class that is called by the *ServletRunner* utility (also included in the JSDK).

- The `ServletDebug` class can be used with almost any Java IDE, including the popular Visual Café and JBuilder products. This chapter described servlet debugging using both of these tools.

- The latest versions of JBuilder include integrated servlet debugging facilities that simplify the servlet debugging process.

CHAPTER 10

Beyond Servlet API Basics

In Chapter 6, we learned about the most fundamental classes and interfaces necessary to build a servlet. Many servlets can be developed using only the classes and interfaces previously described. However, there are additional objects in the Servlet API that could also be classified as fundamental. We explore these objects in this chapter.

Although not required by every servlet, the classes and interfaces presented here are commonly used to build servlets that are more functional and complex than anything we have seen so far. In this chapter, the following objects are presented:

- `ServletInputStream` class
- `ServletOutputStream` class
- `ServletConfig` interface
- `ServletContext` interface
- `ServletException` class
- `UnavailableException` class

These classes and interfaces, although not required by every servlet, are essential to building more advanced servlets. Keep in mind that only the most common methods of each object are discussed here. For a complete list of methods supported by these objects, see Chapter 20. All of the classes and interfaces presented here reside in the `javax.servlet` package.

ServletInputStream **Class**

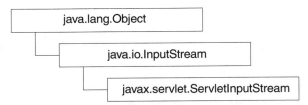

The ServletInputStream class provides an input stream for reading data from a client request. ServletInputStream directly extends java.io.InputStream and, therefore, supports all of its methods. In addition to the functionality inherited from InputStream, ServletInputStream provides a simple readLine() method for reading one line of text at a time from the request. The ServletInputStream is accessed through the getInputStream() method of the ServletRequest object. This class should be used for reading binary data from the content of the client request. A BufferedReader object, returned by the getReader() method of ServletRequest or HttpServletRequest, can be used for reading text data. The sole method defined by ServletInputStream is readLine().

readLine

```
public int readLine(byte[] b, int off, int len) throws
    IOException
```

The readLine() method reads the number of bytes specified by the len parameter into the byte array b starting at the offset off. This method reads bytes into the byte array until the number of bytes specified by len has been read or a linefeed ("\n") is encountered. When read, the linefeed is added to the byte array and the read process is terminated. The readLine() method returns an integer representing the number of bytes actually read or -1 if the end of the stream is reached.

ServletOutputStream **Class**

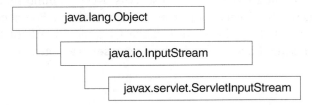

The ServletOutputStream class provides an output stream for writing data out to the client. ServletOutputStream extends java.io.OutputStream and, therefore, supports all of its methods. In addition to the functionality inherited from

OutputStream, ServletOutputStream provides many variations of the print() and println() methods for sending data back to the client. The ServletOutputStream is accessed through the getOutputStream() method of the ServletResponse object. This class should be used for transmitting binary data. The PrintWriter object, returned by the getWriter() method of ServletResponse or HttpServletResponse, can be used for sending text data. The methods defined by ServletInputStream are print() and println().

print

```
print(String s)
print(boolean b)
print(char c)
print(int i)
print(long l)
print(float f)
print(double d)
```

The print() method supports seven different parameters—String, boolean, char, int, long, float, and double. This method simply prints the specified value to the output stream that is tied to the client. There is no white space, carriage return, or linefeed added to the output stream by this method.

println

```
println()
println(String s)
println(boolean b)
println(char c)
println(int i)
println(long l)
println(float f)
println(double d)
```

The println() method supports eight different parameters—none, String, boolean, char, int, long, float, and double. This method prints the value specified in the parameter to the output stream and appends a carriage return/linefeed. Calling the println() method with no parameters sends only a carriage return/linefeed to the client.

ServletConfig Interface

javax.servlet.ServletConfig

The ServletConfig interface is implemented by the servlet engine in order to pass configuration information to a servlet. The server passes an object that implements the ServletConfig interface to the servlet's init() method. Servlet-Config defines three methods that can be used by servlets to gain information regarding configuration settings and the environment in which they are running. The following methods are defined by the ServletConfig interface.

getInitParameter

```
public String getInitParameter(String name)
```

The getInitParameter() method returns a string containing the value of the specified initialization parameter. Initialization parameters can be established before a servlet is started. These values are normally read in the servlet's init() method and used to perform some type of initialization. If the specified parameter does not exist, null is returned.

The following text demonstrates how initialization parameters are defined using Sun's Servlet Runner. Servlet Runner is a simple servlet engine that ships with the JSDK. Servlet Runner was discussed in Chapter 8.

```
servlet.phonelist.code=PhoneListServlet
servlet.phonelist.initArgs=maxRows=100,\
   language=English,\
   verbose=true
```

The preceding text is stored in a file called *servlet.properties*. The first line defines an alias, phonelist, for the servlet PhoneListServlet.class. The rest of the lines define initialization parameters that the server passes to the phonelist servlet. The back-slashes ("\") serve as line continuation characters. The following code demonstrates how the initialization parameters can be read by the servlet. Note that the variables maxRows, languageMode, and verbose are declared outside of the init() method.

```
public void init(ServletConfig config) throws ServletException
{
   super.init(config); //pass ServletConfig to parent class

   //get initialization parameters maxRows, language, verbose
   maxRows = Integer.parseInt(
     config.getInitParameter("maxRows"));

   languageMode = config.getInitParameter("language");

   verbose = config.getInitParameter("verbose").equals("true");
}
```

getInitParameterNames

```
public Enumeration getInitParameterNames()
```

As described in Chapter 6, the getInitParameterNames() method returns the names of all initialization parameters as an enumeration of strings. If no initialization parameters have been defined, an empty enumeration is returned. This method is often used in conjunction with getInitParameter() to retrieve the name and value of all initialization parameters. The following sample code shows how the names and values of the servlet's initialization parameters can be retrieved.

```java
public void init(ServletConfig Config) throws ServletException
{
  String name, value;

  super.init(config); //pass ServletConfig to parent class

  //create Enumeration of initialization parameter names
  Enumeration enum = config.getInitParameterNames();

  //iterate through all initialization parameters
  while (enum.hasMoreElements())
  {
    name = (String)enum.nextElement();
    value = config.getInitParameter(name);
    System.out.println("Name: " + name + ", Value: " + value +
      "\n");
  }
}
```

The init() method shown above extracts the initialization parameter names and values from the ServletConfig object and prints them to standard out.

getServletContext

```
public ServletContext getServletContext()
```

The getServletContext() method returns a ServletContext object. This object contains information regarding the server environment in which the servlet is running.

ServletContext Interface

```
javax.servlet.ServletContext
```

The ServletContext interface provides information to servlets regarding the environment in which they are running. It also provides a standard way for servlets to write events to a log file. An object that implements the `Servlet-Context` interface can be accessed with the `getServletContext()` method of the `ServletConfig` object that is passed to the servlet's `init()` method. Many commonly called methods defined by the `ServletContext` interface are outlined in the following sections.

getRealPath

```
public abstract String getRealPath(String path)
```

The `getRealPath()` method evaluates the virtual path passed as an argument and returns the actual path to the resource (according to the file system or network). If the translation is not possible, a `null` is returned. Passing a "/" to `getRealPath()` will return the server's document root. The following code demonstrates this method.

```
public void service(HttpServletRequest request,
    HttpServletResponse response) throws ServletException,
    IOException
{
    //set MIME type for HTTP header
    response.setContentType("text/plain");

    //get a handle to the output stream
    PrintWriter out = response.getWriter();

    //shows physical path for specified relative path
    out.println(request.getRealPath("/public/html"));

    //shows physical path of requested resource
    out.println(request.getRealPath(request.getPathInfo()));

    out.close(); //always close the output stream
}
```

For example, if the preceding code represented a servlet called `GetPath-Servlet` that was invoked using this URL:

http://localhost:8080/servlet/GetPathServlet/test

the output of the servlet would look like this (under Windows OS):

```
.\servlets\public\html
.\servlets\test
```

getServerInfo

```
public String getServerInfo()
```

The `getServerInfo()` method returns a `String` describing the name and version of the servlet engine that is running the servlet. For example, while a servlet is running under Sun's Servlet Runner, this method returns the following string:

servletrunner/2.1

Servlet Runner was discussed in Chapter 8.

log

```
public void log(String msg)
public abstract void log(String message, Throwable throwable)
```

The first log() method accepts a String that is written to the servlet log file. The name and location of this file are server dependent. This method is useful for logging significant events. The second log() method accepts an exception (i.e., a Throwable object) and a String as parameters. This method writes the stack trace and the message to the servlet log file. This is useful for logging errors.

ServletException Class

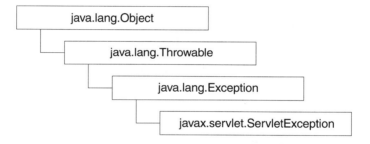

ServletException is thrown by the servlet in response to some type of servlet error. If a ServletException is not caught or is explicitly thrown by the servlet, the error will be handled by the server itself. A well-written servlet should catch most exceptions and handle them in an elegant manner. However, both ServletException and IOException are usually thrown by the primary servlet methods (e.g., init(), service(), doGet(), doPost()). For example, this declaration of the service() method is typical (notice the throws instruction):

```
public void service(HttpServletRequest request,
    HttpServletResponse response) throws ServletException,
    IOException
```

If a ServletException or IOException is caught, the servlet should log the event and explicitly throw the exception to the server (see the following sample service() method). If all exceptions are caught by the servlet, the error can be properly logged. Although many servers will record servlet exceptions in an error log, this action is server dependent and not guaranteed. In addition to the functionality described here, ServletException extends java.lang.Exception and, therefore, inherits all of its methods.

ServletException defines the following two constructors:

```
public ServletException()
public ServletException(String msg)
```

The first constructor is the default constructor that accepts no parameters. The second constructor accepts a descriptive message describing the error that has taken place or some other text. The following pseudocode demonstrates a typical situation in which ServletException is thrown.

```
public void service(HttpServletRequest request,
  HttpServletResponse response) throws ServletException,
  IOException
{
  try
  {
    //...servlet code goes here...
  }
  catch (Exception e)
  {
    log(e, "Error Description: " + e);

    throw new ServletException(e.toString());
  }
}
```

UnavailableException Class

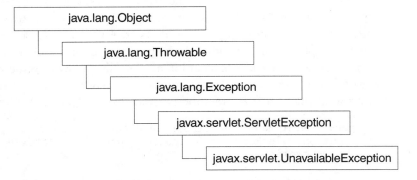

UnavailableException is an exception that extends ServletException and is thrown by the servlet to indicate that it is unavailable. Servlets may be unavailable for any number of reasons including network problems, an error in the servlet configuration, or a lack of system resources (e.g., memory or disk space). A well-written servlet will throw an UnavailableException whenever a condition that makes it inaccessible occurs.

UnavailableException defines the following two constructors:

```
public UnavailableException(Servlet servlet, String msg)
public UnavailableException(int seconds, Servlet servlet,
    String msg)
```

The first constructor accepts a Servlet object and a message describing the problem. Because UnavailableException is thrown by the servlet itself, simply pass "this" for the servlet parameter to reference the current servlet. The second constructor is identical to the first except for the addition of the seconds parameter. The seconds parameter represents the number of seconds the servlet is anticipated to be unavailable. A zero or negative number indicates that no estimate is available.

The first constructor should be used if the servlet requires an administrative action to correct the problem. For instance, the servlet will not be available until an administrator resolves some issue with the server or network (e.g., servlet misconfiguration or network inaccessibility). Use the second constructor when the servlet is temporarily unavailable and an estimate can be made regarding when it will be accessible. A temporarily unavailable condition might be caused by excessive network congestion or server load. In other words, given time, a temporarily unavailable condition should correct itself.

Summary

Though not utilized in every servlet, this chapter introduced several important classes and interfaces that are commonly used to build robust servlets. A strong understanding of these objects, in addition to those presented in Chapter 6, will get you well on your way to writing powerful servlets. The classes and interfaces discussed in this chapter are briefly summarized below.

Chapter Highlights

- The ServletInputStream class class provides an input stream for reading binary data from a client request.
- The ServletOutputStream class provides an output stream for writing binary data out to the client.
- The ServletConfig interface is implemented by the servlet engine in order to pass configuration information to a servlet.

- The `ServletContext` interface provides information to servlets regarding the environment in which they are running.
- A `ServletException` is thrown in response to some type of servlet error.
- An `UnavailableException` is thrown if, for some reason, the servlet becomes unavailable.

This chapter concludes the Introduction to Servlets part of the book. In the next part, Advanced Servlet Concepts, we will examine more complex servlet development issues including state and session management, writing thread safe code, and database access.

PART III

Advanced Servlet Concepts

CHAPTER 11

Writing Thread Safe Servlets

Thread safety is a common concern among Java programmers. Ensuring that two threads do not read or change data inconsistently is a constant challenge. Writing servlets is no different. The servlet interface does not protect the developer against multiple threads accessing servlet class and instance variables simultaneously.

In this chapter, we will explore several techniques for enforcing thread safety in your servlets. Specifically, the following four topics are covered:

- What is thread safety?
- Synchronization
- `service()`, `doGet()`, and `doPost()` local variables
- `SingleThreadModel` interface

Although these topics will provide you with sufficient information to write thread safe servlets, for an in-depth understanding of Java threads please see one of the many excellent books on the subject.

What Is Thread Safety?

An application is *thread safe* if it always behaves predictably regardless of the number of concurrent threads running in its process space. To achieve this predictable behavior, the servlet writer must ensure that no thread can read a variable while another thread is in the process of changing it. Although this may sound simple, thread safety is often difficult to achieve. The following scenario illustrates a common mistake that can lead to inconsistent behavior within an application.

This example may be trite, but it does a good job of conveying the importance of thread safety. Consider the following sequence of events regarding the use of a bank's automatic teller machine (ATM). We are assuming that this ATM system does not properly enforce thread safety.

1. A bank customer with a balance of $1000 in checking withdraws $800. To process this transaction, the ATM program first checks the balance of the checking account to confirm that at least $800 exists. After verifying a sufficient balance, the checking account is debited $800 and the cash is dispensed to the customer.

2. At another ATM, the customer's spouse simultaneously attempts to withdraw $500 from checking. Since the ATM program is not thread safe, it is possible for the second ATM to read the balance of the checking account after the first ATM checked the balance but before it actually debited the account. Since the second ATM verified a sufficient balance before the first ATM could debit the account, the account is debited another $500 and the cash is dispensed to the customer.

3. Because the ATM program is not thread safe, deductions of $500 and $800 were made to an account containing only $1000, leaving the account overdrawn.

This example contains a thread safety error known as a race condition. A *race condition* occurs when the proper behavior of the program relies on one thread completing execution before another. This timing requirement can result in inconsistent program behavior since there is usually no guarantee that one thread will finish before another. You may now understand the importance of enforcing thread safety in your own code. Listing 11.1 demonstrates a simple servlet that is not thread safe.

Listing 11.1   Example of a servlet that is not thread safe.

```
import javax.servlet.*;
import javax.servlet.http.*;
import java.io.*;

/**
 * The BankAccount servlet is an example of a servlet that
 * is not thread safe. A race condition is created between
 * the time that the checking account balance is read and
 * the time the account is debited.
 *
 * @author Dustin R. Callaway
 * @version 1.0, 06/06/98
 */
public class BankAccount extends HttpServlet
{
```

```
    //instance variables
    float checkingBalance;

    /**
     * init method is called when servlet is first loaded.
     */
    public void init(ServletConfig config) throws ServletException
    {
      super.init(config); //pass ServletConfig to parent

      checkingBalance = 1000; //start with $1000 in checking
    }


    /**
     * service method is invoked by any request to this
     * servlet. Displays the current value of the checking
     * and savings account.
     */
    public void service(HttpServletRequest request,
      HttpServletResponse response) throws ServletException,
      IOException
    {
      response.setContentType("text/plain");
      PrintWriter out = response.getWriter();

      if (checkingBalance >= 100) //always withdraw $100
      {
        //...some processing code may run here

        checkingBalance -= 100; //deduct $100 from checking

        out.println("Amount in Checking: " + checkingBalance);
      }
      else
      {
        out.println("Sorry, you only have " + checkingBalance +
          " dollars in your account.");
      }

      out.close();
    }
  }
```

The code that makes this servlet unsafe is shown here:

```
    if (checkingBalance >= 100) //always withdraw $100
    {
      //...some processing code may run here

      checkingBalance -= 100; //deduct $100 from checking

      out.println("Amount in Checking: " + checkingBalance);
    }
```

A race condition occurs between the time the thread verifies sufficient funds (the `if` statement) and the time the `checkingBalance` variable is decremented. If another thread executes the `if` statement after the first thread checked the balance but before the balance is decremented, the servlet may perform improperly.

NOTE: Race conditions only occur when reading or modifying shared objects. For example, since static class variables are shared across all requests to a servlet (and all threads that service these requests), race conditions may occur when class variables are used. Later in the chapter, we will see that objects declared inside the `service()`, `doGet()`, or `doPost()` method are automatically thread safe because they are not shared between threads.

However, there are many times when the use of shared objects is safe and appropriate. For example, opening a shared database connection that is used by all threads can often improve servlet performance. Because this database connection is not modified by any thread, there are no thread safety concerns.

So, the question remains: how do we make the preceding servlet thread safe? The Java `synchronized` keyword provides the answer. The next section describes the proper use of the `synchronized` keyword.

Synchronization

Synchronization in Java is the process of locking a variable so that it can be read and modified by only a single thread at a time. It allows the servlet engine to call the `service()`, `doGet()`, or `doPost()` method without having to wait for all prior executions of these methods to finish. The `synchronized` keyword eliminates race conditions by locking variables for a specified duration. The following code demonstrates how it can be used by the preceding servlet.

```
synchronized (this)
{
  if (checkingBalance >= 100) //always withdraw $100
  {
    //...some processing code may run here

    checkingBalance -= 100; //deduct $100 from checking

    out.println("Amount in Checking: " + checkingBalance);
  }
}
```

This code ensures that the `checkingBalance` variable cannot be read or altered by another thread while the synchronized block is executing. This eliminates the race condition and makes the servlet thread safe.

> **NOTE:** It is possible to synchronize the entire `service()` method rather than specific blocks of code within it. In this way, only one thread at a time can execute the method, ensuring that no other thread could read or modify the protected variables. The declaration of a synchronized `service()` method looks like this:
>
> ```
> public synchronized void service(HttpServletRequest
>     request, HttpServletResponse response) throws
>     ServletException, IOException
> ```
>
> However, this approach often incurs a large performance penalty. Synchronized blocks of code create a performance bottleneck since all other threads have to "wait in line" for the current thread to complete its execution of synchronized code. The more code that is synchronized, the greater the performance penalty. To avoid this penalty, minimize the amount of code that is synchronized by using the "`synchronized (this)`" technique shown in the text. This practice will reduce the bottleneck effect of synchronization by ensuring that variables remain locked for the least amount of time necessary.

When writing servlets, pay close attention to the way you handle class and instance level variables. It is not necessary to synchronize shared variables if they cannot be altered. For instance, if a shared database connection is instantiated in the `init()` method, it can be used by all threads without concern. However, if a shared object can be both read and modified, it may be a candidate for synchronization.

This concludes our very brief discussion about Java synchronization. Since this topic is not particular to writing servlets, this book does not attempt to fully educate the reader on writing thread safe Java code. For a more in-depth review on the subject, please see one of the many books on the market that focus on Java threads.

service(), doGet(), and doPost() Local Variables

In most server implementations, a new servlet object is not instantiated for each new client request. Rather, a single servlet object usually services all requests. This behavior explains how instance variables can often be shared.

So now you may be wondering, if a single servlet object services all requests, how are requests processed simultaneously? The answer is that each call to service(), doGet(), or doPost() acquires its own thread from the servlet thread pool. Though the servlet is instantiated only once, each request is processed by its own thread.

NOTE: Although this example assumes that the server uses a single servlet instance to handle all requests, remember that other server implementations may create multiple servlet instances. Because of this, it is a good practice to use static class variables rather than instance variables for shared resources. In this way, class variables can be shared between service() threads as well as between different instances of the servlet class. Regardless, for demonstration purposes, we use instance variables in this example (assuming that the server services all requests with a single servlet instance).

Because every call to service(), doGet(), or doPost() is executed in its own thread, variables local to these methods are not shared between requests and are automatically thread safe. Objects that are not meant to be shared between requests should be declared in either the service(), doGet(), or doPost() methods. These request-specific variables should then be passed to supporting functions in order to maintain thread safety. Consider the servlet in Listing 11.2. Can you find the thread safety problems in this code? The HTML form that invokes this servlet is shown in Listing 11.3.

Listing 11.2   This servlet's instance variable is not thread safe.

```
import javax.servlet.*;
import javax.servlet.http.*;
import java.io.*;

public class Greetings extends HttpServlet
{
  //instance variables
  String userName; //stores client's name


  /**
   * service method is called in response to any servlet request
   */
  public void service(HttpServletRequest request,
    HttpServletResponse response) throws ServletException,
    IOException
  {
    response.setContentType("text/plain");
    PrintWriter out = response.getWriter();
```

```
        userName = request.getParameter("name");
        printGreeting(out);

        out.close();
    }


    /**
     * printGreeting sends a simple message to the client
     *
     * @param out Client output stream
     */
    private void printGreeting(PrintWriter out)
    {
        out.println("Hello, " + userName);
    }
}
```

Listing 11.3 HTML form that sends the client's name to a servlet

```
<HTML>
<HEAD><TITLE>Enter Your Name</TITLE></HEAD>
<BODY>
<FORM METHOD="POST" ACTION="/servlet/Greetings">
<P>Name: <INPUT TYPE="TEXT" NAME="name" SIZE="25"></P>
<P><INPUT TYPE="SUBMIT" VALUE="Submit">
</FORM>
</BODY>
</HTML>
```

In a single user environment, this servlet would operate as expected. However, there is a thread safety concern when concurrent requests are received. Notice that the user's name is extracted from a Web variable that was submitted by the user. The problem arises when the user's name is assigned to the shared variable, userName. Because this variable is declared outside of the service() method, it is shared between all requests. You may now see the problem and the race condition that is created when multiple requests are received. Consider the following sequence of events.

1. A request is received from user "Bob" and the service() method is invoked to process the request.

2. The shared variable, userName, is assigned the value "Bob."

3. A second request is received from user "Fred" and the service() method is invoked to process the request.

4. Before the thread for the first request is able to call the printGreeting() function, the second thread sets userName to "Fred."

5. The first thread now calls the printGreeting() method which returns the message "Hello, Fred" rather than "Hello, Bob."

6. As long as no other request is processed between the time the second request sets the value of `userName` and the time the greeting is returned to the client, the second request will receive the message "Hello, Fred" as expected.

As you can see, a race condition is created between the time the value of `userName` is set and the time the greeting is returned to the client. Listing 11.4 demonstrates how this race condition can be eliminated by using variables declared within the `service()` method.

Listing 11.4   Servlet is made thread safe by eliminating instance variable.

```
import javax.servlet.*;
import javax.servlet.http.*;
import java.io.*;

public class Greetings extends HttpServlet
{
  /**
   * service method is called in response to any servlet request
   */
  public void service(HttpServletRequest request,
    HttpServletResponse response) throws ServletException,
    IOException
  {
    String userName; //stores client's name

    response.setContentType("text/plain");
    PrintWriter out = response.getWriter();

    userName = request.getParameter("name");

    printGreeting(out, userName);

    out.close();
  }


  /**
   * printGreeting sends a simple message to the client
   *
   * @param out Client output stream
   * @param userName Name of user
   */
  private void printGreeting(PrintWriter out, String userName)
  {
    out.println("Hello, " + userName);
  }
}
```

This servlet eliminates the race condition by eliminating the shared variable. Notice that userName is now declared inside of the service() method. Because each call to service() is handled by its own thread, this variable is protected (each request has its own copy) and cannot be modified by other requests. However, since userName is no longer globally visible, it must now be passed as a parameter to the printGreeting() function. The practice of declaring request-specific variables in the service(), doGet(), or doPost() methods and passing them to other functions is a powerful technique that ensures servlet thread safety.

SingleThreadModel Interface

The simplest way to ensure that a servlet is thread safe is to implement the SingleThreadModel interface. This interface defines no methods and simply serves as a flag to the server. If a servlet implements the SingleThreadModel interface, the server guarantees that no more than one thread can execute the service(), doGet(), or doPost() method at a time for a particular servlet instance. This restriction effectively guarantees that your servlet will be thread safe.

If the service() method cannot be executed concurrently, you may have concerns regarding the performance of servlets that implement the SingleThreadModel interface. These concerns are valid. However, some of the performance penalties are alleviated by maintaining a pool of servlet instances. When the servlet engine loads a servlet that implements SingleThreadModel, the engine automatically creates a pool of servlet instances to service concurrent requests. The size of this pool is usually configurable on the server. For example, the JRun servlet engine described in Chapter 8 provides a *SingleThreadModel Pool Size* setting (see Figure 11.1).

Although the SingleThreadModel technique is resource intensive, it is the simplest way to ensure thread safety and may be appropriate in many circumstances when servlet traffic is expected to be low. The servlet that is shown in Listing 11.5 implements the SingleThreadModel interface to provide thread safety.

NOTE: If excessive concurrent requests arrive such that the servlet instance pool is exhausted, the excess requests will be queued until an instance is available. This will usually have a strong negative impact on performance.

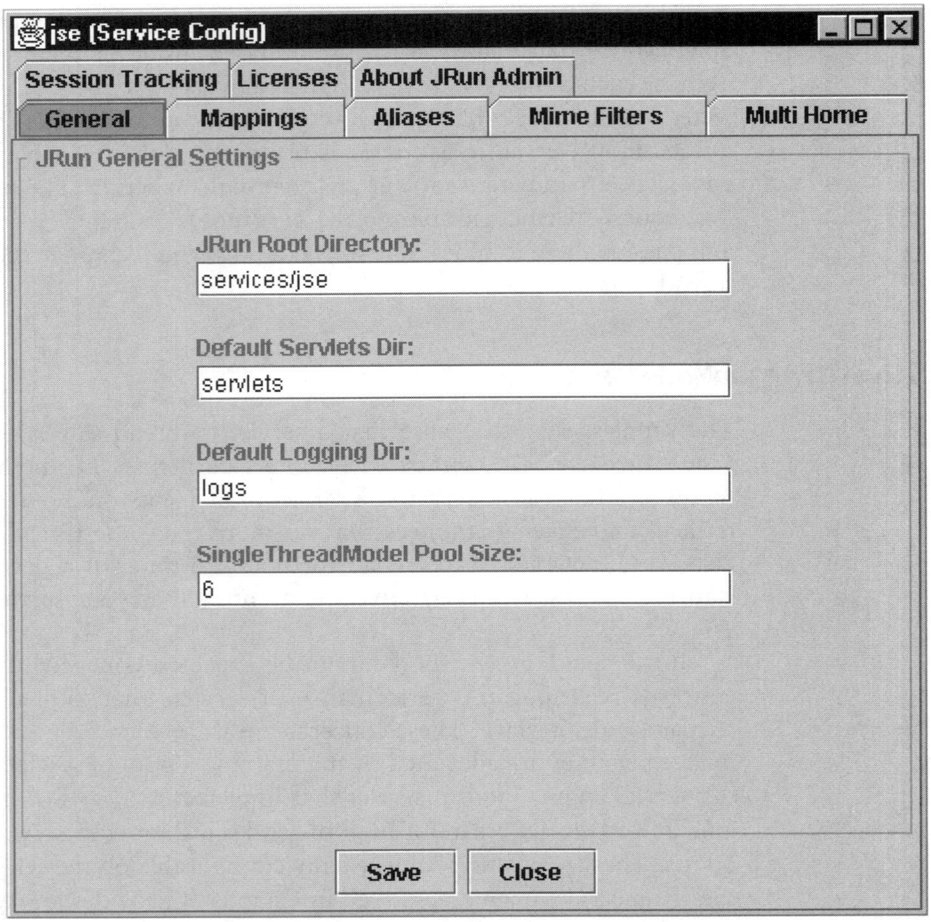

Figure 11.1   JRun Allows User to Specify Size of Servlet Instance Pool

Listing 11.1   SingleThreadModel guarantees thread safety.

```
import javax.servlet.*;
import javax.servlet.http.*;
import java.io.*;

public class Greetings extends HttpServlet implements
   SingleThreadModel
{
  //instance variables
  String userName; //stores client's name


  /**
   * service method is called in response to any servlet request
```

```
      */
   public void service(HttpServletRequest request,
      HttpServletResponse response) throws ServletException,
      IOException
   {
      response.setContentType("text/plain");
      PrintWriter out = response.getWriter();

      userName = request.getParameter("name");

      printGreeting(out);

      out.close();
   }


   /**
    * printGreeting sends a simple message to the client
    *
    * @param out Client output stream
    */
   private void printGreeting(PrintWriter out)
   {
      out.println("Hello, " + userName);
   }
}
```

It's that simple! Although earlier in the chapter we showed how the preceding servlet is not thread safe, thread safety can be achieved by simply implementing the SingleThreadModel interface.

Summary

This chapter introduced you to the inherent dangers of running servlets that are not thread safe as well as several techniques that ensure thread safety. Whenever you encounter seemingly random, infrequent, or otherwise perplexing bugs in your servlets, evaluate your servlet for any code that may violate the rules of thread safety. At first, if you are not accustomed to dealing with threads, this may seem a bit unnatural. However, once you become accustomed to always asking yourself the question, "How will this portion of code respond to multiple concurrent calls?" you will be well on your way to writing thread safe code.

In addition, remember that testing servlets in a single-user environment is not a true indication of how they will perform under load. If you develop servlets with multiple users in mind and simulate multiple users when testing, the aggravations resulting from race conditions and other thread safety violations will be greatly reduced. In the next chapter, we will explore a very useful mechanism known as an HTTP redirect.

Chapter Highlights

- An application is *thread safe* if it always behaves in a predictable manner regardless of the number of concurrent threads running in its process space.

- To achieve thread safety the servlet writer must ensure that no thread can read a variable while another thread is in the process of changing it.

- A *race condition* occurs when the proper behavior of the program relies upon one thread to complete execution before another. This timing requirement can result in inconsistent program behavior.

- *Synchronization* in Java is the process of locking variables so that they can only be read and modified by a single thread at a time. The `synchronized` keyword eliminates race conditions by locking variables for a specified duration.

- Typically, a new servlet object is not instantiated for each client request. Rather, a single servlet object usually services all requests. Each call to `service()`, `doGet()`, or `doPost()` acquires its own thread from the servlet thread pool. Even though the servlet is instantiated only once, each request is processed by its own thread.

- Because every call to `service()`, `doGet()`, or `doPost()` is executed in its own thread, variables local to these methods are not shared between requests and are automatically thread safe.

- The simplest way to ensure that a servlet is thread safe is to implement the `SingleThreadModel` interface. If a servlet implements `SingleThreadModel`, the server guarantees that no more than one thread can execute the `service()`, `doGet()`, or `doPost()` method at a time. This restriction effectively guarantees thread safety within your servlet.

CHAPTER 12

HTTP Redirects

This chapter covers an important mechanism supported by the HTTP proto-col—HTTP redirects. An HTTP redirect allows the server to respond to a client request with instructions to load a resource at a different location. Most browsers will automatically request the new resource in response to a redirect. Specifically, the following topics are discussed in this chapter:

- What is an HTTP redirect?
- HTTP header syntax for a redirect
- Sending a redirect with the Servlet API

What Is an HTTP Redirect?

An *HTTP redirect* is a set of instructions included in the header of an HTTP response that instructs the browser to issue a new request to a new URL. Though you may not notice them, redirects are extremely common on the Web and are useful in a number of different circumstances. For example, consider the following scenario.

The Web site for the Acme Company was originally hosted at *http://www.isp.com/~acme*. However, as Acme's Web site traffic and online sales increased, they decided to acquire their own domain name and host the site themselves. Acme's new URL is:

http://www.acmesite.com

But what about the people still referencing Acme's old URL? An obvious solu-tion would be to display a page at the old URL containing a hyperlink to the new URL. This method is very effective but still requires the user to take action in order to visit the new site.

HTTP redirects offer a more seamless way to transfer a user from one URL to another. Rather than simply displaying a page containing a hyperlink to the new URL, Acme decides to implement an HTTP redirect. Whenever a user references the old URL, the response will include the proper redirect instructions such that the browser will automatically request the page at the new location. Once the browser receives the redirect, the user is seamlessly transferred to the new site (most likely unaware that a redirect has taken place).

Although redirects are supported by practically all current browsers, it is good practice to include a hyperlink to the new URL in the body of the redirect response in case the user's browser does not support automatic HTTP redirects. The next two sections will examine redirect syntax and how redirects can be issued from within a Java servlet.

HTTP Header Syntax for a Redirect

We have established that a redirect is an HTTP response from the server instructing the client to request a resource at a different URL. There are two key elements in the header of an HTTP response that convey a redirect to the client. These elements are the HTTP status code and the Location header.

An HTTP redirect response uses an HTTP status code of either "301 Moved Permanently" or "302 Moved Temporarily" accompanied by a Location header containing a valid URL. If the client receives an HTTP response with status code 301 or 302, it will immediately request the resource at the URL designated by the Location header. If no Location header exists, the browser will display the status code message (indicating that the item has moved) and perhaps a more detailed description of the problem. The browser should respond identically to either HTTP status code 301 or 302 with one exception; in response to a "301 Moved Permanently" status code, the browser should update any bookmarks pointing to the old location. A typical redirect response (including all HTTP headers) is shown here:

```
HTTP/1.1 301 Moved Permanently
Date: Sat, 11 Jul 1998 19:45:12 GMT
Server: Apache/1.3.0 (Unix)
Location: http://www.acmesite.com/index.html
Content-Type: text/html

<HTML>
<HEAD><TITLE>301 Moved Permanently</TITLE></HEAD>
<BODY>
<H1>Moved Permanently</H1>
Document has moved <A HREF="http://www.acmesite.com">here.</A>
</BODY>
</HTML>
```

Let's take a moment to examine this redirect response. First, the response indicates a "301 Moved Permanently" HTTP status code. At this point, the client will search the response for a Location header. If found, the client immediately requests the resource at the new URL (as specified by the Location header). In addition to the status code and Location header, notice that an HTML document is included in the response. This document provides an informative message and a hyperlink for browsers that do not support automatic redirects. This message may also be useful for browsers that do support redirects if it takes more than a few seconds to load the resource from the new URL.

Finally, it should also be noted that the URL stored in the Location header need not be fully qualified. For instance, to redirect a request from the document index.html to welcome.html in the same directory, the value of the Location header may simply contain welcome.html. If no domain or path information is specified in the Location header, the domain and path of the originally requested resource are assumed.

Now that we understand how redirects are constructed at the HTTP header level, we will examine how to issue redirects from within a servlet. For more information on HTTP status codes and headers, see Appendices H and I, or RFC 2068.

Sending a Redirect with the Servlet API

There are two ways for a servlet to send an HTTP redirect. The first way is to manually set the HTTP status code and add the Location header to the response. The following service() method demonstrates how this is done.

```
public void service(HttpServletRequest request,
  HttpServletResponse response) throws ServletException,
  IOException
{
  String newURL = "http://www.acmesite.com/index.html";

  response.setContentType("text/html");

  response.setStatus(
    HttpServletResponse.SC_MOVED_PERMANENTLY);

  response.setHeader("Location", newURL);

  PrintWriter out = response.getWriter();

  out.println("<HTML>");
  out.println("<HEAD>");
  out.println("<TITLE>301 Moved Permanently</TITLE>");
```

```
        out.println("</HEAD>");
        out.println("<BODY>");
        out.println("Document moved to <A HREF=\"" + newURL +
          "\">here.</A>");
        out.println("</BODY>");
        out.println("</HTML>");

        out.close();
    }
```

Let's examine this code. The setStatus() method of HttpServletResponse sets the HTTP response code to "301 Moved Permanently." This is the first step in issuing the redirect. Next, the setHeader() method of HttpServletResponse is used to add a Location header to the response that includes the new URL information. Finally, an HTML document is added to the body of the response for clients that do not support automatic redirects.

That may have seemed pretty easy. However, using a specialized method, the Servlet API can make certain types of redirects even easier. The HttpServletResponse object includes the following method for sending temporary redirects:

```
public void sendRedirect(String location) throws IOException
```

The sendRedirect() method accepts a single parameter—a String describing the new location of the requested resource.

This method automatically sets the HTTP status code of the response to "302 Moved Temporarily," adds the appropriate Location header, and generates a generic HTML message. Keep in mind that the sendRedirect() method requires a fully qualified URL. Relative URLs are not permitted. Thus, the sendRedirect() method is limited to sending temporary redirects using fully qualified URLs. For permanent redirects or redirects requiring relative URLs, use the manual redirect method demonstrated previously. The following service() method illustrates the simplicity of the sendRedirect() method.

```
public void service(HttpServletRequest request,
    HttpServletResponse response) throws ServletException,
    IOException
{
    response.sendRedirect("http://www.acmesite.com/");
    return; //good practice to exit immediately after redirect
}
```

One line is all it takes. The HTTP response (including headers) looks like this:

```
HTTP/1.1 302 Moved Temporarily
Server: servletrunner/2.1
Content-Type: text/html
```

```
Location: http://www.acmesite.com/
Content-Length: 152
Date: Sat, 11 Jul 1998 21:06:38 GMT

<head><title>Document Moved</title></head>
<body><h1>Document Moved</h1>
This document has moved <a href="http://www.acmesite.com">here
</a>.<p>
</body>
```

Notice that the sendRedirect() method created all of the essential elements of an HTTP redirect. The "302 Moved Temporarily" status code was set, the Location header was added to the response, and an HTML message was included for older browsers. For temporary redirects that use absolute URLs, the HttpServletResponse object's sendRedirect() method is quick and easy.

NOTE: The sendRedirect() method should be executed before any data is sent to the output stream. Likewise, no data should be sent to the output stream after the sendRedirect() method is called. In fact, it is a good practice to immediately exit the service(), doGet(), or doPost() method after execution of the sendRedirect() method.

Summary

This chapter introduced an extremely useful HTTP mechanism. HTTP redirects allow a server to seamlessly redirect clients to another location. Among other possibilities, redirects allow Web sites to temporarily or permanently change URLs without affecting users. In the next chapter, we will examine another useful HTTP mechanism—cookies.

Chapter Highlights
- An HTTP redirect is a set of instructions included in the header of an HTTP response that instructs the browser to issue a new request to a new URL.
- There are two key elements in the header of an HTTP response that convey a redirect to the client. These elements are the HTTP status code and the Location header. An HTTP redirect response uses an HTTP status code of either "301 Moved Permanently" or "302 Moved Temporarily" accompanied by a Location header containing a valid URL.

- A servlet can send a redirect in two steps. First, set the HTTP status code of the response to 301 or 302 using the `HttpServletResponse` object's `setStatus()` method. Second, use the `HttpServletResponse` object's `setHeader()` method to add a `Location` header indicating the new URL.

- The Servlet API contains a shortcut method for sending temporary redirects that use fully qualified URLs. The `sendRedirect()` method of the `HttpServletResponse` object automatically sets the HTTP response status code to 302, adds the necessary `Location` header, and constructs a simple HTML message for browsers that do not support automatic redirects.

CHAPTER 13

Cookies

A cookie is an HTTP mechanism that is useful for maintaining specific user settings and managing state. State management is necessary in order to "track" individual users as they traverse a Web site and store user-specific information such as the contents of an electronic shopping cart. State management is covered in depth in the next chapter.

This chapter explains:

- What is a cookie?
- HTTP header syntax for a cookie
- Setting cookies with the Servlet API

What Is a Cookie?

Consider an electronic commerce Web site that allows users to order products from an online catalog. As customers browse the catalog, they are given the option of adding products to their virtual shopping cart. When they have completed shopping, they may then proceed to the virtual checkout line where their purchases are totaled and their credit card is charged.

You may be wondering how this sort of functionality is accomplished. After all, in Chapter 3 we learned that HTTP is a stateless protocol. Once a user issues a request and receives a response, the server has no memory of the transaction. Furthermore, when the same user makes another request, the server has no way to distinguish this user from any other. So, how can the server remember the contents of each user's shopping cart? This is where the concept of a cookie comes to the rescue.

A *cookie* is a simple mechanism used to store and retrieve user-specific[1] information on the Web. When an HTTP server receives a request, in addition to the requested document, the server may choose to return some state information that is stored by a cookie-enabled client. This state information includes a URL range within which the information should be returned to the server. The URL range is composed of the server's domain and some path information. Whenever the client issues an HTTP request, it checks the URL of the request against the URL ranges of all stored cookies. If a match is found, the state information is included in the client's request. In this way, the server can effectively overcome the stateless nature of the Web and track a client from request to request.

In the electronic commerce Web site example cited earlier, a cookie may have been used to store the items in a customer's shopping cart. When the customer requests to check out, the selected items (which are stored in a cookie) are transmitted back to the server for processing. Another common solution to the shopping cart problem is to store the contents of each customer's shopping cart on the server (either in memory or in a database) and send a cookie containing only a unique customer identification number. In this manner, when the customer attempts to check out, the database can be queried for the shopping cart contents using the customer's ID number that was returned in a cookie. We will discuss this type of state management in detail in the next chapter.

Before investigating how cookies are passed in the HTTP header, let's briefly examine the history of the cookie concept. Netscape Communications first proposed the idea of a cookie and they proceeded to add cookie support to their popular browser (Netscape Navigator). Netscape states that this mechanism is called a "cookie" for "no compelling reason." You may view the original cookie spec on Netscape's Web site at:

> *http://home.netscape.com/newsref/std/cookie_spec.html*

Since Netscape first proposed the cookie, the cookie specification has been improved and expanded (see RFC 2109). Today, cookies are a very popular method for managing state on the Web.

HTTP Header Syntax for a Cookie

In this section, we will examine how cookies are passed in the header of HTTP requests and responses. Let's start with the server response that sets the cookie.

---

[1]Actually, cookies are often client-specific rather than user-specific. This means that they store information particular to a specific client (i.e., a Web browser running on a particular machine) without regard to which user is actually operating the client software. However, some browsers, such as Netscape Navigator, do support multiple user profiles. These profiles allow the browser to store cookie information for each user separately and maintain a distinction between users. Profiles serve to make cookies more user-specific.

The HTTP header syntax for setting a cookie is shown here (assume the entire instruction is on one line).

```
Set-Cookie: <NAME>=<VALUE>; expires=<DATE>;
   domain=<DOMAIN_NAME>; path=<PATH>; secure
```

The Set-Cookie instruction is included in the header of the server's HTTP response to instruct the client to store a cookie. Multiple Set-Cookie headers can be included in a single HTTP response. When a cookie-enabled browser encounters the Set-Cookie header in the server's response, it stores the cookie for future use. An explanation of each attribute of the Set-Cookie header is given in Table 13.1.

A typical HTTP header for a response that sets a client-side cookie is shown here:

```
HTTP/1.0 200 OK
Server: Netscape-Enterprise/2.01
Content-Type: text/html
Content-Length: 87
Set-Cookie: customerID=1234; domain=acmesite.com; path=/orders
```

The cookie set by this HTTP header will be returned whenever the client makes a request to the /orders path of the acmesite.com domain. For instance, a request to the following URL would return the cookie:

http://www.acmesite.com/orders/checkout.html

Now that we have discovered how the server stores a cookie on the client, let's take a look at how the cookie information is returned to the server. Similar to the manner in which the server sets a cookie, the client sends the cookie information within the HTTP header. However, rather than Set-Cookie, the header that returns state information is simply called Cookie. The syntax of the Cookie header is as follows:

```
Cookie: <NAME1>=<VALUE1>; <NAME2>=<VALUE2> ...
```

Whenever a client issues a request, it first attempts to match the domain and path information of the request against all stored cookies. If a match is found, the name/value pair of the cookie is added to the Cookie header. A typical example of a client request that contains cookie information follows.

```
GET /login.html HTTP/1.0
User-Agent: Mozilla/4.02 [en] (Win95; I)
Accept: image/gif, image/x-xbitmap, image/jpeg, */*
Cookie: customerID=1234; color=blue
```

This cookie will allow the server to extract the user's customer ID number as well as their background color preference. In this manner, the server can identify users, maintain user-defined preferences, and enforce security policies.

Table 13.1   Attributes of the `Set-Cookie` Header

Attribute	Description
`<NAME>=<VALUE>`	The name/value pair for a cookie is similar to the name/value pair for a Web variable transmitted in an HTTP POST operation. `NAME` is the name of the cookie variable and `VALUE` is the value stored in this variable. This is the only required attribute of the `Set-Cookie` header. The following is an example of a name/value pair within a `Set-Cookie` header: `Set-Cookie: customerID=1234`.
`expires=<DATE>`	The `expires` attribute indicates when the cookie is no longer valid. When a cookie expires, it should be removed from storage and no longer given out. If no `expires` attribute exists, then the cookie will expire at the conclusion of the user's session (when the browser is closed). The date should be in the following format (according to RFC 822): `Weekday, DD-Mon-YYYY HH:MM:SS GMT`. An example of setting a cookie with an `expires` attribute is: `Set-Cookie: customerID=1234; expires=Saturday, 04-Jul-98 23:59:59 GMT`.

`domain=`
`<DOMAIN_NAME>`
	The `domain` attribute indicates the domain to which the cookie should be returned. If the domain of a client request matches the `domain` attribute of a cookie, then the request's path is compared to the cookie's `path` attribute. If there is a match, the cookie is transmitted to the server along with the request.
	
	A successful domain match for the domain attribute *sourcestream.com* would include the following:
	
	    www.sourcestream.com
	    orders.sourcestream.com
	    info.sourcestream.com
	
	In addition, a server cannot arbitrarily set a cookie for any domain. It can only set cookies for its own domain.
	
	For the seven top-level domains including "COM", "EDU", "NET", "ORG", "GOV", "MIL", and "INT", the `domain` attribute must contain at least two periods. This prevents a server from setting a cookie using a generic domain such as ".com."
	
	The default value of the `domain` attribute is the host name of the server that requested the cookie. An example `domain` attribute is shown here.
	
	`Set-Cookie: customerID=1234; domain=sourcestream.com`

`path=<PATH>`	The `path` attribute indicates the URLs within a domain for which the cookie is valid. If a domain match is made, then the client compares the request's path information to the cookie's `path` attribute. If the request's path falls into the cookie's path range, the cookie is valid and is returned to the server with the request. If no `path` attribute is specified in the `Set-Cookie` header, the path is assumed to be the same as the resource that is being returned by the server. The most general, or root, path is specified by "/". Here is an example `path` attribute: `Set-Cookie: customerID=1234; domain=sourcestream.com; path=/`
`secure`	The `secure` attribute indicates that this cookie should only be sent across a secure (i.e., encrypted) connection such as HTTPS. If a secure connection has not been established, the cookie is not sent.

Here are a few other notes about cookies. To learn more about cookies, see Netscape's original cookie specification at *http://home.netscape.com/newsref/std/cookie_spec.html* or RFC 2109, "HTTP State Management Mechanism."

- It is possible to have multiple `Set-Cookie` headers in a single HTTP response. If two cookies are set with identical names and paths, the second will overwrite the first. However, if two cookies with identical names but separate paths are set, the two name/value pairs will coexist and the appropriate cookie will be returned when there is a path match.
- Cookies with more specific paths should be sent before cookies with more general paths. For instance, a cookie using the path "/orders" should be set before a cookie using the path "/".
- The Netscape cookie specification indicates that the client should store a maximum of 300 cookies, with each cookie having a maximum size of 4 kilobytes. Also, the client should store no more than 20 cookies per domain. This limit helps to ensure that cookies cannot exhaust the client's storage capacity.

Setting Cookies with the Servlet API

Now that we understand the syntax for setting a cookie on the client, it becomes a rather simple task to add the `Set-Cookie` instruction to the HTTP response header. Let's first take a look at how this can be done manually using the Servlet API.

As we discovered in Chapter 6, the `HttpServletResponse` interface defines a method called `setHeader()` that allows a servlet to add HTTP headers to the response. The declaration for the `setHeader()` method looks like this:

```
public abstract void setHeader(String name, String value)
```

The `name` parameter sets the name of the header and the `value` parameter specifies a `String` value. The following sample code demonstrates how this method can be used to send cookies.

```
public void service(HttpServletRequest request,
  HttpServletResponse response) throws ServletException,
  IOException
{
  response.setContentType("text/plain");

  response.setHeader("Set-Cookie", "customerID=1234");
  response.setHeader("Set-Cookie", "color=blue");
```

```
        PrintWriter out = response.getWriter();

        out.println("You just received a cookie.");

        out.close();
    }
```

The preceding code sends the client two cookies—one named `customerID` having a value `1234` and the other named `color` having a value of `blue`. These cookies may be used to identify the user and set user-defined preferences. Though the method shown above appears rather simple and straightforward, the Servlet API provides a better, more object-oriented, way to send cookies.

Let's start by examining the `javax.servlet.http.Cookie` class. This class provides an object representation of a cookie. In essence, it encapsulates the state information contained in a cookie, thus allowing for easy modification and retrieval of this information. The `Cookie` class also simplifies the process of setting other cookie attributes such as `domain` and `path`.

The constructor for the `Cookie` class looks like this:

```
public Cookie(String name, String value)
```

Therefore, a `Cookie` object can be instantiated easily with the following line of code:

```
Cookie myCookie = new Cookie("customerID", "1234");
```

That was simple! Setting the rest of the attributes is just as easy. The following code demonstrates how a typical `Cookie` object may be created. Table 13.2 describes the methods of the `Cookie` class.

```
Cookie myCookie = new Cookie("password", "joshua");
myCookie.setDomain("sourcestream.com");
myCookie.setPath("/");
myCookie.setSecure(true);
```

Once we have created a `Cookie` object, we need to send it to the client. Again, the Servlet API provides a simple method for accomplishing this task. The `HttpServletResponse` object (passed to the `service()`, `doGet()`, and `doPost()` methods) provides the following method for transmitting cookies to the client:

```
public void addCookie (cookie)
```

The `addCookie()` method can be called multiple times with multiple `Cookie` objects. However, keep in mind that the original cookie specification indicates that no more than twenty cookies from any single domain should be stored.

Table 13.2 Methods of the Cookie Class

Method	Description
setComment()	Sends a comment describing the purpose of the cookie. Some clients may use this comment when advising the user that a cookie is being set.
getComment()	Returns the comment set by the setComment() method.
setDomain()	Sets the domain for which this cookie is valid.
getDomain()	Returns the domain set by the setDomain() method.
setMaxAge()	Sets the maximum amount of time the cookie should persist. This method accepts an integer value representing the number of seconds before the cookie expires. A zero value will delete an existing cookie. A negative value indicates that the cookie should expire when the user session ends (the browser is closed).
getMaxAge()	Returns the number of seconds before the cookie expires as set by the setMaxAge() method.
setPath()	Sets the path portion of the URL in which the cookie is valid.
getPath()	Returns the path portion of the URL set by the setPath() method.
setSecure()	Specifies whether the cookie information should be transmitted across an unsecure connection. If true is passed to the setSecure() method, cookie information will only be sent if the client has established a secure link (such as HTTPS) with the server.
getSecure()	Returns the boolean value set by the setSecure() method.
getName()	Returns the name of the cookie set in the constructor when the cookie was first instantiated (this name cannot be changed). Represents the name portion of the name/value pair. For example, consider this cookie: Cookie: customerID=1234 The name of this cookie is customerID.
setValue()	Sets the cookie's value. Represents the value portion of the name/value pair. For example, consider the cookie shown here: Cookie: customerID=1234 The value of this cookie is 1234.
getValue()	Returns the value of the cookie set in the constructor or by the setValue() method.
setVersion()	Sets the version of the cookie protocol being used.
getVersion()	Returns the version of the cookie protocol set by the setVersion() method.

The `service()` method that follows demonstrates how multiple cookies can be set using `Cookie` objects and the `addCookie()` method. For the code to execute as shown, it is assumed that the `java.io.*` and `javax.servlet.http.*` packages have been imported.

```
public void service(HttpServletRequest request,
   HttpServletResponse response) throws IOException
{
   response.setContentType("text/plain");
   PrintWriter out = response.getWriter();

   Cookie customerID = new Cookie("customerID", "1234");
   Cookie color = new Cookie("color", "blue");

   response.addCookie(customerID);
   response.addCookie(color);

   out.println("This response sets 2 cookies.");

   out.close();
}
```

NOTE: To delete a cookie, simply create a new `Cookie` object having the same name as the cookie you wish to delete and set its maximum age to zero (0). Add this cookie to the response and the matching cookie on the client will be deleted. The sample code below demonstrates how to delete an existing cookie from the client's browser (assuming that a cookie named "customerID" already exists on the client).

```
Cookie customerID = new Cookie("customerID", "");
customerID.setMaxAge(0);
response.addCookie(customerID);
```

Figure 13.1
*Cookie Setting
Dialog Box*

Note that when no domain or path information is specified for a cookie, the default is the domain of the server that sent the cookie and the path of the Web server's root ("/"), respectively. After constructing your first servlet to implement cookies, you may need a way to test it. A simple way to test cookies generated by your servlet is to enable your browser's "Warn me before accepting cookies" option before requesting the servlet. This option should aid in troubleshooting cookies by displaying a dialog box similar to the one shown in Figure 13.1. This dialog box will be repeated for all cookies included in the response.

Another way to test a servlet that sets cookies is to use the *Protocol Explorer* utility described in Chapter 3 and provided on the accompanying CD-ROM. This utility allows you to view the entire HTTP header returned by the servlet (including the Set-Cookie headers). In the screen shot shown in Figure 13.2, you can see the cookie being set in the HTTP header.

Cookies provide a simple and efficient way to manage state on the Web. Cookies enrich the Web experience by allowing users to customize Web sites to their own preferences and enable other exciting features such as virtual shopping carts, Web site tracking and statistics, and security.

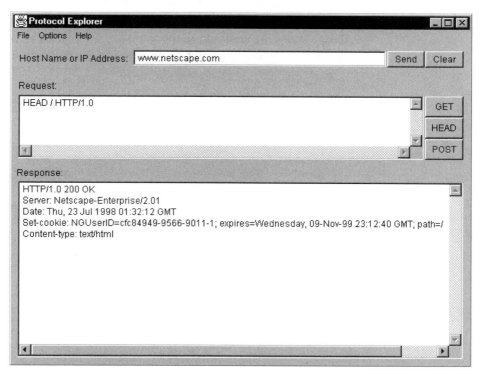

Figure 13.2 The Set-Cookie Header as Displayed by *Protocol Explorer*

Summary

Cookies provide a simple solution to state management and security. Cookies can be used to enhance the Web experience by "remembering" user preferences or storing items in an electronic shopping cart. Although we touched on the subject of state management during our discussion on cookies, the next chapter will dig far deeper into this important subject. We will also examine the new state management mechanisms included in the Servlet API.

Chapter Highlights

- A *cookie* is a simple mechanism used to store and retrieve user-specific information on the Web.

- A cookie can be transmitted to the client by adding the `Set-Cookie` header to the HTTP response using the `HttpServletResponse` object's `setHeader()` method.

- The `javax.servlet.http.Cookie` class provides an object representation of a cookie. In essence, it encapsulates the state information contained in a cookie, thus allowing for easy modification and retrieval of this information.

- The `addCookie()` method of the `HttpServletResponse` object allows one or more `Cookie` objects to be added to the response.

CHAPTER 14

State and Session Management

We have already established that HTTP is a stateless protocol. In the first section of this chapter, we will review what it means to be "stateless." Though stateless protocols have many advantages over those that are stateful, they also present some significant technical challenges. For instance, the lack of state prevents the server from uniquely identifying each user. This limitation inhibits the implementation of user-defined preferences since the server cannot distinguish one user from another. In addition, security policies cannot be enforced if the server does not know who is requesting a particular resource. Fortunately, several methods exist that effectively add state to the HTTP protocol. This chapter explores some of these methods as well as introduces the state and session management mechanisms built into the Servlet API.

At the end of this chapter, you should have a strong understanding of stateless protocols and some common methods that allow state to be added. You should also understand how state can be added to HTTP using several specialized objects from the Servlet API. Specifically the following topics are covered in this chapter:

- What is a stateless protocol?
- What is a session?
- State and session management defined
- State and session management methods
- Session management with the Servlet API

What Is a Stateless Protocol?

HTTP is a stateless protocol. A protocol is said to be *stateless* if it has no memory of prior connections and cannot distinguish one client's request from that of another. In contrast, FTP is a *stateful* protocol because the connection is not opened and closed with every request. After the initial login, the FTP server maintains the user's credentials throughout the session. On the other hand, due to its stateless nature, there is no inherent method in HTTP for tracking a client's traversal of a Web site. Every request uses a new connection from an anonymous client. State is extremely useful for secure sites that require a user to log in or for electronic commerce sites that provide customers with a virtual shopping cart.

The stateless nature of HTTP is both a strength and a weakness. It is a strength in that its stateless nature keeps the protocol simple and straightforward. It also consumes fewer resources on the server and can support more simultaneous users since there are no client credentials and connections to maintain. The disadvantage is the increased overhead required to create a new connection with each request and the inability to track a single user as he traverses a Web site. The rest of this chapter will discuss ways to overcome these disadvantages.

What Is a Session?

There is more than one definition of the term session. In the traditional sense, a *session* is a persistent network connection between two hosts (usually a client and a server) that facilitates the exchange of information. When the connection is closed, the session is over. However, we are not interested in this type of session. Rather, let's focus on another type of session known as an *HTTP session* or a *virtual session*. This type of session involves a virtual connection between the client and server rather than a physical one. Let's first examine what is meant by a "virtual connection" as we attempt to understand an HTTP session.

In an HTTP transaction, each connection between the client and server is very brief. This is an inherent trait of a stateless protocol. To illustrate, a typical stateless protocol transaction goes like this: the client establishes a connection to the server, issues a request, receives a response, and then closes the connection. Because a persistent connection between the client and server is not maintained between requests, the server's tie to the client is severed once the connection is closed. If the same client issues a new request, the server cannot associate this connection with the client's previous one. The fact that the server "forgets about" the client after the connection is closed presents significant challenges to the HTTP protocol. If not remedied, this disconnect between client and server can lead to the following problems and limitations:

- If the server requires client authentication (e.g., a client must log in), the client must reauthenticate with every request. The server does not realize that it has already authenticated this client because the connection between the two was lost.

- Storing user-specific information, such as the contents of a shopping cart or user-defined preferences, is not possible because the server cannot distinguish one client from another.

The solution to these problems is to establish a persistent "virtual connection" between the client and server. A virtual connection associates each request received by the server with the client that issued it. This association is accomplished by requiring the client to return a piece of state information with each new request. The server uses this piece of information (usually called a session ID or user ID) to uniquely identify the client and associate the current request with the client's previous requests. By allowing the server to identify the client, virtual connections alleviate the problems presented above. These virtual connections are commonly referred to as sessions. Sessions are used to maintain state and client identity across multiple requests.

In a traditional session, all client requests are associated by virtue of the fact that they share the same network connection. In contrast, an HTTP session associates client requests by virtue of the fact that they all share the same session ID. A traditional session refers to the duration of time that a network connection is open. Similarly, an HTTP session refers to the duration of time that a virtual connection is active. In short, an *HTTP session* is a series of associated requests in which the client can be uniquely identified. This association between the HTTP client and the HTTP server persists across multiple requests and/or connections for a specific period of time.

We know that the traditional type of session expires when the network connection is closed. However, since an HTTP session persists between requests (with each request opening and closing a connection), you might be asking, "When does an HTTP session expire?" The duration of an HTTP session is configurable on the server. A common approach is to instruct the server to expire any sessions that have been inactive for more than a specified amount of time, say fifteen minutes. In this case, the session will persist between a client's requests as long as they are received no more than fifteen minutes apart. If the client waits more than fifteen minutes before issuing a new request, the server will expire the client's session and the client will be required to log in again (the server usually issues a valid session ID with each log in). Automatically expiring sessions after a period of inactivity ensures that server resources are not consumed by old sessions.

Now let's consider the question "What does it mean for an HTTP session to expire?" Essentially, this means that the unique session ID used to identify a client is removed from storage along with any associated data (e.g., shopping cart contents). Session IDs are usually stored in memory or in a database. Once a session ID expires and is removed from storage, the client that utilized this session ID must log in again in order to be assigned a new session ID.

NOTE: For security purposes, it is good practice to allow users to immediately expire their sessions. This is usually accomplished by providing a log out option on the Web site's menu bar. When the user chooses to log out, the session ID should be deleted. In this way, if someone else uses the same browser before the session would have timed out, they will not be able to utilize the previous user's session (and therefore, the previous user's security privileges).

Likewise, the reason that you should automatically expire sessions that are stale (inactive for a period of time) is that many users will not log out properly. Rather, they may just close their browser or jump to another site. To prevent storing excess session information, old sessions should be purged regularly.

To illustrate, let's walk through a typical series of events that comprise the lifecycle of an HTTP session. Keep in mind that a network connection is opened before each client request and closed after each server response.

1. The client requests a resource from the server.

2. The server returns an authentication challenge that results in the browser displaying a name/password dialog box.

3. The client returns a valid name and password.

4. The server returns a valid session ID that allows this client to be uniquely identified. In this case, the session ID is sent in a cookie that will be returned by the client with each request. THIS BEGINS THE HTTP SESSION.

5. The client issues any number of requests to the server. The server is able to identify the client and the client's security privileges based on the session ID that accompanies each request.

6. The client closes the browser without explicitly logging out (an explicit logout should immediately expire the session).

7. After fifteen minutes, the server expires the session by deleting the row containing the session ID from a database table. THIS CONCLUDES THE HTTP SESSION.

This example used a cookie to communicate the session ID. In the next section, we will explore different ways that session information can be passed between client and server.

State and Session Management Defined

In this chapter, we often refer to "state/session" management. However, there is a distinct difference between state management and session management.

State management is the ability to maintain a client's current state (e.g., items in a shopping cart or user preferences) by passing client-specific information between the client and server. However, with simple state management, the server may not be able to uniquely identify each client. Allowing clients to select their background color is an example of state management. Once selected, the client will transmit this preferred color to the server with each request.

Although the server can determine the client's preferred background color, it cannot uniquely identify the client. For instance, assume that two clients select blue as their preferred background color. Each time either of these clients issues a request, the request will include a piece of state information such as `bcolor=blue` that will convey their preference. Although the server can determine the preferred background color for each of these clients, it cannot distinguish one client from the other. State management can be useful for storing small amounts of state information when the client's identity is not relevant.

In contrast, *session management* maintains both state and identity. Session management provides an association between the client and the server that allows the server to uniquely identify each client. This association persists across requests for a specified period of time. In essence, session management is a superset of state management (in fact, these two terms are often used interchangeably). However, in addition to managing state, it also keeps track of client identity. For example, assume that two clients select blue as their preferred background color. Rather than sending a piece of state information, such as the preferred background color, to the client, the server will send a unique session ID.

This session ID, which uniquely identifies each client, is returned to the server with each request. The server uses the session ID to identify the client. After the client's identity is established, the server can determine the client's preferred background color, which may be stored in memory or in a database associated with the client's session ID.

Session management is useful for storing large amounts of state information because only a session ID is passed between the client and server. All other state information can be stored on the server. Finally, session management can be used to enforce security policies because the client can be identified with every request.

State and Session Management Methods

There are multiple methods that facilitate the exchange of session IDs or state information between the client and the server. In this section, we will explore three of the most commonly used techniques. These techniques include storing the session ID in the URL path, implementing rewritten URLs and hidden variables, and utilizing cookies to pass session information.

Storing Session Information in the URL Path

When adding state to a stateless protocol like HTTP, every technique has one trait in common; the state-enabling mechanism must allow the server to send state information to the client with the guarantee that this information will be returned with every client request. The URL path method of managing state accomplishes this two-way communication by embedding a session ID (or other state information) in the URL path. For instance, consider the following sequence of events.

1. The client requests the document located at *http://www.sourcestream. com/login.html*. This screen includes an HTML form that allows the client to submit a name and password.

2. Upon receiving a valid name and password, the server generates a unique session ID, say 122893, and immediately redirects the client to *http://www.sourcestream.com/sessionID/122893/welcome.html*.

3. The server parses the path portion of all requested URLs for a valid session ID. If no session ID exists or the session ID is invalid, the client is redirected to the login screen described in step 1.

4. From this point forward, the hyperlinks within all documents returned to the client use only relative URLs (rather than absolute URLs). Recall from Chapter 2 that the browser stores the protocol, host, and path information from the most recent absolute URL request. After requesting an absolute URL, every subsequent relative URL request uses the same protocol, host, and path information as the absolute URL. The browser automatically fills in the missing protocol, host, and path information for every relative URL. Notice how this browser behavior will effectively return the client's session ID with every new request.

5. Each time the client follows a relative URL hyperlink within the site, the browser will return the full path information (including the session ID) to the server. The server can then use this session information to identify the client, enforce security policies, and store client-specific information like personal preferences and shopping cart contents.

This procedure, as with all techniques for adding state to HTTP, has both advantages and disadvantages. The advantages of storing the session ID in the URL path is that no special browser features are required. This method will work with all browsers, including those that do not support cookies.

There are also several disadvantages to this approach. First, the requirement of using only relative URLs throughout an entire Web site can be limiting. Remember, if an absolute URL is ever used without explicitly including the session ID in the path, state information will be lost. Second, the client's unique session ID is visible in the browser's location window. This could present a security risk if another user were to copy the visible session ID. With this session ID a malicious user could then violate security by referencing a resource on the server using the stolen session ID as follows:

http://www.sourcestream.com/sessionID/122893/catalog.html

Of course, the attacker would have to access the Web site in a timely manner before the session expired (a timeout period on the server automatically expires sessions after a period of inactivity).

Lastly, it can be more difficult to process URLs that contain session information. Every request must be parsed for session information and the appropriate resource (specified in the path after the session ID) must be returned. Cookies, for instance, do not require the URL to be parsed. In addition, when using cookies, the virtual path within the URL can be easily converted to the physical file system path using the Servlet API (see the `getRealPath()` method of the `ServletContext` interface).

NOTE: Storing the session ID within the URL path can frustrate search engines. For example, when a search engine visits a site that stores the session ID in the URL path, it will index the Web site's pages using each page's full URL including the session ID. If at a later time the search engine presents this URL to a user looking for your site, the link will not be valid because the session ID will have long since expired.

Rewritten URLs and Hidden Variables

Another popular method of sharing state information between the client and server involves the use of rewritten URLs and hidden HTML form variables. Although they serve similar purposes, rewritten URLs and hidden variables are only effective within the appropriate context. Let's examine these two mechanisms and discuss when each should be used.

Rewritten URLs

Using rewritten URLs is an effective method for managing state on the Web. Rewritten URLs pass state information between the client and server by embedding information in the URL of all hyperlinks within an HTML document. Recall from Chapter 2 that information can be passed in the query string of a URL in the form of name/value pairs with each pair separated by an ampersand ("&"). For example, entering the following URL into your browser's location field will pass search criteria to the WebCrawler search engine:

```
http://www.webcrawler.com/cgi-bin/WebQuery?searchText=servlets
```

The query string immediately follows the question mark ("?") in the URL. The name/value pairs within the query string are passed to the server as Web variables. With the Servlet API, these variables can be read using the getParameter() or getParameterValues() method of the HttpServletRequest object.

Now that we understand that information can be passed within a URL, let's examine how we can use this behavior to pass state information between the client and the server. Let's start by demonstrating how hyperlinks within an HTML document can store client-specific state information. The following HTML document allows the client to select a preferred background color.

```
<HTML>

<HEAD>
<TITLE>Select Background Color</TITLE>
</HEAD>

<BODY>

<P>Please select your preferred background color:<BR>
<A HREF="SampleServlet?bcolor=white">White</A><BR>
<A HREF="SampleServlet?bcolor=black">Black</A><BR>
<A HREF="SampleServlet?bcolor=red">Red</A><BR>
<A HREF="SampleServlet?bcolor=green">Green</A><BR>
<A HREF="SampleServlet?bcolor=blue">Blue</A><BR>

</BODY>

</HTML>
```

Notice that each hyperlink requests the same resource (SampleServlet). However, each link passes a different color value. In order to maintain the specified background color for the client's future requests, this information must be transmitted between the client and server with each request and response. This can be accomplished with rewritten URLs. Rewriting URLs is a method whereby the server adds state information to the URL of every hyperlink within an HTML document before it is returned to the client. This process is accomplished in one of two ways. Either the developer explicitly adds state information to each URL as HTML is generated by servlet code or the server parses an HTML file, adding state information to the URL of every hyperlink, before the document is sent to the client.

For example, the following HTML document is returned in response to the client selecting a background color of blue.

```
<HTML>

<HEAD>
<TITLE>Main Menu for Acme Company</TITLE>
</HEAD>

<BODY BGCOLOR="0000FF"> <!-- set background color to blue -->

<P>Please select from the choices below:<BR>
<A HREF="/catalog.html?bcolor=blue">Product Catalog</A><BR>
<A HREF="/info.html?bcolor=blue">Corporate Info</A><BR>
<A HREF="/press.html?bcolor=blue">Press Releases</A><BR>
<A HREF="/employment.html?bcolor=blue">Employment</A><BR>
<A HREF="/search.html?bcolor=blue">Search the Site</A>

</BODY>

</HTML>
```

Notice how the server added the query string bcolor=blue to the URL of every hyperlink in the document. In this way, no matter which option the client selects, the link will always return the preferred background color to the server.

Although this simple example allows state information (i.e., the user's preferred background color) to be shared between the client and server, it does not provide session management. A more efficient way of storing client-specific information is through the use of a session ID. In the case of rewritten URLs, the server typically generates a unique session ID and passes it to the client within the query string of each hyperlink. In turn, the client returns the session ID to the server whenever a hyperlink is followed. In this way, client-specific state information can be stored on the server and only one piece of information (the session ID) need be exchanged. The following HTML document is a typical response from a server that utilizes rewritten URLs for session management.

```
<HTML>

<HEAD>
<TITLE>Main Menu for Acme Company</TITLE>
```

```
</HEAD>

<BODY BGCOLOR="0000FF"> <!-- set background color to blue -->

<P>Please select from the choices below:<BR>
<A HREF="/catalog.html?sessionID=122893">Catalog</A><BR>
<A HREF="/info.html?sessionID=122893">Corporate Info</A><BR>
<A HREF="/press.html?sessionID=122893">Press Releases</A><BR>
<A HREF="/employ.html?sessionID=122893">Employment</A><BR>
<A HREF="/search.html? sessionID=122893">Search the Site</A>

</BODY>

</HTML>
```

It should be noted that rewritten URLs are only effective when the client follows a hyperlink. So, the question remains, "What happens if the client submits an HTML form rather than clicking on a hyperlink?" If a client submits an HTML form, the state information within rewritten URLs is not passed to the server. The solution to this problem is hidden HTML form variables.

Hidden Variables

Hidden HTML form variables are commonly used to store state information. A hidden variable operates like an HTML input field (e.g., text fields, checkboxes, radio buttons) in that when the page is submitted, the client transmits the field's name/value pair to the server. The difference between a hidden variable and a normal HTML input field is that the client cannot see or modify the value of a hidden HTML variable (however, hidden variables are visible in the HTML source). Remember that hidden variables only work when the client submits an HTML form. Following a hyperlink does not return hidden variables to the server.

The following example demonstrates how hidden variables can be used to pass state information between the client and server. Assume that the server presents a client with the following HTML document:

```
<HTML>

<HEAD>
<TITLE>Select Background Color</TITLE>
</HEAD>

<BODY>

<FORM ACTION="SampleServlet" METHOD="POST">
<P>Please select your preferred background color:<BR>
<INPUT TYPE="RADIO" NAME="bcolor" VALUE="white">White<BR>
<INPUT TYPE="RADIO" NAME="bcolor" VALUE="black">Black<BR>
```

```
<INPUT TYPE="RADIO" NAME="bcolor" VALUE="red">Red<BR>
<INPUT TYPE="RADIO" NAME="bcolor" VALUE="green">Green<BR>
<INPUT TYPE="RADIO" NAME="bcolor" VALUE="blue">Blue<BR>
<BR>
<INPUT TYPE="SUBMIT" VALUE="Submit">
</FORM>

</BODY>

</HTML>
```

This HTML form allows the user to select a background color from a list of choices and submit that choice to the server. The client's selection is transmitted to the server in a name/value pair format as part of an HTTP POST operation. The actual POST request generated by the browser looks like this:

```
POST /SampleServlet HTTP/1.0
User-Agent: Mozilla/4.02 [en] (Win95; I)
Accept: image/gif, image/jpeg, image/pjpeg, */*
Content-Length: 11

bcolor=blue
```

On receiving the client's POST request, the server extracts the value of the bcolor Web variable and uses it to construct the next HTML document (recall that Web variables can be read with the getParameter() or getParameter-Values() method of HttpServletRequest). When the document is constructed, the server sets the background color according to the user's preference.

Although this technique works fine to this point, there is still a problem; the user's color preference is available for the first page but not for succeeding pages. How is the server to know the user's preferred background color for all succeeding pages? The solution is to store the user's color preference in a hidden form variable on every page that is sent to the client. This will ensure that the user's preference will always be passed back to the server. The following HTML document illustrates how the server might use a hidden variable in response to the HTTP POST request shown previously.

```
<HTML>
<HEAD>
<TITLE>What's Your Name?</TITLE>
</HEAD>

<BODY BGCOLOR="0000FF"> <!-- set background color to blue -->

<FORM ACTION="SampleServlet" METHOD="POST">
<P>Please enter your first name:<BR>
<INPUT TYPE="TEXT" NAME="name" SIZE="25"><BR>
<INPUT TYPE="HIDDEN" NAME="bcolor" VALUE="blue">
<BR>
```

```
<INPUT TYPE="SUBMIT" VALUE="Submit">
</FORM>

</BODY>

</HTML>
```

Assuming that the user's name is Tyler, the POST request generated by the HTML form looks like this:

```
POST /SampleServlet HTTP/1.0
User-Agent: Mozilla/4.02 [en] (Win95; I)
Accept: image/gif, image/jpeg, image/pjpeg, */*
Content-Length: 11

name=Tyler&bcolor=blue
```

By storing the user's color preference in a hidden form variable on every page, the value can be passed from page to page, thus preserving the user's color preference. Although the example above is effective at managing a single piece of state information, attempting to store all client-specific information in hidden variables or rewritten URLs can become unwieldy. For increased amounts of client-specific information or at times when the client must be uniquely identified, session management should be utilized. Session management is implemented by storing a unique session ID within a hidden variable on every page. This approach allows client-specific information to be stored on the server and accessed whenever necessary via the session ID that accompanies each request.

Using Rewritten URLs and Hidden Variables Together

It is usually necessary to use both rewritten URLs and hidden variables to maintain state and session with HTTP. After all, it is common for an HTML document to contain one or more HTML forms in addition to multiple hyperlinks. To ensure that session information will not be lost, all hyperlinks must include the session ID and all HTML forms must include a hidden variable containing the session ID. In this way, no matter how the user chooses to proceed session information will be preserved. To illustrate, consider the following sequence of events.

1. The user requests a page from a session-enabled Web site.
2. The server returns an HTML form prompting the user to enter his or her name, e-mail address, and preferred background color. The HTML form contains a hidden variable that holds a unique session ID for this client. The unique session ID is stored in a database table on the server.
3. The user completes the form and clicks the *Submit* button.

4. The user's input is transmitted to the server along with the session ID.

5. The server extracts the user's name, e-mail address, and color preference from the request and stores them in a database table along with the user's session ID.

6. An HTML document containing the same unique session ID is returned to the client. This session ID is stored in hidden variables within all HTML forms and within rewritten URLs for all hyperlinks.

7. When the user submits a form or follows a hyperlink, the session ID is returned to the server. The server extracts the session ID and uses it to query the table storing the user's information.

The following HTML document illustrates how rewritten URLs and hidden variables can be used together. Notice that this document contains two HTML forms and multiple hyperlinks.

```
<HTML>

<HEAD>
<TITLE>Computer User Survey</TITLE>
</HEAD>

<BODY>
<A HREF "about.html?sessionID=091896">About Survey</A><BR>
<A HREF "index.html?sessionID=091896">Back to Main Menu</A>

<P>
<FORM ACTION="SurveyServlet" METHOD="POST">
<P>WEB DEVELOPERS FORM
<P>Please select the tool you use most:<BR>
<INPUT TYPE="RADIO" NAME="webtool" VALUE="jb">JBuilder<BR>
<INPUT TYPE="RADIO" NAME="webtool" VALUE="cf">Visual Cafe<BR>
<INPUT TYPE="RADIO" NAME="webtool" VALUE="pj">Power J<BR>
<INPUT TYPE="RADIO" NAME="webtool" VALUE="va">Visual Age<BR>
<INPUT TYPE="RADIO" NAME="webtool" VALUE="ot">Other<BR>
<INPUT TYPE="HIDDEN" NAME="sessionID" VALUE="091896">
<INPUT TYPE="SUBMIT" VALUE="Submit">\
</FORM>

<FORM ACTION="SurveyServlet" METHOD="POST">
<P>CLIENT/SERVER DEVELOPERS FORM
<P>Please select the tool you use most:<BR>
<INPUT TYPE="RADIO" NAME="cstool" VALUE="vc">Visual C++<BR>
<INPUT TYPE="RADIO" NAME="cstool" VALUE="dl">Delphi<BR>
<INPUT TYPE="RADIO" NAME="cstool" VALUE="vb">Visual Basic<BR>
<INPUT TYPE="RADIO" NAME="cstool" VALUE="pb">PowerBuilder<BR>
<INPUT TYPE="RADIO" NAME="cstool" VALUE="ot">Other<BR>
<INPUT TYPE="HIDDEN" NAME="sessionID" VALUE="091896">
<INPUT TYPE="SUBMIT" VALUE="Submit">
</FORM>
```

```
<P><A HREF="SurveyServlet?sessionID=091896">No Response</A>
</BODY>

</HTML>
```

This HTML document will return the client's session ID to the server regardless of the user's action. Both HTML forms include a hidden variable with the session ID and each hyperlink includes the session ID in the URL.

Let's examine the advantages and disadvantages of using rewritten URLs and hidden variables for state and session management. Similar to placing the session ID in the URL path, the primary advantage of this method is that virtually all browsers support both rewritten URLs and hidden variables. Specifically, cookie support is not required.

The primary disadvantage to this method is the amount of processing required on the server in order to implement rewritten URLs and hidden variables. To properly implement these features, the server must parse every HTML document that it serves, adding state information to hyperlink URLs and adding hidden variables to all HTML forms. This increased overhead incurs a performance penalty and requires more complex code.

NOTE: It is good practice to keep the amount of information passed in a rewritten URL to a minimum. Some browsers enforce a limit on the length of URLs and will truncate those that are too long. For example, Microsoft Internet Explorer 3 truncates URLs longer than 255 characters.

Cookies

Cookies present the simplest way to store state information on the client. As discussed in Chapter 13, a *cookie* is a simple mechanism that allows the server to instruct the client to store some amount of state information. In turn, this information is returned to the server with each client request. See Chapter 13 for more detailed information.

The process of using cookies to manage state and session is very straightforward. To illustrate, let's return to the example of how a user might set the preferred background color. Consider the following sequence of events.

1. The user selects a background color from a list of options on an HTML form and submits the form.

2. The server extracts the user's color selection from the HTML form submitted by the client.

3. To ensure that the user's color selection persists across multiple requests, the server sets a cookie on the client that stores the user's color preference. This information is returned to the server with each client request. (For more information on how to set cookies using the Servlet API, see Chapter 13.)

4. The server constructs an HTML document, setting its background color to the user's choice, and returns it to the client.

5. Each time the server receives a request, it extracts the user's color preference from the cookie information. The HTML document returned to the client is constructed according to the user's background color selection.

6. This process continues as long as the client issues requests and the cookie does not expire.

As you can see, using cookies to manage state is a very simple process. As in the previously discussed state management methods, cookies can also be used to manage sessions by replacing the color information with a unique session ID. Session management with cookies allows client-specific information, such as color preference, to be stored on the server rather than the client. In turn, communication with the client is more efficient because only a single cookie (the session ID) is returned with each request rather than numerous client-specific preferences.

Finally, let's examine the advantages and disadvantages to using cookies for state and session management. The advantages of using cookies are many. First, cookies are the simplest way to store state information on the client because this information need only be stored once. It is not required to keep returning this information to the client, as is the case with rewritten URLs and hidden variables. And unlike storing the session ID in the URL path, either relative or absolute URLs may be used without losing state. Also, in contrast to either of the previous two methods, cookies do not require parsing of the requested URL or the HTML document. Cookie information can be extracted from the client request using a very simple Servlet API method (the `getCookies()` method of `HttpServletRequest`). Thus, server-side processing is kept to a minimum. Cookies provide a simple method of maintaining state and session with very low overhead.

Despite the many benefits provided by cookies, there is one distinct disadvantage. The primary problem with cookies is that they are not supported by all browsers. This lack of cookie support may result from one of two causes: either the client is using an older browser that does not recognize cookies or the user has instructed the browser not to accept cookies. Some users may, often out of ignorance, turn off cookie support in their browser for fear that cookies may somehow compromise security or exhaust their system's resources (or some other unfounded fear). Considering that virtually all current browsers support cookies, the chance that a user is running a browser that does not recognize cookies is small. The possibility that a user might manually disable cookie support and, in turn, disable a Web site's mechanism for state and session management is of greater concern. Therefore, some sites may choose to use an alternate session management mechanism due to the possibility that a user may not accept cookies.

Session Management with the Servlet API

Although we could use any of the methods discussed previously to manually implement our own session management, there is a simpler way. Fortunately, session management support is built into the Servlet API and can be implemented using a few simple objects and methods. In this section, we will explore how to manage sessions using the Servlet API.

The session management implementation in the Servlet API revolves around an interface called HttpSession. An HttpSession object encapsulates the essential information of an HTTP session, such as a unique session ID and other client-specific information. An object that implements HttpSession can be retrieved from HttpServletRequest using the getSession() method. Table 14.1 briefly describes the methods supported by an HttpSession object.

Table 14.1   Methods Defined by the HttpSession Interface

Method	Description
getCreationTime()	Returns the time that the session was created. The time is returned as the number of milliseconds since midnight, January 1, 1970 UTC.
getId()	Returns the unique session ID assigned to this session.
getLastAccessedTime()	Returns the time of the client's last request using the current session ID. The time is returned as the number of milliseconds since midnight, January 1, 1970 UTC.
getMaxInactiveInterval()	Returns the maximum number of seconds that a session is guaranteed to be valid without a request from the client. After the maximum inactive interval expires, the session may be expired by the servlet engine. If the session never expires, a -1 is returned.
getValue()	Returns a client-specific object that is bound to the current session. Objects are bound to a session using the putValue() method. Returns null if no such object exists.
getValueNames()	Returns a String array containing the names of all objects bound to this session.

Method	Description
`invalidate()`	Expires the current session.
`isNew()`	Returns `true` if this is a new session. When the `getSession()` method of `HttpServletRequest` is called, it either returns a valid session ID or, if the client has not yet established a session, it creates a new session.
`putValue()`	Stores an object and binds it to the current session. This session-specific object can be retrieved during future requests using the `getValue()` method.
`removeValue()`	Unbinds an object from the session and makes it available for garbage collection (which removes the object from memory).
`setMaxInactiveInterval()`	Sets the maximum number of seconds that a session is guaranteed to be valid without a request from the client. After the maximum inactive interval expires, the session may be expired by the servlet engine.

The `HttpSession` object contains the majority of the methods that you'll use to manage session, but the `HttpServletRequest` object also contains several useful methods. Table 14.2 describes several methods supported by the `HttpServletRequest` object that are used to implement session management.

By default, the session management mechanisms in the Servlet API use cookies. Cookies are used because of the increased overhead required to implement rewritten URLs. However, the Servlet API does provide methods to determine if the client lacks cookie support, in which case rewritten URLs can be used instead. The servlet in Listing 14.1 uses cookies to establish a session with the client and returns session information with each request.

Listing 14.1 Servlet displaying session information.

```
import javax.servlet.*;
import javax.servlet.http.*;
import java.io.*;

/**
 * The SessionInfoServlet demonstrates the session management
 * mechanisms built into the servlet API.
 *
 * @author Dustin R. Callaway
 * @version 1.0, 06/06/98
 */
public class SessionInfoServlet extends HttpServlet
{
    /**
```

Table 14.2 Session Management Methods of `HttpServletRequest`

Method	Description
`getRequestedSessionId()`	Returns the session ID that accompanied the client's request. This may or may not be the same as the current session ID. For instance, if the client's session has expired, this method will return the expired session ID even if the client is issued a new session ID with this request.
`getSession()`	Returns a handle to the client's `HttpSession`. If the client has not yet established a session or the client's session is invalid, this method may return a handle to a new session. `getSession()` accepts a `boolean` parameter indicating whether to create a new session if one does not currently exist.
`isRequestedSessionIdFromCookie()`	Returns `true` if the session ID was returned by a cookie.
`isRequestedSessionIdFromURL()`	Returns `true` if the session ID was returned by a rewritten URL.
`isRequestedSessionIdValid()`	Returns `true` if the client's session ID represents a valid session. Returns `false` if the session is invalid (i.e., session has expired).

```
 * init method is called when servlet is first loaded.
 */
public void init(ServletConfig config) throws ServletException
{
  super.init(config); //pass ServletConfig to parent
}


/**
 * service method builds an HTML document containing session
 * information and returns it to the client.
 */
public void service(HttpServletRequest request,
  HttpServletResponse response) throws ServletException,
  IOException
{
  //get current session or, if necessary, create a new one
  HttpSession mySession = request.getSession(true);

  //MIME type to return is HTML
  response.setContentType("text/html");
```

```
                    //get a handle to the output stream
                    PrintWriter out = response.getWriter();

                    //generate HTML document
                    out.println("<HTML>");
                    out.println("<HEAD>");
                    out.println("<TITLE>Session Info Servlet</TITLE>");
                    out.println("</HEAD>");
                    out.println("<BODY>");
                    out.println("<h3>Session Information</h3>");
                    out.println("New Session: " + mySession.isNew());
                    out.println("<br>Session ID: " + mySession.getId());
                    out.println("<br>Session Creation Time: " +
                        mySession.getCreationTime());
                    out.println("<br>Session Last Accessed Time: " +
                        mySession.getLastAccessedTime());

                    out.println("<h3>Request Information</h3>");
                    out.println("Session ID from Request: " +
                        request.getRequestedSessionId());
                    out.println("<br>Session ID via Cookie: " +
                        request.isRequestedSessionIdFromCookie());
                    out.println("<br>Session ID via rewritten URL: " +
                        request.isRequestedSessionIdFromURL());
                    out.println("<br>Valid Session ID: " +
                        request.isRequestedSessionIdValid());

                    out.println("</BODY></HTML>");

                    out.close(); //close output stream
                }


                /**
                 * getServletInfo returns a brief description of this servlet
                 */
                public String getServletInfo()
                {
                    return "Servlet returns session information.";
                }
            }
```

Figure 14.1 displays the response to the client's first request to `Session-InfoServlet`, and Figure 14.2 shows the response to the client's second request to `SessionInfoServlet`. Notice that the first request passed an old session ID that is no longer valid (see Figure 14.1).

The code in Listing 14.2 illustrates session management with a slightly more involved servlet. This servlet prompts users to select a background color and enter their name. The servlet then demonstrates how, through session management mechanisms, it can remember each user's name, color preference, and the number of times the user has requested the servlet. Again, this example uses

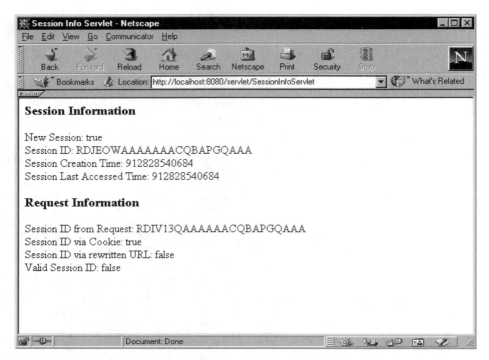

Figure 14.1   HTML Generated by First Request to `SessionInfoServlet`

cookies for session management. A future example will demonstrate how rewritten URLs can be used if the client does not support cookies.

Listing 14.2   Servlet using session management to remember client information.

```java
import javax.servlet.*;
import javax.servlet.http.*;
import java.io.*;

/**
 * The ColorSessionServlet demonstrates the session management
 * mechanisms built into the servlet API. A session is
 * established and the client's preferred background color
 * as well as the number of times they have requested the
 * servlet are stored.
 *
 * @author Dustin R. Callaway
 * @version 1.0, 08/05/98
 */
public class ColorSessionServlet extends HttpServlet
{
```

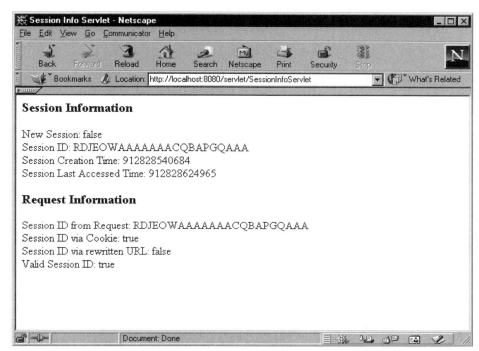

Figure 14.2 HTML Generated by Second Request to `SessionInfoServlet`

```
/**
 * init method is called when servlet is first loaded.
 */
public void init(ServletConfig config) throws
  ServletException
{
  super.init(config); //pass ServletConfig to parent
}


/**
 * service generates HTML pages that allows the client to
 * choose a color and then remembers the color on future
 * requests.
 */
public void service(HttpServletRequest request,
  HttpServletResponse response) throws ServletException,
  IOException
{
  String name; //name of user
  String color; //user's color preference
  Integer hitCount; //# of times user has requested servlet
```

```java
//get current session, create if it doesn't exist
HttpSession mySession = request.getSession(true);

//MIME type to return is HTML
response.setContentType("text/html");

//get a handle to the output stream
PrintWriter out = response.getWriter();

if (mySession.isNew()) //first time client requests page
{
  //generate HTML form requesting name and color preference
  out.println("<HTML>");
  out.println("<HEAD>");
  out.println("<TITLE>Color Selector</TITLE>");
  out.println("</HEAD>");
  out.println("<BODY>");
  out.println("<FORM METHOD=\"POST\" " +
    "ACTION=\"ColorSessionServlet\">");
  out.println("Please select background color:<BR>");
  out.println("<INPUT TYPE=\"RADIO\" NAME=\"bcolor\" " +
    "VALUE=\"white\">White<BR>");
  out.println("<INPUT TYPE=\"RADIO\" NAME=\"bcolor\" " +
    "VALUE=\"red\">Red<BR>");
  out.println("<INPUT TYPE=\"RADIO\" NAME=\"bcolor\" " +
    "VALUE=\"green\">Green<BR>");
  out.println("<INPUT TYPE=\"RADIO\" NAME=\"bcolor\" " +
    "VALUE=\"blue\">Blue<P>");
  out.println("Please enter your name:<BR>");
  out.println("<INPUT TYPE=\"TEXT\" NAME=\"name\" " +
    "SIZE=\"25\"><P>");
  out.println("<INPUT TYPE=\"SUBMIT\" VALUE=\"Submit\">");
  out.println("</BODY>");
  out.println("</HTML>");
}
else //client has already established a session
{
  if (request.getParameter("bcolor") != null)
  {
    //client is submitting the color preference form
    String bcolor; //for user's preferred background color
    bcolor = request.getParameter("bcolor");

    //get HEX code for color
    if (bcolor.equals("red"))
    {
      color = "#FF0000";
    }
    else if (bcolor.equals("green"))
    {
      color = "#00FF00";
    }
    else if (bcolor.equals("blue"))
```

```
                        {
                           color = "#0000FF";
                        }
                        else //if nothing selected, default to white
                        {
                           color = "#FFFFFF";
                        }

                        name = request.getParameter("name"); //get user name
                        hitCount = new Integer(1); //requested 1 time so far

                        mySession.putValue("bcolor", color); //store color
                        mySession.putValue("hitCount", hitCount);
                        mySession.putValue("name", name); //store user name
                     }
                     else //user has previously submitted HTML form
                     {
                        //get color, name, and hit count from session
                        color = (String)mySession.getValue("bcolor");
                        name = (String)mySession.getValue("name");
                        hitCount = (Integer)mySession.getValue("hitCount");
                     }

                     //increment hit count and store in session
                     mySession.putValue("hitCount",
                        new Integer(hitCount.intValue() + 1));

                     out.println("<HTML>");
                     out.println("<HEAD>");
                     out.println("<TITLE>Color Selected</TITLE>");
                     out.println("</HEAD>");
                     out.println("<BODY BGCOLOR=\"" + color + "\">");
                     out.println("<H2>Hello " + name + "!</H2>");
                     out.println("<H3>You have requested this page " +
                        hitCount.toString() + " times.<BR>");
                     out.println("Notice how session management allows me " +
                        "to remember<BR>");
                     out.println("who you are, how many times you've " +
                        "requested this page,<BR>");
                     out.println("and your preferred background color.<P>");
                     out.println("<A HREF=\"ColorSessionServlet\">Next " +
                        "Screen</A></H3>");
                     out.println("</BODY>");
                     out.println("</HTML>");
                  }
               out.close();
            }

            /**
             * getServletInfo returns a brief description of this servlet
             */
            public String getServletInfo()
            {
```

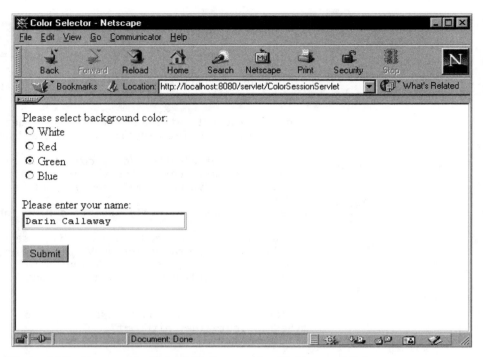

Figure 14.3　Generated by Listing 14.2, Prompts User for Name and Color

```
        return "Servlet uses session management to maintain color.";
    }
}
```

Figure 14.3 shows the HTML form generated by Listing 14.2 that prompts the user for a name and color preference. When the form shown in Figure 14.3 is submitted, the page shown in Figure 14.4 is displayed. Each time the *Next Screen* hyperlink is clicked, the page hit counter increases by one.

So far, we have seen how cookies are used to provide state and session management. Now let's examine how the Servlet API simplifies the process of implementing rewritten URLs for session management. The following servlet (see Listing 14.3) uses the `encodeURL()` method of the `HttpServletResponse` object to add the session ID to all URLs.

Listing 14.3　Servlet using rewritten URLs for session management.

```
import javax.servlet.*;
import javax.servlet.http.*;
import java.io.*;
```

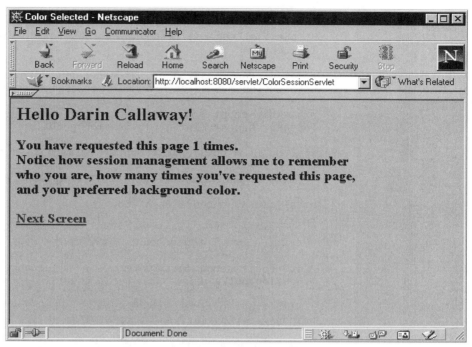

Figure 14.4 Page Demonstrates How Listing 14.2 Uses Session Management

```
/**
 * The URLSessionServlet demonstrates how the servlet API
 * makes it easy to use rewritten URLs for session
 * management rather than cookies.
 *
 * @author Dustin R. Callaway
 * @version 1.0, 08/08/98
 */
public class URLSessionServlet extends HttpServlet
{
  /**
   * init method is called when servlet is first loaded.
   */
  public void init(ServletConfig config) throws ServletException
  {
    super.init(config); //pass ServletConfig to parent
  }


  /**
   * service uses session object to track the number of times
   * each user has requested this servlet.
```

```java
*/
public void service(HttpServletRequest request,
  HttpServletResponse response) throws ServletException,
  IOException
{
  //get current session or, if necessary, create a new one
  HttpSession mySession =request.getSession(true);

  //get hit count from session
  Integer count = (Integer)mySession.getValue("hitCounter");

  if (count == null) //hitCounter value not in session
  {
    count = new Integer(1); //start hit count at 1
  }
  else //session contains hitCounter
  {
    //increment hit counter
    count = new Integer(count.intValue() + 1);
  }
  //store hit count in session
  mySession.putValue("hitCounter", count);

  //MIME type to return is HTML
  response.setContentType("text/html");

  //get a handle to the output stream
  PrintWriter out = response.getWriter();

  //generate HTML document to send to client
  out.println("<HTML>");
  out.println("<HEAD>");
  out.println("<TITLE>Sessions with URLs</TITLE>");
  out.println("</HEAD>");
  out.println("<BODY>");
  out.println("You have visited this page " + count +
    " times.<P>");

  out.println("Click <A HREF=\"" +
    response.encodeURL("URLSessionServlet") +
    "\">here</A> to load page again.");

  out.println("</BODY>");
  out.println("</HTML>");

  out.close(); //close output stream
}

/**
 * getServletInfo returns a brief description of this servlet
 */
public String getServletInfo()
{
```

```
            return "Manages session with rewritten URLs.";
    }
}
```

That's all there is to it. To encode the session ID into a hyperlink, simply pass the URL to the `encodeURL()` method of the `HttpServletResponse` object. In fact, the `URLSessionServlet` shown in Listing 14.3 works with cookies or rewritten URLs. The implementation of the `encodeURL()` method checks to see if encoding is required. If URL rewriting is not required (e.g., the client supports cookies or session tracking is off), the URL is returned unchanged. Otherwise, the session ID is added to the query string of the URL. For example, if cookie support on the client is turned off, the HTML generated by the `URLSessionServlet` looks like this:

```
<HTML>
<HEAD>
<TITLE>Session Management with URLs</TITLE>
</HEAD>
<BODY>
You have visited this page 1 times.<P>
Click
<A HREF="URLSessionServlet?session=GJ2FH4QAAAAAQCQBAPGQAAA">
here</A> to load page again.
</BODY>
</HTML>
```

Notice how the session ID is appended to the URL's query string. When using rewritten URLs for session management, the URL in all hyperlinks should be encoded using the `encodeURL()` method. This practice will ensure that no matter where the user travels, session integrity will be maintained.

NOTE: The `HttpServletResponse` object also supports a method called `encodeRedirectURL()`. This method adds the session ID to the URL to which the client is being redirected. The following code demonstrates how a client can be redirected to a new URL without losing session:

```
hsrsResponse.sendRedirect(hsrsResponse.encodeRedirectURL(
    "http://www.sourcestream.com/orders.html"));
```

The implementation of the `encodeRedirectURL()` method determines whether or not session encoding is necessary. If encoding is unnecessary (e.g., the client supports cookies), the URL is returned unchanged. Since the rules regarding whether a URL requires encoding may differ between a redirect and a normal link, this method is provided separately. The following HTTP header illustrates how the session ID is passed in a redirect.

```
HTTP/1.1 301 Moved Permanently
Date: Sat, 11 Jul 1998 19:45:12 GMT
Server: Apache/1.3.0 (Unix)
Location: http://www.sourcestream.com/orders.html?session=
GJ2FH4QAAAAAQCQBAPGQAAA
Content-Type: text/html
```

Notice that the session ID is appended to the redirect URL designated by the Location header.

Since we have only demonstrated the encodeURL() method using hyper-links, you may be wondering how session information is passed back to the server when the user submits an HTML form rather than clicking on a hyper-link. Actually, in this case, session information would be lost if we only encoded the URLs in the hyperlinks and not in the form itself. Therefore, the solution to this problem is to always encode the URL within the ACTION attribute of the <FORM> tag. For example, an HTML form that maintains state using rewritten URLs can be created by using the encodeURL() method as follows:

```
out.println("<FORM METHOD=\"POST\" ACTION=\"" +
    response.encodeURL("URLSessionServlet") + "\">");
```

Although the Servlet API supports other methods of managing state and session, it is recommended that cookies be used when available. Since cookies require less coding and lower overhead, they are the preferred session manage-ment mechanism.

Summary

As demonstrated in this chapter, the Servlet API provides a simple and straight-forward method of implementing session management. With the addition of these mechanisms, the Servlet API allows the developer to build Web applica-tions that provide an unsurpassed level of user interaction. Session management provides a richer Web experience by enabling user-specific preferences, elec-tronic shopping carts, enforcement of security policies, and much more.

This concludes our discussion of state and session management. In the next chapter, we will learn how to invoke a servlet from within an HTML document using a mechanism called server-side includes.

Chapter Highlights

- HTTP is a stateless protocol. A protocol is said to be *stateless* if it has no memory of prior connections and cannot distinguish one client's request from that of another.

- An HTTP session associates each request received by the server with the client that issued it. This association is accomplished by requiring the client to return a piece of state information with each new request. Sessions are used to maintain state and client identity across multiple requests.

- In this chapter, we often refer to "state/session" management. However, there is a distinct difference between state management and session management. *State management* is the ability to maintain a client's current state by passing client-specific information between the client and server. In contrast, *session management* maintains both state and identity. Session management provides an association between the client and the server that allows the server to uniquely identify each client. This association persists across requests for a specified period of time.

- There are multiple methods that facilitate the exchange of session IDs between the client and the server. These techniques include storing the session ID in the URL's path, implementing hidden variables and rewritten URLs, and utilizing cookies to pass session information.

- The session management implementation in the Servlet API revolves around an interface called `HttpSession`. An `HttpSession` object encapsulates the essential information of an HTTP session, such as a unique session ID and other client-specific information.

- By default, the session management mechanisms in the Servlet API use cookies. Cookies are used by default because of the increased overhead required to implement rewritten URLs. However, the Servlet API does provide methods to determine if the client lacks cookie support, in which case rewritten URLs can be used instead.

CHAPTER 15

Server-Side Includes and Request Forwarding

Sun Microsystems has defined a standard environment for running servlets. This environment specification, known as the *JavaServer architecture,* defines the functionality that must be supported by a fully compliant server. For instance, a full JavaServer architecture implementation supports advanced features such as server-side includes and servlet chaining. In this chapter, we will examine both of these features. In addition, we will learn how to programatically forward requests to and include content from other server resources using the RequestDispatcher object.

Although primarily focusing on server-side includes and request forwarding, we will briefly examine the concept of servlet chaining at the end of this chapter. The following topics are covered in this chapter:

- Server-side includes
- Using the RequestDispatcher object
- Servlet chaining

Server-Side Includes

Server-side includes (SSIs) allow you to embed servlet calls within an HTML document using a special <servlet> tag. By convention, these documents should use the .shtml file extension. This extension indicates to the server that the HTML document includes SSI directives and, therefore, should be passed to a specialized SSI servlet for processing. This servlet, called SSIncludeServlet when using the Java Web Server, parses the HTML document searching for

<servlet> tags. When a <servlet> tag is encountered, SSIncludeServlet loads the servlet specified by the <servlet> tag (if not already loaded), executes it (passing any parameters included in the <servlet> tag), and includes the servlet's output in the HTML page returned to the client. The following sequence of events may help clarify the SSI process.

1. The server receives a request for the file *index.shtml*.

2. The Java-enabled server maps all *.shtml files to the SSI servlet by default. Thus, when using the Java Web Server, the client's request for *index.shtml* is passed to SSIncludeServlet for processing. (Although the extension .shtml is mapped to the SSI servlet by default, custom aliases may also be defined that map other extensions to the SSI servlet.)

3. SSIncludeServlet parses the requested HTML document searching for <servlet> tags. When a <servlet> tag is located, SSIncludeServlet first reads any initialization parameters and loads the servlet referenced by the tag (if necessary). It then reads any parameters included in the tag and passes them to the specified servlet.

4. The servlet specified by the <servlet> tag generates data that is included in the HTML page returned to the client. Essentially, the <servlet> tag is replaced by the specified servlet's output.

NOTE: The Java Web Server uses a servlet called SSIncludeServlet to process server-side includes. However, each servlet engine implements its own Server-Side Include servlet and may name it something other than SSIncludeServlet. For example, the Server-Side Include servlet implemented by the JRun servlet engine is called JRunSSI.

Now that you understand how the process works, let's take a look at the syntax of the <servlet> tag.

```
<servlet name=SERVLET_NAME
  code=CLASS_NAME
  codebase=CLASS_LOCATION_URL
  INIT_PARAM1=VALUE1
  INIT_PARAM2=VALUE2
  INIT_PARAMn=VALUEn>
<param name=SERVLET_PARAM1 value=VALUE1>
<param name=SERVLET_PARAM2 value=VALUE2>
<param name=SERVLET_PARAMn value=VALUEn>
</servlet>
```

Using the `<servlet>` tag, servlets can be referenced by alias name or class name. To specify a servlet by alias, use the `name` attribute. To reference a servlet by its class name (with or without the `.class` extension), use the `code` attribute instead of the `name` attribute. When a `<servlet>` tag is located, the SSI servlet attempts to load the servlet specified by the `name` attribute first. If the `name` attribute does not exist or the named servlet cannot be found, the servlet specified by the `code` attribute is loaded. The `codebase` attribute is optional but useful if the servlet must be loaded from a remote location.

All other name/value pairs within the `<servlet>` tag are passed as initialization parameters (i.e., they can be retrieved using the `ServletConfig` object's `getInitParameter()` method). Additionally, any number of `param` tags may be included between `<servlet>` and `</servlet>`. These name/value pairs are passed to the specified servlet as parameters (i.e., they can be retrieved using the `HttpServletRequest` object's `getParameter()` method).

Now let's put server-side includes to work. Our goal is to standardize all of our company's Web pages by applying a standard header and footer to each. Listings 15.1 and 15.2 show two servlets that generate this header and footer.

Listing 15.1 Servlet that returns a standard header.

```
import javax.servlet.*;
import javax.servlet.http.*;
import java.io.*;
import java.util.Date;
import java.text.DateFormat;

/**
 * Header Servlet
 *
 * This servlet returns a standard header
 * @author Dustin R. Callaway
 * @version 1.0, 10/10/1998
 */
public class HeaderServlet extends HttpServlet
{
  public void service(HttpServletRequest request,
    HttpServletResponse response) throws ServletException,
    IOException
  {
    response.setContentType("text/html"); //HTML output

    //get handle to output stream
    PrintWriter out = response.getWriter();

    //create a DateFormat object to format our Date object
    DateFormat longDate = DateFormat.getDateInstance(
      DateFormat.LONG);
```

```
            //generate header HTML
            out.println("<CENTER><FONT SIZE=6><B>SourceStream</B>" +
              "</FONT><BR>");
            out.println(longDate.format(new Date()) +
              "</ALIGN></CENTER><HR>");
            out.close();
        }
    }
```

Listing 15.2   Servlet that returns a standard footer.

```
import javax.servlet.*;
import javax.servlet.http.*;
import java.io.*;

/**
 * Footer Servlet
 *
 * This servlet returns a standard footer
 * @author Dustin R. Callaway
 * @version 1.0, 10/10/1998
 */
public class FooterServlet extends HttpServlet
{
    public void service(HttpServletRequest request,
      HttpServletResponse response) throws ServletException,
      IOException
    {
      response.setContentType("text/html"); //HTML output

      //get handle to output stream
      PrintWriter out = response.getWriter();

      //generate footer HTML
      out.println("<HR><CENTER><FONT SIZE=2>Copyright &copy 1998"+
        "SourceStream. All Rights Reserved.</FONT></CENTER>");
      out.close();
    }
}
```

Let's use these two servlets to add a consistent "look and feel" to the HTML document shown in Listing 15.3. Be sure to notice the placement of the <servlet> tags. This HTML document, in conjunction with the header and footer servlets, produces the display shown in Figure 15.1 on page 284.

Listing 15.3   HTML page using server-side includes to add a header and footer.

```
<HTML>
<HEAD>
<TITLE>Servlet API Support</TITLE>
</HEAD>
<BODY>
```

```
<SERVLET CODE="HeaderServlet"></SERVLET>
<BR>
These servers support the Java Servlet API:<P>
<LI>Acme Acme.Serve
<LI>Apache Web Server
<LI>ATG Dynamo Application Server
<LI>IBM Internet Connection Server
<LI>IBM VisualAge WebRunner Toolkit
<LI>jo!
<LI>KonaSoft Enterprise Server
<LI>Live Softeware JRun
<LI>Lotus Domino Go Webserver
<LI>Mort Bay Jetty
<LI>Novocode NetForge
<LI>Paralogic WebCore
<LI>ServletFactory
<LI>Sun WebServer
<LI>Tandem iTP WebServer
<LI>W3C Jigsaw
<LI>WebEasy WEASEL
<LI>WebLogic Tengah Application Server
<LI>Zeus Web Server
<BR><BR>
<SERVLET CODE="FooterServlet"></SERVLET>

</BODY>
</HTML>
```

You may be starting to recognize the power of server-side includes. The example above demonstrated that, through server-side includes, the standard header and footer displayed on all HTML pages can be changed by simply altering the servlets that generate them. This technique ensures a consistent "look and feel" across an entire Web site and greatly simplifies the task of changing headers and footers used by numerous pages.

Of course, this example demonstrates only one possible application of server-side includes. In addition to establishing a consistent "look and feel," server-side includes can provide flexible customization. For example, an SSI servlet might check the time of day in order to include a "Good Morning," "Good Afternoon," or "Good Evening" message to users. Or perhaps after a user logs in, a Server-Side Include servlet checks a database and displays a customized message if it is the user's birthday. As you can see, there are countless uses for this powerful feature.

Using the `RequestDispatcher` Object

New with Servlet API 2.1, the `RequestDispatcher` object allows you to forward requests to or include output from other server resources. This is the sole pur-

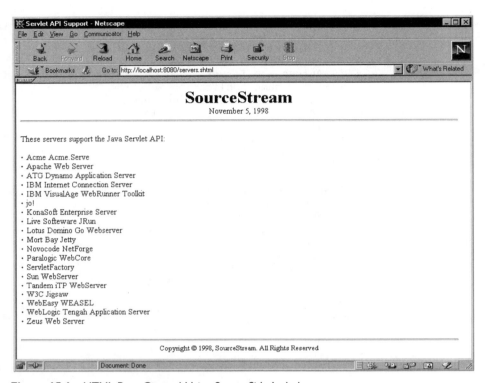

Figure 15.1   HTML Page Created Using Server-Side Includes

pose of the `RequestDispatcher` object, which includes only two methods—
`forward()` and `include()`. In this section, we will examine both of these
methods.

RequestDispatcher is a Java interface. An object that implements this interface can be acquired using the `getRequestDispatcher()` method of the
ServletContext object as demonstrated below. This example assumes that a
servlet called `AccountBalance` already exists.

```
public void service(HttpServletRequest request,
  HttpServletResponse response) throws ServletException,
  IOException
{
  //create a string object with URL to server resource
  String url = "/servlet/AccountBalance?cust_id=1234";

  //get a reference to the ServletContext
  ServletContext context = getServletContext();

  //create a new RequestDispatcher object
  RequestDispatcher rd = context.getRequestDispatcher(url);
}
```

The `getRequestDispatcher()` method accepts a URL designating the server resource to which this request will be forwarded or from which content will be read. The `RequestDispatcher` object essentially serves as a "wrapper" around a server resource in order to provide forwarding and server-side include functionality. Once you have created a `RequestDispatcher` object, you can use its `forward()` and `include()` methods to forward requests or include content generated by another server resource. Let's examine these methods now.

forward

```
public abstract void forward(ServletRequest request,
    ServletResponse response) throws ServletException, IOException
```

The `forward()` method of the `RequestDispatcher` object allows you to programatically forward a request to another servlet (or other server resource) known as a *delegate*. Because forwarding passes all control to the new resource, you should not disrupt its communication with the client by retrieving a handle to the output stream (i.e., using the `getWriter()` or `getOutputStream()` method) or setting any HTTP headers (i.e., using the `setHeader()` or `setStatus()` method). These tasks should be left to the servlet to which the request is forwarded. However, the current servlet may do some type of preprocessing before the request is forwarded.

Let's take a look at a simple example of forwarding a request from one servlet to another. Again, this example assumes that a servlet called `AccountBalance` already exists.

```
public void service(HttpServletRequest request,
    HttpServletResponse response) throws ServletException,
    IOException
{
    //...execute all request preprocessing here...

    String url = "/servlet/AccountBalance?cust_id=1234";
    ServletContext context = getServletContext();
    RequestDispatcher rd = context.getRequestDispatcher(url);

    rd.forward(request, response); //forward request
}
```

The `forward()` method of the `RequestDispatcher` object passes the current request to the servlet designated by the specified URL. Unlike the `include()` method, control will never return to the servlet that forwards the request. The `forward()` method passes all control to the delegate servlet which will generate the response. Notice that both the `request` and `response` objects are passed to the delegate to allow it to read from the request and generate an appropriate response.

You may have noticed that the URL designated here includes a query string to pass information to the Delegate servlet. This information can be read by the delegate using the request object's getParameter() method. However, there is a better way to pass information to a delegate servlet. Servlet API 2.1 adds a new method to the ServletRequest object called setAttribute(). This method allows any number of Java objects to be stored in the request object. These stored objects can then be read by the Delegate servlet using the request object's getAttribute() method. In addition, you may use the getAttribute-Names() method to determine the names of all attributes stored in the request (it returns an Enumeration).

Therefore, rather than just passing string criteria using the URL's query string, it is now possible to pass Java objects to the Delegate servlet. The following sample code demonstrates the use of attributes rather than passing information in the query string. Once the object is stored in the request using the setAttribute() method, the Delegate servlet can extract the object using getAttribute("ATTRIBUTE_NAME") and finish processing the request.

```
public void service(HttpServletRequest request,
   HttpServletResponse response) throws ServletException,
   IOException
{
   //...execute all request preprocessing here...

   Customer cust = new Customer(1234); //create customer object
   request.setAttribute("customer", cust);

   String url = "/servlet/AccountBalance";
   ServletContext context = getServletContext();
   RequestDispatcher rd = context.getRequestDispatcher(url);

   rd.forward(request, response); //forward request
}
```

include

```
public abstract void include(ServletRequest request,
   ServletResponse response) throws ServletException, IOException
```

The include() method of the RequestDispatcher object allows you to pro-gramatically include content generated by another servlet (or other server resource) within the body of the calling servlet's response. The included servlet cannot change the status of the response or set HTTP headers.

Setting the proper response status code and headers is the calling servlet's responsibility. Unlike the `forward()` method, control is returned to the calling servlet once the Delegate servlet completes its processing. The delegate's response is then added to the body of the calling servlet's response. The following sample code demonstrates how a customer's balance is calculated by a Delegate servlet and included in the output of the Calling servlet.

```
public void service(HttpServletRequest request,
  HttpServletResponse response) throws ServletException,
  IOException
{
  PrintWriter out = response.getWriter();

  Customer cust = new Customer(1234); //create customer object
  request.setAttribute("customer", cust);

  String url = "/servlet/AccountBalance";
  ServletContext context = getServletContext();
  RequestDispatcher rd = context.getRequestDispatcher(url);

  out.println("Your account balance is:<BR>");

  rd.include(request, response); //get content from delegate

  out.println("<BR>Thank you for your business!");
}
```

Like `forward()`, the `include()` method passes the `request` and `response` objects to the Delegate servlet so that it can process the request and generate a response (which is included in the Calling servlet's response). The `Request-Dispatcher` object's `include()` method makes it simple to generate server-side includes programmatically.

Servlet Chaining

Servlet chaining is the process of passing the output of one servlet to the input of another. This feature is very similar to piping in UNIX or DOS. As shown in Figure 15.2, servlet chaining works as follows. The client request is sent to the first servlet in the chain. Once the request has been processed by the servlet, it passes its output to the next servlet in the chain. This process continues through any number of servlets until the last servlet's output is returned to the client. The `getInputStream()` method of `HttpServletRequest` can be used to read the previous servlet's output.

Because the servlet chain configuration is server-specific, chaining is only briefly described here. It is presented primarily to make you aware of the feature's existence and purpose. Please refer to the documentation that came with

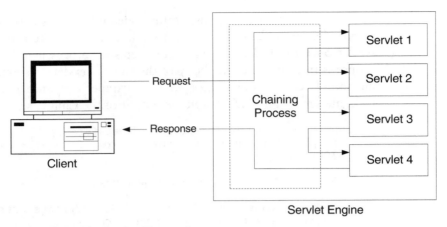

Figure 15.2   The Servlet Chaining Process

your Java-enabled server or servlet engine to learn how to properly configure servlet chaining.

Summary

This chapter demonstrated a powerful technique called server-side includes that allows servlet calls to be embedded within an HTML document. In addition, the concept of servlet chaining was discussed. In the next chapter, we will learn how to add database connectivity to a servlet using JDBC.

Chapter Highlights

- Sun Microsystems has defined a standard environment for running servlets. This environment specification, known as the *JavaServer architecture,* defines the functionality that must be supported by a fully compliant server.

- *Server-side includes* allow you to embed servlet calls within an HTML document using a special <servlet> tag. By convention, these documents should use the .shtml file extension. All .shtml files are passed to a special SSI servlet for processing.

- When a <servlet> tag is encountered, the SSI servlet loads the servlet specified in the <servlet> tag (if necessary), executes it (passing any parameters included in the <servlet> tag), and includes the servlet's output in the HTML page returned to the client.

- New with Servlet API 2.1, the `RequestDispatcher` object allows you to forward requests to or include output from other server resources.
- The `forward()` method of the `RequestDispatcher` object allows you to programatically forward a request to another servlet (or other server resource) known as a *delegate*.
- The `include()` method of the `RequestDispatcher` object allows you to programatically include content generated by another servlet (or other server resource) within the body of the calling servlet's response.
- *Servlet chaining* is the process of passing the output of one servlet to the input of another.
- Servlet chaining works as follows. The client request is sent to the first servlet in the chain. Once the request has been processed by the servlet, it passes its output to the next servlet in the chain. This process continues through any number of servlets until the last servlet's output is returned to the client.

CHAPTER 16

Database Access with JDBC

Storing and retrieving database information is one of the most common operations performed by servlets. In this chapter, we will examine Sun's Java Database Connectivity (JDBC) API and demonstrate database connectivity within a servlet. This chapter provides a very brief overview of a topic that could easily consume an entire book. In fact, there are many books currently available that focus completely on JDBC programming. I recommend *JDBC™ Database Access with Java™* from Addison Wesley Longman.[1] Specifically, the following topics are covered:

- JDBC architecture
- Accessing a database
- Sample JDBC servlet

JDBC Architecture

JDBC is an API specification developed by Sun that defines a uniform interface for accessing different relational databases. JDBC is a core part of the Java platform and is included in the standard JDK distribution.

The primary function of the JDBC API is to allow the developer to issue SQL statements and process the results in a consistent, database-independent manner. JDBC provides rich, object-oriented access to databases by defining classes and interfaces that represent the following:

---

[1]Hamilton, G., R.G.G. Catell, and M. Fisher, *JDBC™ Database Access with Java™: A Tutorial and Annotated Reference*. Reading, MA: Addison Wesley Longman, 1997.

- Database connections
- SQL statements
- Result sets
- Database metadata
- Prepared statements
- SQL arrays
- Binary Large Objects (BLOBs)
- Character Large Objects (CLOBs)
- Callable statements
- Database drivers
- Driver manager

The JDBC API uses a driver manager and database-specific drivers to provide transparent connectivity to heterogeneous databases. The *JDBC driver manager* ensures that the correct driver is used to access each data source. The driver manager is capable of supporting multiple concurrent drivers connected to multiple heterogeneous databases. The location of the driver manager with respect to the JDBC drivers and the servlet is shown in Figure 16.1.

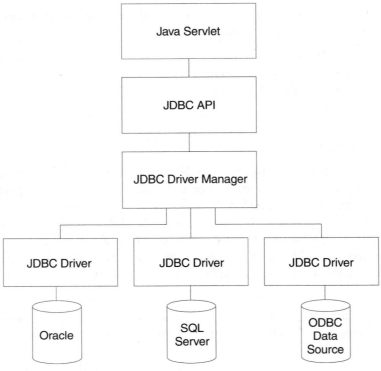

Figure 16.1   Layers of the JDBC Architecture

A *JDBC driver* translates standard JDBC calls into a network protocol or client API call that facilitates communication with the database. This translation provides JDBC applications with database independence. If the back-end database changes, only the JDBC driver must be replaced with few code modifications required. There are four distinct types of JDBC drivers.

Type 1 *JDBC-ODBC Bridge.* Type 1 drivers act as a "bridge" between JDBC and another database connectivity mechanism such as ODBC. The JDBC-ODBC bridge provides JDBC access using most standard ODBC drivers. This driver is included in the Java 2 SDK within the sun.jdbc.odbc package. Finally, the JDBC-ODBC bridge requires that the native ODBC libraries, drivers, and required support files be installed and configured on each client employing a Type 1 driver. This requirement may present a serious limitation for many applications. (See Figure 16.2.)

Type 2 *Java to Native API.* Type 2 drivers use the Java Native Interface (JNI) to make calls to a local database API. Type 2 drivers are usually faster than Type 1 drivers. Like Type 1 drivers, Type 2 drivers require native database client libraries to be installed and configured on the client machine. (See Figure 16.3.)

Type 3 *Java to Network Protocol.* Type 3 drivers are pure Java drivers that use a proprietary network protocol to communicate with JDBC middleware on the server. The middleware then translates the network protocol to database-

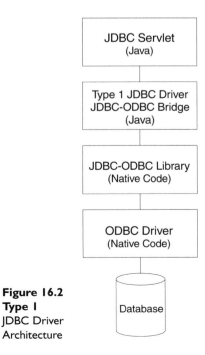

Figure 16.2
Type 1
JDBC Driver
Architecture

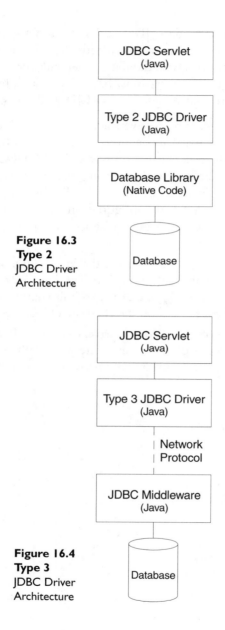

Figure 16.3
Type 2
JDBC Driver
Architecture

Figure 16.4
Type 3
JDBC Driver
Architecture

specific function calls. Type 3 drivers are the most flexible JDBC solution because they do not require any native database libraries on the client and can connect to many different databases on the back-end. Type 3 drivers can be deployed over the Internet without any client installation required. (See Figure 16.4.)

Type 4 *Java to Database Protocol.* Type 4 drivers are pure Java drivers that implement a proprietary database protocol (like Oracle's SQL*Net) to communicate directly with the database. Like Type 3 drivers, they do not require any native database libraries and can be deployed over the Internet without any client installation required. One drawback to Type 4 drivers is that they are database specific. Unlike Type 3 drivers, if your back-end database changes, you may have to purchase and deploy a new Type 4 driver. However, because Type 4 drivers communicate directly with the database engine rather than through middleware or a native library, they are usually the fastest JDBC drivers available. (See Figure 16.5.)

So, you may be asking yourself, "Which is the right type of driver for my application?" Well, that depends on the requirements of your particular project. If you do not have the opportunity or inclination to install and configure software on each client, you can rule out Type 1 and Type 2 drivers. However, if the cost of Type 3 or Type 4 drivers is prohibitive, Type 1 and Type 2 drivers may become more attractive because they are usually available free of charge. Price aside, the debate will often boil down to whether to use a Type 3 or Type 4 driver for a particular application. In this case, you may need to weigh the benefits of flexibility and interoperability against performance. Type 3 drivers offer your application the ability to transparently access different types of databases, while Type 4 drivers usually exhibit better performance.

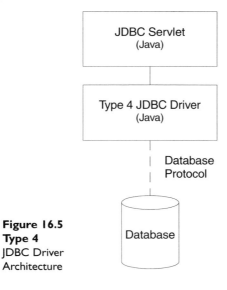

Figure 16.5
Type 4
JDBC Driver
Architecture

Accessing a Database

The basic process of connecting to a database via JDBC looks like this:

1. Register the JDBC driver with the driver manager.
2. Establish a database connection.
3. Execute an SQL statement.
4. Process the results.
5. Close the database connection.

Let's examine how each of these steps is accomplished.

Register the JDBC Driver

Before a JDBC driver can be used to establish a database connection, it must first be registered with the driver manager. The driver manager's job is to maintain all driver objects that are available to JDBC clients. A JDBC driver automatically registers itself with the driver manager when it is loaded. To load a JDBC driver, use the `Class.forName()` method call as demonstrated here:

```
Class.forName("sun.jdbc.odbc.JdbcOdbcDriver");
```

`Class.forName()` is a `static` method that instructs the Java virtual machine to dynamically locate, load, and link the specified class (if not already loaded). If the class cannot be located, a `ClassNotFoundException` is thrown.

As you can see from this example, a JDBC driver is simply a Java class that resides in a valid CLASSPATH. In this case, we are loading the JDBC-ODBC bridge driver located in the `sun.jdbc.odbc` package.

Establish a Database Connection

Once a valid driver is loaded, we can use it to establish a connection to the database. A JDBC connection is identified by a "database URL" that tells the driver manager which driver and data source to use. The most common syntax for a database URL is shown here:

```
jdbc:<SUBPROTOCOL>:<DATABASE_IDENTIFIER>
```

The first part of the URL indicates that JDBC is being used to establish the connection. The *subprotocol* is the name of a valid JDBC driver or other database connectivity solution. The *database identifier* is typically a logical name, or alias, that maps to a physical database. To illustrate, the following URL uses ODBC to connect to the *Northwind* data source. (Northwind is the sample database that ships with Microsoft Access.) We will demonstrate how to create ODBC data sources a little later in this chapter.

```
jdbc:odbc:Northwind
```

A database connection is established using the `static` method, `get-Connection()`, of the `DriverManager` object like this:

```
Connection dbConn = DriverManager.getConnection(
  "jdbc:odbc:Northwind");
```

Or, for databases that require authentication, the connection can be established like this:

```
String username = "Erin", password = "secret";
Connection dbConn = DriverManager.getConnection(
  "jdbc:odbc:Northwind", username, password);
```

NOTE: To improve performance of JDBC servlets, define your database connection as a class or instance variable and open the connection within the `init()` method (see sample code below). In this way, the database connection will be established only once (when the servlet is first loaded) and will be shared across all requests.

```
public class JdbcServlet extends HttpServlet
{
  //database connection is shared by all requests
  Connection dbConn;

  public void init() throws ServletException
  {
    //open database connection (dbConn) here
  }
}
```

Execute an SQL Statement

Once established, the database connection can be used to submit SQL statements to the database. An SQL statement performs some operation on the database such as retrieving, inserting, updating, or deleting rows. To execute an

SQL statement, a `Statement` object must be created using the `Connection` object's `createStatement()` method. The `Statement` object provides methods to perform various operations against the database including executing SQL queries. A `Statement` object is created as shown here:

```
Statement stat = dbConn.createStatement();
```

Using the `Statement` object's `executeQuery()` method, information can be retrieved from the database. The `executeQuery()` method accepts an SQL select statement and returns a `ResultSet` object containing the database rows extracted by the query. For inserts, updates, or deletes, use the `executeUpdate()` method. The `ResultSet` object is created like this:

```
ResultSet set = stat.executeQuery("select * from orders");
```

NOTE: In addition to the `Statement` object, there are two other types of statements—prepared statements and callable statements.

A *prepared statement* is used for an SQL statement that will be executed multiple times. When a prepared statement is created, the SQL statement is sent to the database for precompilation (if supported by the JDBC driver). Because they are precompiled, prepared statements execute much faster than standard statements. Methods are provided that allow the query parameters to be modified.

A `PreparedStatement` object is created like this:

```
PreparedStatement ps = dbConn.prepareStatement("insert into
    orders (order_id, cust_id) values (?,?)");
```

The question marks in the SQL statement above represent dynamic query parameters. These parameters can be changed each time the prepared statement is called.

A *callable statement* is used to execute SQL stored procedures. Methods are provided to specify input parameters and retrieve return values. The `Callable-Statement` object extends `PreparedStatement` and, therefore, inherits its methods. A `CallableStatement` object that calls the `getOrder()` stored procedure is created like this:

```
CallableStatement cs = dbConn.prepareCall(
    "{call getOrder(?, ?)}");
```

Process the Results

To process the results, you can iterate through the rows of the result set using the `ResultSet` object's `next()` and `previous()` methods. The following sample code creates a `Statement` object, executes a query, and iterates through the result set. The `ResultSet` object's `getString()` method is used to extract the value of specific fields.

```
Statement stat = dbConn.createStatement();
ResultSet set = stat.executeQuery("select * from orders");

while (set.next())
{
  System.out.println(set.getString("OrderID") + " - " +
    set.getString("Customer"));
}
```

Close the Database Connection

Because database connections are a valuable and limited resource, you should always close the connection when processing is complete. The `Connection` object provides a simple `close()` method for this purpose.

In addition to closing the database connection, you should also explicitly close all `Statement` and `ResultSet` objects using their `close()` method. Although the Java virtual machine's garbage collector will eventually release resources that are no longer in scope, it is always a good practice to manually release these objects as soon as they are no longer useful. The `close()` method is used like this:

```
set.close();
stat.close();
dbConn.close();
```

Sample JDBC Servlet

OK, let's put it all together by writing a simple JDBC servlet. This example requires a Microsoft Windows operating system. To complete this exercise, you will need to install Microsoft Access including the sample databases or separately install the Microsoft Access ODBC driver and Northwind database. Let's start by reviewing how to create an ODBC data source.

Within a Windows operating system, ODBC data sources are created using the *ODBC Data Source Administrator*. This utility, found in the *Control Panel*, is shown in Figure 16.6. Let's create a new data source for the Northwind

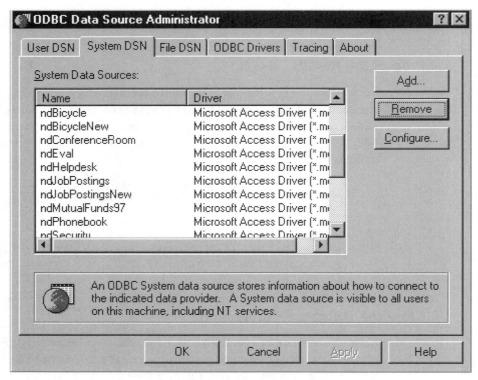

Figure 16.6　The ODBC Data Source Administrator for Windows

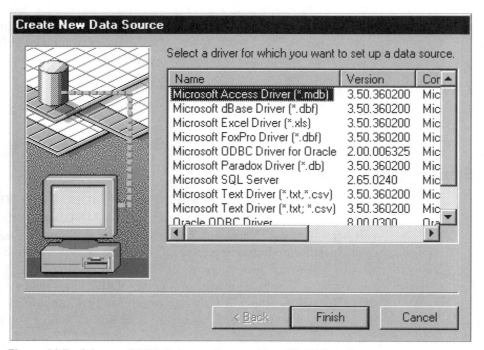

Figure 16.7　Select an ODBC Driver to Create a New ODBC Data Source

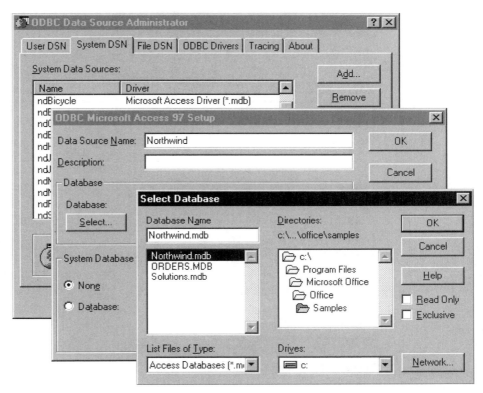

Figure 16.8 Create the Northwind Data Source

database. We will create this data source as a *System DSN* (Data Source Name) so that it will be available to all users on this machine (see Figure 16.6). Start by clicking the *Add* button and select the Microsoft Access driver (see Figure 16.7). Name the data source "Northwind" and select the database from the file system as shown in Figure 16.8.

That's it. Now we're ready to look at the code. When invoked, the following servlet reads customer data from an ODBC data source, formats it into an HTML table, and returns it to the client (see Listing 16.1). The servlet output is shown in Figure 16.9.

Listing 16.1 Sample JDBC servlet.

```
import javax.servlet.*;
import javax.servlet.http.*;
import java.io.*;
import java.sql.*;
```

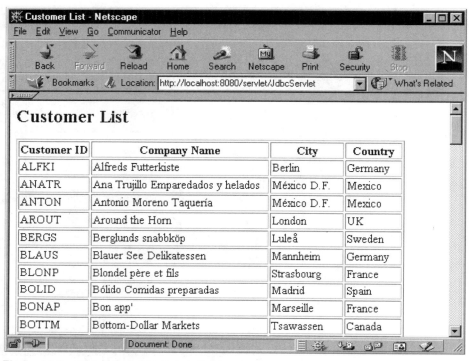

Figure 16.9   Output From the Sample Servlet

```
/**
 * JdbcServlet reads customer information from an ODBC data
 * source and presents it to the client in an HTML table.
 *
 * @author Dustin R. Callaway
 * @version 1.0, 10/01/98
 */
public class JdbcServlet extends HttpServlet
{
  //database connection is shared by all requests
  Connection dbConn;

  /**
   * init method is called when servlet is initialized.
   * Establishes a database connection when servlet is initially
   * loaded that can be shared across all requests.
   */
  public void init(ServletConfig config) throws ServletException
  {
    super.init(config); //pass ServletConfig to parent
```

```java
    try
    {
      //load JDBC-ODBC Bridge driver
      Class.forName("sun.jdbc.odbc.JdbcOdbcDriver");
      //establish database connection to Northwind using ODBC
      dbConn = DriverManager.getConnection(
        "jdbc:odbc:Northwind");
    }
    catch (ClassNotFoundException e) //Class.forName throws
    {
      System.out.println("JDBC-ODBC bridge not found!");
      return;
    }
    catch (SQLException e) //DriverManager.getConnection throws
    {
      System.out.println("SQL exception thrown in init!");
      return;
    }
  }


  /**
   * doGet method is called in response to a GET request
   */
  public void doGet(HttpServletRequest request,
    HttpServletResponse response) throws ServletException,
    IOException
  {
    try
    {
      response.setContentType("text/html"); //returns HTML

      //get handle to output stream
      PrintWriter out = response.getWriter();

      //create statement
      Statement stat = dbConn.createStatement();
      //query database for result set
      ResultSet customers = stat.executeQuery(
        "SELECT CustomerID, CompanyName, City, Country FROM " +
        "Customers");

      //generate HTML document to return to client
      out.println("<HTML>");
      out.println("<HEAD><TITLE>Customer List</TITLE></HEAD>");
      out.println("<BODY>");
      out.println("<H2>Customer List</H2>");
      out.println("<TABLE BORDER=1>"); //create an HTML table
      out.println("<TR><TH>Customer ID</TH>");
      out.println("<TH>Company Name</TH>");
      out.println("<TH>City</TH>");
      out.println("<TH>Country</TH></TR>");
```

```
        while (customers.next()) //iterate through all records
        {
          //add a table row for each record
          out.println("<TR><TD>" +
            customers.getString("CustomerID")+ "</TD><TD>" +
            customers.getString("CompanyName") + "</TD><TD>" +
            customers.getString("City") + "</TD><TD>" +
            customers.getString("Country") + "</TD></TR>");
        }

        out.println("</TABLE>");
        out.println("</BODY></HTML>");
        out.close();
      }
      catch (Exception e)
      {
        e.printStackTrace();
      }
    }

    /**
     * Tells the server about this servlet
     */
    public String getServletInfo()
    {
      return "Sample JDBC servlet";
    }
  }
```

The short tutorial and sample code presented here barely scratch the sur-
face of the full capabilities of JDBC, but I hope that you were able to catch a
glimpse of the great potential of using JDBC in your servlets.

Summary

This chapter defined the purpose of the Java Database Connectivity API and illustrated the basic JDBC architecture. The four types of JDBC drivers were also
described. Finally, the process of connecting to a database was discussed in detail and a sample JDBC servlet was presented.

Chapter Highlights

- JDBC is an API specification developed by Sun Microsystems that defines a uniform interface for accessing different relational databases. The
  primary function of the JDBC API is to allow the developer to issue
  SQL statements and process the results in a consistent, database-
  independent manner.

- The JDBC API uses a driver manager and database-specific drivers to provide transparent connectivity to heterogeneous databases.

- The *JDBC driver manager* ensures that the correct driver is used to access each data source. The driver manager is capable of supporting multiple concurrent drivers connected to multiple heterogeneous databases.

- A *JDBC driver* translates standard JDBC calls into a network protocol or client API call that facilitates communication with the database. This translation provides JDBC applications with database independence.

- The basic process of connecting to a database via JDBC looks like this: register the JDBC driver, establish a database connection, execute an SQL statement, process the results, close the database connection.

This concludes the Advanced Servlet Concepts part of the book. The next part, Sample Servlets, offers useful servlet examples.

PART IV

Sample Servlets

CHAPTER 17

Diagnostics Servlet

The Diagnostics servlet presented in this chapter may serve as a helpful troubleshooting tool as well as a useful programming reference. This servlet utilizes many Servlet API methods to reveal information concerning an HTTP request and the server environment in which the servlet is executing. Much of this information may be useful to the servlet developer when debugging and troubleshooting HTTP communications.

The following list enumerates some of the information revealed by the Diagnostics servlet:

- Requested resource
- HTTP method utilized by request (GET, POST, etc.)
- Request query string
- Server and servlet information (name, IP address, port, initialization parameters, etc.)
- Request HTTP headers
- Request parameters (Web variables)

This information, particularly the request's HTTP headers and Web variables, may be very useful when building servlets that respond to client requests. Figure 17.1 shows a screen shot of the servlet responding to a typical HTTP request.

Listing 17.1 provides the full source code for the Diagnostics servlet. In-line documentation provides further information regarding the code.

Listing 17.1   Diagnostics servlet source code.

```
import java.io.*;
import java.util.*;
import javax.servlet.*;
import javax.servlet.http.*;
```

Figure 17.1 Diagnostics Servlet's Response to a Typical HTTP Request

```java
/**
 * Diagnostics servlet. Displays various information concerning
 * the client's request and the state of the servlet
 * environment. This information includes init parameters,
 * request HTTP method, request parameters, and request headers.
 * This servlet is useful when troubleshooting.
 *
 * @author Dustin R. Callaway
 * @version 1.0, 08/15/1998
 */
public class Diagnostics extends HttpServlet
{
  /**
   * init method is called when servlet is first loaded.
   */
  public void init(ServletConfig config) throws ServletException
  {
    super.init(config); //pass ServletConfig to parent
  }


  /**
   * Called in response to any request to this servlet
   */
  public void service(HttpServletRequest request,
```

```
            HttpServletResponse response) throws ServletException,
            IOException
{
   response.setContentType("text/html"); //HTML output

   //get handle to output stream
   PrintWriter out = response.getWriter();

   //generate HTML to return to client
   out.println("<HTML>");
   out.println("<HEAD>");
   out.println("<TITLE>Diagnostics Servlet</TITLE>");
   out.println("</HEAD>v);
   out.println("<BODY>");
   out.println("<H1>Diagnostics Servlet</H1>v);

   //Request Properties
   out.println("<H2>Request Properties</H2>");
   out.println("<BLOCKQUOTE><PRE>");
   out.println("Request URL: " +
      HttpUtils.getRequestURL(request).toString());
   out.println("Request URI: " + request.getRequestURI());
   out.println("Request Method: " + request.getMethod());
   out.println("Request Protocol: " + request.getProtocol());
   out.println("Request Scheme: " + request.getScheme());
   out.println("Content Type: " + request.getContentType());
   out.println("Content Length: " +
      request.getContentLength());
   out.println("Query String: " + request.getQueryString());
   out.println("Authorization Scheme: " +
      request.getAuthType());
   out.println("</PRE></BLOCKQUOTE><BR>");

   //REQUEST INFORMATION
   out.println("<H2>Request Information</H2>");
   out.println("<BLOCKQUOTE><PRE>");
   out.println("Servlet Path: " + request.getServletPath());
   out.println("Path Information: " + request.getPathInfo());
   out.println("Path Translated: " +
      request.getPathTranslated());
   out.println("Server Name: " + request.getServerName());
   out.println("Server Port: " + request.getServerPort());
   out.println("Remote User: " + request.getRemoteUser());
   out.println("Remote Address: " + request.getRemoteAddr());
   out.println("Remote Host: " + request.getRemoteHost());
   out.println("Character Encoding: " +
      request.getCharacterEncoding());
   out.println("</PRE></BLOCKQUOTE><BR>");

   //REQUEST HEADERS
   //create Enumeration of headers
   Enumeration headers = request.getHeaderNames();
   if (headers.hasMoreElements()) //check for headers
   {
```

```java
      out.println("<H2>Request Headers</H2>");
      out.println("<BLOCKQUOTE><PRE>");
      //iterate through header names
      while (headers.hasMoreElements())
      {
        //get header name
        String header = (String)headers.nextElement();
        //generate HTML to display header name and value
        out.println(header + ": " + request.getHeader(header));
      }
      out.println("</PRE></BLOCKQUOTE><BR>");
    }

    //REQUEST PARAMETERS (web variables)
    //create Enumeration of parameter names
    Enumeration paramNames = request.getParameterNames();
    if (paramNames.hasMoreElements()) //check for param names
    {
      out.println("<H2>Request Parameters</H2>");
      out.println("<BLOCKQUOTE><PRE>");
      while (paramNames.hasMoreElements()) //iterate thru params
      {
        //get parameter name
        String paramName = (String)paramNames.nextElement();
        //get parameter value
        String paramValues[] =
          request.getParameterValues(paramName);
        if (paramValues != null)
        {
          //print parameter name and first value
          out.print(paramName + ": " + paramValues[0]);
          //print remaining parameter values (if any)
          for (int i = 1; i < paramValues.length; i++)
          {
            out.print(", " + paramValues[i]);
          }
          out.println("");
        }
      }
      out.println("</PRE></BLOCKQUOTE><BR>");
    }

    //INITIALIZATION PARAMETERS
    //create Enumeration of initialization parameters
    Enumeration initParams =
      getServletConfig().getInitParameterNames();
    if (initParams.hasMoreElements()) //check for init params
    {
      out.println("<H2>Initialization Parameters</H2>");
      out.println("<BLOCKQUOTE><PRE>");
      while (initParams.hasMoreElements()) //iterate thru params
      {
```

```
            //get param name
            String initParam = (String) initParams.nextElement();
            //generate HTML to display init parameter name and value
            out.println(initParam + ": " +
               getInitParameter(initParam));
         }
         out.println("</PRE></BLOCKQUOTE><BR>");
      }

      out.println("</BODY>");
      out.println("</HTML>");
      out.close(); //close output stream
   }


   /**
    * Allows server to identify this servlet
    */
   public String getServletInfo()
   {
      return "Servlet returns various request information.";
   }
}
```

CHAPTER 18

Form Mailer Servlet

The Form Mailer servlet provides a convenient way to e-mail information entered on an HTML form. This servlet extracts the required e-mail data (i.e., sender, recipient, subject, message) from a basic HTML form, opens a socket to the mail server, and transmits the message via the SMTP protocol. After the message is successfully sent, the client is redirected to a page specified by a hidden field on the HTML form. Likewise, the client may be redirected to a different page if an error occurs and the e-mail is not sent. This servlet is thread safe and can be utilized by any number of HTML forms concurrently.

The successful operation of the Form Mailer servlet is dependent on the proper naming of the HTML form elements. Table 18.1 shows the correct names of each HTML form element. The naming of each element is critical because the servlet queries for these parameters by name when extracting the mail information from the form.

The simple HTML document shown in Listing 18.1 uses the naming conventions described in Table 18.1 and works well with the Form Mailer servlet. Notice the hidden fields within the HTML form that instruct the server where to redirect the client after the mail has been sent (NextPage and ErrorPage). Figure 18.1 shows how the HTML looks when rendered by a browser.

Listing 18.1   HTML form that invokes the Form Mailer servlet.

```
<HTML>

<HEAD>
<TITLE>Mail Form</TITLE>
</HEAD>

<BODY>
```

Table 18.1   HTML Form Element Naming Scheme Required by Form Mailer Servlet

HTML Form Element	Correct Element Name
Mail recipient (*To* field)	To
Mail sender (*From* field)	From
Subject text	Subject
Message text	Message
Success URL (page to which client is redirected if mail is sent successfully)	NextPage
Error URL (page to which client is redirected if mail is not sent successfully)	ErrorPage

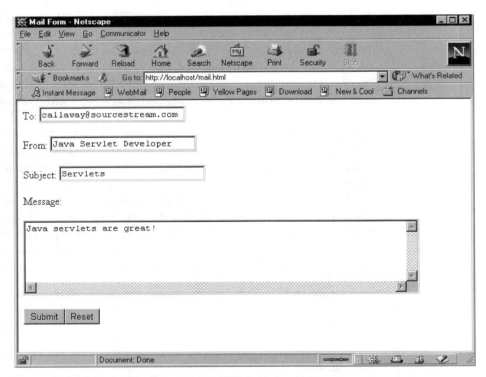

Figure 18.1   Browser Rendering of the HTML in Listing 18.1

```
<FORM ACTION="http://localhost:8080/servlet/FormMailer"
  METHOD="POST">

<P>To: <INPUT TYPE="TEXT" NAME="To" SIZE="25"></P>
<P>From: <INPUT TYPE="TEXT" NAME="From" SIZE="25"></P>
<P>Subject: <INPUT TYPE="TEXT" NAME="Subject" SIZE="25"></P>
<P>Message:</P>
<P><TEXTAREA NAME="Message" ROWS="5" COLS="70"></TEXTAREA></P>

<INPUT TYPE="HIDDEN" NAME="NextPage"
  VALUE="http://localhost/mailsent.html">
<INPUT TYPE="HIDDEN" NAME="ErrorPage"
  VALUE="http://localhost/mailerror.html">

<P><INPUT TYPE="SUBMIT" NAME="Submit" VALUE="Submit">
<INPUT TYPE="RESET" NAME="Reset" VALUE="Reset">
</FORM>

</BODY>

</HTML>
```

Listing 18.2 contains the full source code for the Form Mailer servlet. In-line documentation is provided within the code.

Listing 18.2   Form Mailer servlet source code.

```
import javax.servlet.*;
import javax.servlet.http.*;
import java.io.*;
import java.util.*;
import java.net.*;

/**
 * Form mailer servlet. Accepts the input from an HTML form
 * and e-mails it to the specified recipient. The form should
 * contain a hidden variable specifying the page to which the
 * client should be redirected after the mail is sent.
 *
 * @author Dustin R. Callaway
 * @version 1.0, 08/20/1998
 */
public class FormMailer extends HttpServlet
{
  private static final int PORT = 25;
  private static final int LINELENGTH = 72;
  private static final String MAILSERVER =
    "mail.sourcestream.com";

  /**
   * init method is called when servlet is first loaded.
   */
  public void init(ServletConfig config) throws ServletException
  {
```

```
    super.init(config); //pass ServletConfig to parent
}


/**
 * doPost processes the information submitted by the client.
 */
public void doPost(HttpServletRequest request,
  HttpServletResponse response) throws IOException
{
  String from, to, subject, message, host;
  String nextPage, errorPage;

  //get info from HTML form submitted by user
  host = request.getServerName(); //host name of this server
  from = request.getParameter("From");
  to = request.getParameter("To");
  subject = request.getParameter("Subject");
  message = request.getParameter("Message");
  message = wordWrap(message); //wrap message
  nextPage = request.getParameter("NextPage");
  errorPage = request.getParameter("ErrorPage");

  if (sendMail(from, to, subject, message, host))
  {
    //mail was sent successfully, redirect client
    response.sendRedirect(nextPage);
  }
  else //mail NOT sent successfully
  {
    //mail was not sent due to error, redirect to error page
    response.sendRedirect(errorPage);
  }
}


/**
 * Simple implementation of SMTP protocol to send e-mail.
 *
 * @param from The message sender address
 * @param to The message recipient address
 * @param subject The subject of the message
 * @param message The message body
 * @param host The name of server that is processing request
 */
boolean sendMail(String from, String to, String subject,
  String message, String host)
{
  String line; //line of text received from mail server
  Socket mailSocket; //socket to mail server
  BufferedReader mailIn; //used to read input from mail server
  PrintWriter out=null; //handle to output stream
```

```
try
{
  //open socket to mail server
  mailSocket = new Socket(MAILSERVER, PORT);

  //get output stream to mail server
  out = new PrintWriter(new OutputStreamWriter(
    mailSocket.getOutputStream()));

  //get input stream from mail server
  mailIn = new BufferedReader(new InputStreamReader(
    mailSocket.getInputStream()));
  if (!checkResponse(mailIn, "220"))
  {
    return false; //operation failed
  }

  //send HELO handshake
  out.print("HELO " + host + "\r\n");
  out.flush();
  if (!checkResponse(mailIn, "250"))
  {
    return false; //operation failed
  }

  //sender information
  out.print("MAIL FROM: " + from + "\r\n");
  out.flush();
  if (!checkResponse(mailIn, "250"))
  {
    return false; //operation failed
  }

  //recipient information
  out.print("RCPT TO: " + to + "\r\n");
  out.flush();
  if (!checkResponse(mailIn, "250"))
  {
    return false; //operation failed
  }

  //beginning of message's data portion
  out.print("DATA\r\n");
  out.flush();
  if (!checkResponse(mailIn, "354"))
  {
    return false; //operation failed
  }

  //send date information
  out.print("Date: " + new Date().toString() + "\r\n");
  out.flush(); //flush output stream
```

```
            //send from information
            out.print("From: " + from + "\r\n");
            out.flush(); //flush output stream

            //send subject information
            out.print("Subject: " + subject + "\r\n\r\n");
            out.flush(); //flush output stream

            //tokenize each line of the message body
            StringTokenizer stMessage = new
              StringTokenizer(message, "\n");

            //send message
            while (stMessage.hasMoreTokens())
            {
              line = stMessage.nextToken(); //get next line (or token)
              if (line.equals(".")) //replace single period with colon
              {
                line = ":"; //prevents user from ending message
              }

              out.println(line); //send message to mail server
              out.flush(); //flush the output stream
            }

            out.print("\r\n.\r\n"); //end message
            out.flush(); //flush the output stream
            if (!checkResponse(mailIn, "250"))
            {
              return false; //operation failed
            }

            //close session with mail server
            out.print("QUIT\r\n");
            out.flush(); //flush the output stream
            if (!checkResponse(mailIn, "221"))
            {
              return false; //operation failed
            }
          }
          catch (UnknownHostException e)
          {
            return false;
          }
          catch (IOException e)
          {
            return false;
          }
          finally
          {
            try
            {
              out.close(); //close socket
            }
```

```
         catch (Exception e)
         {}
      }

    return true;
  }

  /**
   * Verifies that the mail server's response is correct
   *
   * @param mailIn Input stream from mail server
   * @param valid Indicates valid response code
   */
  boolean checkResponse(BufferedReader mailIn, String valid)
  {
    String line; //stores the next line from mail server

    try
    {
      line = mailIn.readLine(); //read next line from server

      //return false if line doesn't start with expected code
      if (!line.startsWith(valid))
      {
        return false;
      }
    }
    catch (IOException e)
    {
      return false;
    }

    return true;
  }


  /**
   * Wraps message lines longer than LINELENGTH
   *
   * @param message The message content
   */
  String wordWrap(String message)
  {
    String word; //individual word
    int column=0, length;
    StringBuffer messageBuffer = new StringBuffer();
    //tokenize the message by spaces (break into single words)
    StringTokenizer words = new StringTokenizer(message," ");

    while (words.hasMoreTokens()) //iterate through each word
    {
      word = words.nextToken(); //set word to next token

      length = word.length(); //set length of word
```

```java
            //word exceeds line length, print on next line
            if (column > 0 && (column + length) > LINELENGTH)
            {
              messageBuffer.append("\n" + word + " ");
              column = length + 1; //increase column pointer
            }
            else if (word.endsWith("\n")) //word ends current line
            {
              messageBuffer.append(word);
              column = 0; //set column pointer to zero
            }
            else //word does not exceed line length or end line
            {
              messageBuffer.append(word + " ");
              column += length + 1; //increase column pointer
            }
         }

     return messageBuffer.toString(); //return processed message
  }


  /**
   * Allows server to identify this servlet
   */
  public String getServletInfo()
  {
    return "Servlet sends e-mail based on info from HTML form";
  }
}
```

CHAPTER 19

File Upload Servlet

The File Upload servlet enables the client to upload files to the server via a simple HTML form. This servlet requires a Web browser that supports the form-based upload specification documented in RFC 1867. Fortunately, the latest versions of Netscape Navigator and Microsoft Internet Explorer both support form-based file uploads.

Let's start by briefly reviewing form-based uploads. An HTML form can specify that a file is to be uploaded to the server by indicating an encryption type of "`multipart/form-data`" and including an `INPUT` page element of type "`FILE`." The following HTML demonstrates a simple HTML form that facilitates file uploads.

```
<FORM ENCTYPE="multipart/form-data"
   ACTION="http://localhost:8080/servlet/UploadServlet"
   METHOD="POST">

<B>File Name: </B>
<INPUT TYPE="FILE" NAME="Filename" VALUE="" MAXLENGTH=255><P>
<INPUT TYPE="SUBMIT" Value="Upload">

</FORM>
```

Notice that the form's encoding type (`ENCTYPE`) is set to `multipart/form-data`. This encoding type indicates to the browser that the data corresponding to each form element should be separated within the request (see Listing 19.2). The data from each form element is separated by a unique string known as a *boundary marker*. This marker allows the server to parse the request and extract the data from each element. Also notice the new form element called `FILE`. This `INPUT` element is similar to a normal textbox except that a *Browse* button is displayed to its immediate right (see Figure 19.1). The *Browse* button displays a standard file dialog box. After the user chooses a file, the

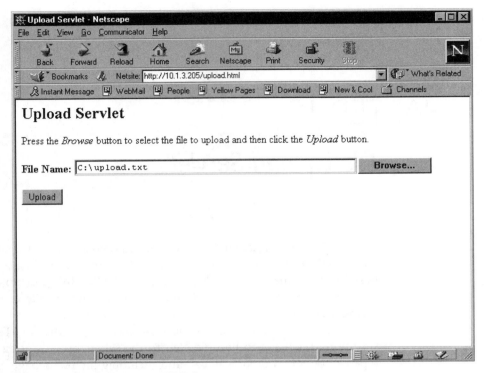

Figure 19.1   Upload Servlet HTML Page

textbox portion of the FILE element is populated with the path and filename of the selected file. Finally, when the user submits the form, the browser packages the data corresponding to each form element into separate sections (or parts) within the request and sends the request to the server (see Listing 19.2). The data that comprises the selected file is included within one of these sections.

NOTE: The browser will package each section of the multipart request in the order that the form elements appear on the HTML page. However, the order of these elements is not critical and does not affect the operation of the Form Upload servlet.

To provide maximum flexibility, many File Upload servlet options can be set by hidden variables on the HTML form. This allows the servlet to be customized without recompiling. The names and descriptions of each of these variables are documented in Table 19.1.

Table 19.1 Names and Descriptions of Form Elements Used by the File Upload Servlet

Element Name	Description
`Directory`	The directory in which the uploaded file should be stored. To prevent a user from uploading a file to any location, this directory exists or is created under the root specified by the servlet. The root can be set with a servlet initialization parameter. The value of this element should always end with a slash ("/") but not begin with one (e.g., "`temp/`").
`SuccessPage`	Contains the URL to which the client should be redirected if the file is uploaded successfully.
`OverWrite`	Serves as a flag to indicate whether to overwrite existing files. Files will only be overwritten if the `OverWrite` variable is set to `true`. If `OverWrite` is not enabled, the upload operation will be canceled and the servlet will redirect the client to the page specified by `OverWritePage`.
`OverWritePage`	Contains the URL to which the client will be redirected if the file they are uploading already exists and the `OverWrite` flag is not set to `true` or is nonexistent.

Listing 19.1 provides a sample HTML form that implements form-based file uploads. Notice the hidden variables in Listing 19.1. Keep in mind that the form elements must be named exactly as they appear in Table 19.1. Figure 19.1 illustrates how a browser renders this HTML document.

Listing 19.1 Sample HTML document that implements form-based file uploads.

```
<HTML>
<HEAD>
<TITLE>Upload Servlet</TITLE>
</HEAD>
<BODY>
<H2>Upload Servlet</H2>

<FORM ENCTYPE="multipart/form-data"
  ACTION="http://localhost:8080/servlet/UploadServlet"
  METHOD="POST">

Press the <I>Browse</I> button to select the file to upload and
then click the <I>Upload</I> button.<P>
<B>File Name: </B>
<INPUT TYPE="FILE" NAME="Filename" VALUE="" MAXLENGTH=255
  SIZE=50><P>
<INPUT TYPE="SUBMIT" Value="Upload">
<INPUT TYPE="HIDDEN" NAME="Directory" VALUE="temp/">
```

```
<INPUT TYPE="HIDDEN" NAME="SuccessPage"
  VALUE="http://localhost/success.html">
<INPUT TYPE="HIDDEN" NAME="OverWrite" VALUE="false">
<INPUT TYPE="HIDDEN" NAME="OverWritePage"
  VALUE="http://localhost/overwrite.html">

</FORM>

</BODY>
</HTML>
```

Now that we have seen how form-based file uploads are accomplished from the HTML side, let's take a look at the format of the multipart/form-data request. Listing 19.2 shows the request generated by the browser when the preceding HTML form is submitted (including the HTTP headers).

Listing 19.2   Format of the multipart/form-data request.

```
POST /servlet/UploadServlet HTTP/1.0
Content-Type: multipart/form-data; boundary=--------------------
-------166801948522407
Content-Length: 802

---------------------------166801948522407
Content-Disposition: form-data; name="Filename";
filename="C:\upload.txt"
Content-Type: text/plain

This text comprises the entire contents of the sample upload
file called "upload.txt" read from the "c:\" directory.
---------------------------166801948522407
Content-Disposition: form-data; name="Directory"

temp/
---------------------------166801948522407
Content-Disposition: form-data; name="SuccessPage"

http://localhost/success.html
---------------------------166801948522407
Content-Disposition: form-data; name="OverWrite"

false
---------------------------166801948522407
Content-Disposition: form-data; name="OverWritePage"

http://localhost/overwrite.html
---------------------------166801948522407--
```

Listing 19.2 should give you a good idea of how the browser packages a file upload request. The file information is stored in the first part of this request immediately following the first boundary marker. Keep in mind that the upload file could just as easily have been composed of binary data rather than ASCII text.

The boundary marker is identified in the Content-Type HTTP header field. The boundary marker for this request is:

```
---------------------------166801948522407
```

This marker is used by the File Upload servlet to find the beginning and end of the upload file as well as to extract the values of the hidden variables.

NOTE: Uploading data can be extremely taxing on server resources. For this reason, the sample servlet presented here prevents clients from uploading files greater than 100K in size. However, this setting can be configured by changing the MAX_SIZE variable. It is recommended that uploaded files be limited to a reasonable size based on available server resources.

Listing 19.3 contains the full source code for the File Upload servlet. In-line documentation is provided within the code.

Listing 19.3 File Upload servlet source code.

```java
import javax.servlet.*;
import javax.servlet.*;
import javax.servlet.http.*;
import java.io.*;

/**
 * UploadServlet works in conjunction with a browser's form-
 * based file upload capability to allow the client to
 * transfer a file (binary or ASCII) to the server and store
 * it in the file system.
 *
 * @author Dustin R. Callaway
 * @version 1.0, 8/30/98
 */
public class UploadServlet extends HttpServlet
{
    //default maximum allowable file size is 100k
    static final int MAX_SIZE = 102400;

    //instance variables to store root and success message
    String rootPath, successMessage;

    /**
     * init method is called when servlet is initialized.
     */
```

```
public void init(ServletConfig config) throws ServletException
{
  super.init(config);

  //get path in which to save file
  rootPath = config.getInitParameter("RootPath");
  if (rootPath == null)
  {
    rootPath = "/";
  }

  /*Get message to show when upload is complete. Used only if
    a success redirect page is not supplied.*/
  successMessage = config.getInitParameter("SuccessMessage");
  if (successMessage == null)
  {
    successMessage = "File upload complete!";
  }
}


/**
 * doPost reads the uploaded data from the request and writes
 * it to a file.
 */
public void doPost(HttpServletRequest request,
  HttpServletResponse response)
{
  ServletOutputStream out=null;
  DataInputStream in=null;
  FileOutputStream fileOut=null;

  try
  {
    /*set content type of response and get handle to output
      stream in case we are unable to redirect client*/
    response.setContentType("text/plain");
    out = response.getOutputStream();
  }
  catch (IOException e)
  {
    //print error message to standard out
    System.out.println("Error getting output stream.");
    System.out.println("Error description: " + e);
    return;
  }

  try
  {
    //get content type of client request
    String contentType = request.getContentType();
```

```
//make sure content type is multipart/form-data
if(contentType != null && contentType.indexOf(
  "multipart/form-data") != -1)
{
  //open input stream from client to capture upload file
  in = new DataInputStream(request.getInputStream());

  //get length of content data
  int formDataLength = request.getContentLength();

  //check for maximum size violation
  if (formDataLength > MAX_SIZE)
  {
    out.println("Sorry, file is too large to upload.");
    out.flush(); //flush output buffer
    return;
  }

  //allocate a byte array to store content data
  byte dataBytes[] = new byte[formDataLength];

  //read file into byte array
  int bytesRead = 0;
  int totalBytesRead = 0;
  while (totalBytesRead < formDataLength)
  {
    bytesRead = in.read(dataBytes, totalBytesRead,
      formDataLength);

    //keep track of total bytes read from input stream
    totalBytesRead += bytesRead;
  }

  //create string from byte array for easy manipulation
  String file = new String(dataBytes, "IS08859_1");
  //since byte array is stored in string, release memory
  dataBytes = null;

  /*get boundary value (boundary is a unique string that
    separates content data)*/
  int lastIndex = contentType.lastIndexOf("=");
  String boundary = contentType.substring(lastIndex+1,
    contentType.length());

  //get Directory web variable from request
  String directory="";
  if (file.indexOf("name=\"Directory\"") > 0)
  {
    directory = file.substring(
      file.indexOf("name=\"Directory\""));
    //remove carriage return
    directory = directory.substring(
      directory.indexOf("\n")+1);
```

```
                 //remove carriage return
                 directory = directory.substring(
                   directory.indexOf("\n")+1);
                 //get Directory
                 directory = directory.substring(0,
                   directory.indexOf("\n")-1);
                 /*make sure user didn't select a directory higher in
                   the directory tree*/
                 if (directory.indexOf("..") > 0)
                 {
                   out.println("Security Error: You can't upload " +
                     "to a directory higher in the directory tree.");
                   return;
                 }
               }

               //get SuccessPage web variable from request
               String successPage="";
               if (file.indexOf("name=\"SuccessPage\"") > 0)
               {
                 successPage = file.substring(
                   file.indexOf("name=\"SuccessPage\""));
                 //remove carriage return
                 successPage = successPage.substring(
                   successPage.indexOf("\n")+1);
                 //remove carriage return
                 successPage = successPage.substring(
                   successPage.indexOf("\n")+1);
                 //get success page
                 successPage = successPage.substring(
                   0, successPage.indexOf("\n")-1);
               }

               //get OverWrite flag web variable from request
               String overWrite;
               if (file.indexOf("name=\"OverWrite\"") > 0)
               {
                 overWrite = file.substring(
                   file.indexOf("name=\"OverWrite\""));
                 //remove carriage return
                 overWrite = overWrite.substring(
                   overWrite.indexOf("\n")+1);
                 //remove carriage return
                 overWrite = overWrite.substring(
                   overWrite.indexOf("\n")+1);
                 //get overwrite flag
                 overWrite = overWrite.substring(0,
                   overWrite.indexOf("\n")-1);
               }
               else
               {
                 overWrite = "false";
               }
```

```
//get OverWritePage web variable from request
String overWritePage="";
if (file.indexOf("name=\"OverWritePage\"") > 0)
{
  overWritePage = file.substring(
    file.indexOf("name=\"OverWritePage\""));
  //remove carriage return
  overWritePage = overWritePage.substring(
    overWritePage.indexOf("\n")+1);
  //remove carriage return
  overWritePage = overWritePage.substring(
    overWritePage.indexOf("\n")+1);
  //get overwrite page
  overWritePage = overWritePage.substring(0,
    overWritePage.indexOf("\n")-1);
}

//get filename of upload file
String saveFile = file.substring(
  file.indexOf("filename=\"")+10);
saveFile = saveFile.substring(0,
  saveFile.indexOf("\n"));
saveFile = saveFile.substring(
  saveFile.lastIndexOf("\\")+1,
  saveFile.indexOf("\""));

/*remove boundary markers and other multipart/form-data
  tags from beginning of upload file section*/
int pos; //position in upload file
//find position of upload file section of request
pos = file.indexOf("filename=\"");
//find position of content-disposition line
pos = file.indexOf("\n",pos)+1;
//find position of content-type line
pos = file.indexOf("\n",pos)+1;
//find position of blank line
pos = file.indexOf("\n",pos)+1;

/*find the location of the next boundary marker
  (marking the end of the upload file data)*/
int boundaryLocation = file.indexOf(boundary,pos)-4;

//upload file lies between pos and boundaryLocation
file = file.substring(pos,boundaryLocation);

//build the full path of the upload file
String fileName = new String(rootPath + directory +
  saveFile);

//create File object to check for existence of file
File checkFile = new File(fileName);
if (checkFile.exists())
{
```

```
            /*file exists, if OverWrite flag is off, give
              message and abort*/
            if (!overWrite.toLowerCase().equals("true"))
            {
              if (overWritePage.equals(""))
              {
                /*OverWrite HTML page URL not received, respond
                  with generic message*/
                out.println("Sorry, file already exists.");
              }
              else
              {
                //redirect client to OverWrite HTML page
                response.sendRedirect(overWritePage);
              }
              return;
            }
          }

          /*create File object to check for existence of
            Directory*/
          File fileDir = new File(rootPath + directory);
          if (!fileDir.exists())
          {
            //Directory doesn't exist, create it
            fileDir.mkdirs();
          }

          //instantiate file output stream
          fileOut = new FileOutputStream(fileName);

          //write the string to the file as a byte array
          fileOut.write(file.getBytes("IS08859_1"),0,
            file.length());

          if (successPage.equals(""))
          {
            /*success HTML page URL not received, respond with
              generic success message*/
            out.println(successMessage);
            out.println("File written to: " + fileName);
          }
          else
          {
            //redirect client to success HTML page
            response.sendRedirect(successPage);
          }
        }
        else //request is not multipart/form-data
        {
          //send error message to client
          out.println("Request not multipart/form-data.");
        }
      }
    }
```

```
        catch(Exception e)
        {
          try
          {
            //print error message to standard out
            System.out.println("Error in doPost: " + e);
            //send error message to client
            out.println("An unexpected error has occurred.");
            out.println("Error description: " + e);
          }
          catch (Exception f) {}
        }
        finally
        {
          try
          {
            fileOut.close(); //close file output stream
          }
          catch (Exception f) {}
          try
          {
            in.close(); //close input stream from client
          }
          catch (Exception f) {}
          try
          {
            out.close(); //close output stream to client
          }
          catch (Exception f) {}
        }
      }
    }
```

PART V

Servlet API Quick Reference

CHAPTER 20

javax.servlet *Package*

The javax.servlet package contains interfaces and classes used to build generic servlets. Unlike the javax.servlet.http package, this package does not contain protocol-specific functionality and can be used to implement any standard or custom protocol. The javax.servlet package contains the interfaces and classes shown in Table 20.1.

Table 20.1 Interfaces and Classes of the javax.servlet Package

Interfaces	RequestDispatcher
	Servlet
	ServletConfig
	ServletContext
	ServletRequest
	ServletResponse
	SingleThreadModel
Classes	GenericServlet
	ServletInputStream
	ServletOutputStream
	ServletException
	UnavailableException

Interface RequestDispatcher

javax.servlet.RequestDispatcher

Definition

```
public interface RequestDispatcher
```

Serves as a "wrapper" around a server resource providing request forwarding and server-side include functionality. Use the getRequestDispatcher() method of the ServletContext object to get a RequestDispatcher object.

Methods

forward

```
public abstract void forward(ServletRequest request,
    ServletResponse response) throws ServletException, IOException
```

Forwards a request from a servlet to another server resource. Since the forwarding servlet should generate all content, the servlet that calls the forward() method should not acquire a reference to the output stream (i.e., use the getWriter() or getOutputStream() method) or attempt to set HTTP headers (i.e., use the setHeader() or setStatus() method).

include

```
public abstract void include(ServletRequest request,
    ServletResponse response) throws ServletException, IOException
```

Allows the output generated by another server resource to be included in the servlet's response. The included servlet should not attempt to set the response status code or any HTTP headers (i.e., use the setStatus() or setHeader() method). Setting response codes and headers is the responsibility of the calling servlet.

Interface Servlet

> javax.servlet.Servlet

Definition

```
public interface Servlet
```

All servlets implement the Servlet interface in order to enforce a common set of functionality.

Methods

destroy

```
public abstract void destroy()
```

Called by the servlet engine when the servlet is unloaded. Should be used to free any resources held by the servlet. Returns nothing.

getServletConfig

```
public abstract ServletConfig getServletConfig()
```

Returns a ServletConfig object which contains servlet initialization parameters and other server configuration settings.

getServletInfo

```
public abstract String getServletInfo()
```

Returns a String containing a brief description of the servlet.

init

```
public abstract void init(ServletConfig config) throws
    ServletException
```

Called when the servlet is loaded. One-time initialization should be performed here. Returns nothing.

service

```
public abstract void service(ServletRequest req, ServletResponse
    res) throws ServletException, IOException
```

Called in response to each request. A Java-enabled server passes objects to this method representing the client's request and the server's response. Returns nothing.

Interface ServletConfig

> javax.servlet.ServletConfig

Definition

```
public interface ServletConfig
```

The ServletConfig interface is implemented by the server in order to provide configuration parameters to a servlet when it is initialized. This interface may also be implemented by a servlet (see GenericServlet later in this chapter). A ServletConfig object is passed into the servlet's init() method.

Methods

getInitParameter

```
public abstract String getInitParameter(String name)
```

Returns a String containing the value of the specified initialization parameter or null if the parameter does not exist.

getInitParameterNames

```
public abstract Enumeration getInitParameterNames()
```

Returns an Enumeration of String objects containing the names of the servlet's initialization parameters or null if no initialization parameters exist.

getServletContext

```
public abstract ServletContext getServletContext()
```

Returns a ServletContext object containing information about the environment in which the servlet is running.

Interface ServletContext

> javax.servlet.ServletContext

Definition

```
public interface ServletContext
```

The ServletContext interface is implemented by the server in order to allow the servlet to obtain information about the environment in which it is running as well as log events in a server-specific manner. A handle to a ServletContext object may be obtained using the getServletContext() method of the ServletConfig object.

Methods

getAttribute

```
public abstract Object getAttribute(String name)
```

Returns an Object of the specified name that has been stored in the servlet context or null if the attribute does not exist. The object can be stored using the setAttribute() method. This method is useful for passing objects between servlets within the same context.

getAttributeNames

```
public abstract Enumeration getAttributeNames()
```

Returns an Enumeration of String objects representing the names of attributes available within this servlet context.

getContext

```
public abstract ServletContext getContext(String uripath)
```

Returns a ServletContext object related to a given URI path or null if there is no ServletContext associated with this path.

getMajorVersion

```
public abstract int getMajorVersion()
```

Returns the major version number of the Servlet API supported by this server.

getMimeType

```
public abstract String getMimeType(String file)
```

Returns a String describing the MIME type of the specified file or null if unknown.

getMinorVersion

```
public abstract int getMinorVersion()
```

Returns the minor version number of the Servlet API supported by this server.

getRealPath

```
public abstract String getRealPath(String path)
```

Returns a String describing the physical (file system) path corresponding to the specified virtual path. Returns null if the translation fails.

getRequestDispatcher

```
public abstract RequestDispatcher getRequestDispatcher(String
    urlpath)
```

Returns a RequestDispatcher object. This object provides request forwarding and server-side include functionality.

getResource

```
public abstract URL getResource(String path) throws
    MalformedURLException
```

Returns a URL object that provides access to the content of the specified resource or null if the resource is not found.

getResourceAsStream

```
public abstract InputStream getResourceAsStream(String path)
```

Returns an input stream to the specified resource or null if the resource is not found.

getServerInfo

```
public abstract String getServerInfo()
```

Returns a String containing the server's name and version.

log

```
public abstract void log(String msg)
```

Writes the specified message to the servlet log file. Returns nothing.

```
public abstract void log(String message, Throwable throwable)
```

Writes the specified message and the stack trace to the servlet log file. Useful for logging exceptions. Returns nothing.

removeAttribute

```
public abstract void removeAttribute(String name)
```

Removes the attribute bound to the specified name within the current servlet context. Returns nothing.

setAttribute

```
public abstract void setAttribute(String name, Object object)
```

Binds the specified `Object` to the specified name within the current servlet context. The object can be retrieved using the `getAttribute()` method. This method is useful for passing objects between servlets within the same context. Returns nothing.

Interface ServletRequest

javax.servlet.ServletRequest

Definition

```
public interface ServletRequest
```

The ServletRequest interface encapsulates information pertaining to a service request. This interface is implemented by the server and passed as a parameter into the servlet's service() method. Some of the request information contained in the ServletRequest object includes content length, content type, and protocol. In addition, the ServletRequest object provides a handle to the client's input stream. Although ServletRequest is protocol independent, other interfaces may extend this interface in order to provide better support for a specific protocol. For instance, the HttpServletRequest interface extends Servlet-Request and provides additional HTTP information and services.

Methods

getAttribute

```
public abstract Object getAttribute(String name)
```

Returns an Object corresponding to the specified attribute name or null if the attribute does not exist. This method is used to obtain information about the request that is not already provided by another method or to retrieve objects stored in the request by another servlet. The naming convention for attributes should be the same as packages. For example, Table 20.2 describes three request attributes that provide information regarding a secure SSL connection. This method is useful for passing objects between servlets. It is often used in conjunction with the forward() and include() methods of the Request-Dispatcher interface.

Table 20.2   Secure SSL Connection Request Attributes

Attribute Name	Attribute Object Type
javax.net.ssl.cipher_suite	String
javax.net.ssl.peer_certificates	javax.security.cert.X509Certificate array
javax.net.ssl.session	javax.net.ssl.SSLSession

getAttributeNames

```
public abstract Enumeration getAttributeNames()
```

Returns an Enumeration of String objects containing the names of the attributes included in this request.

getCharacterEncoding

```
public abstract String getCharacterEncoding()
```

Returns a String description of the request's character set encoding (e.g., ISO-8859-1).

getContentLength

```
public abstract int getContentLength()
```

Returns an integer indicating the size of the request data in bytes or -1 if unknown.

getContentType

```
public abstract String getContentType()
```

Returns a String describing the MIME type of the request's data portion or null if unknown.

getInputStream

```
public abstract ServletInputStream getInputStream() throws
    IOException
```

Returns a handle to the client's input stream as a ServletInputStream object. This input stream should be used for reading binary data. The getReader() method should be used for reading text information.

getParameter

```
public abstract String getParameter(String name)
```

Returns the String value of the specified parameter or null if the parameter does not exist. For example, this method can be used to retrieve a Web variable passed in a query string or within the body of a POST request.

getParameterNames

```
public abstract Enumeration getParameterNames()
```

Returns an Enumeration of String objects containing the names of all parameters passed in this request. If no parameters exist, an empty Enumeration is returned.

getParameterValues

```
public abstract String[] getParameterValues(String name)
```

Returns a String array containing all values of the specified parameter or null if the parameter does not exist. For example, this method can be used to retrieve the values of a Web variable passed in a query string or within the body of a POST request.

getProtocol

```
public abstract String getProtocol()
```

Returns a String describing the name and version of the protocol used by the request. The protocol is displayed in this format:

```
<protocol>/<major version>.<minor version>
```

getReader

```
public abstract BufferedReader getReader() throws IOException
```

Returns a BufferedReader object for reading text information from the data portion of the request. When necessary, character set translation is handled automatically. This method should only be used for text information. Use the getInputStream() method of reading binary data.

getRemoteAddr

```
public abstract String getRemoteAddr()
```

Returns a String containing the client's IP address.

getRemoteHost

```
public abstract String getRemoteHost()
```

Returns a String containing the client's fully qualified hostname.

getScheme

```
public abstract String getScheme()
```

Returns a String that describes the scheme indicated within the requested URL. The scheme usually describes the requested protocol. For example, http, https, ftp, and telnet are common schemes.

getServerName

```
public abstract String getServerName()
```

Returns a String containing the server's hostname.

getServerPort

```
public abstract int getServerPort()
```

Returns an integer indicating the server port on which the request was received.

setAttribute

```
public abstract void setAttribute(String name, Object o)
```

Stores an Object in the request and binds it to the specified name. The object can be retrieved using the getAttribute() method. These attributes are reset with each new request. This method is useful for passing objects between servlets. It is often used in conjunction with the forward() and include() methods of the RequestDispatcher interface. Returns nothing.

Interface ServletResponse

javax.servlet.ServletResponse

Definition

```
public interface ServletResponse
```

The ServletResponse interface encapsulates information pertaining to the server's response. This interface is implemented by the server and passed as a parameter into the servlet's service() method. The ServletResponse object provides a handle to the output stream and allows the servlet to specify the content length and content type of the response. Although ServletResponse is protocol independent, other interfaces may extend this interface in order to provide better support for a specific protocol. For instance, the HttpServlet-Response interface extends ServletResponse and provides additional HTTP services.

Methods

getCharacterEncoding

```
public abstract String getCharacterEncoding()
```

Returns a String description of the response's character set encoding based on the specified content type. If no content type is designated, the default is text/plain.

getOutputStream

```
public abstract ServletOutputStream getOutputStream() throws
    IOException
```

Returns a handle to the output stream as a ServletOutputStream object. This output stream should be used when sending binary data. For text information, use the getWriter() method.

getWriter

```
public abstract PrintWriter getWriter() throws IOException
```

Returns a PrintWriter object for writing text information to the output stream. Use the getOutputStream() method when sending binary data.

setContentLength

```
public abstract void setContentLength(int len)
```

Sets the content length of the response. Returns nothing.

setContentType

```
public abstract void setContentType(String type)
```

Sets the content type of the response. Returns nothing.

Interface `SingleThreadModel`

> javax.servlet.SingleThreadModel

Definition

```
public interface SingleThreadModel
```

The `SingleThreadModel` interface defines no methods and serves only as a flag that conveys to the server that the servlet should run as a single thread. The `SingleThreadModel` interface guarantees that no two threads from this servlet will execute concurrently. The `SingleThreadModel` is the simplest way to ensure thread safety within a servlet.

To help offset the performance penalty incurred by executing only a single thread, a pool of servlet instances is created for each `SingleThreadModel` servlet. As requests arrive for a servlet that implements the `SingleThreadModel` interface, the request is routed to a free servlet instance. Keep in mind that this method of enforcing thread safety does require additional server resources.

Class GenericServlet

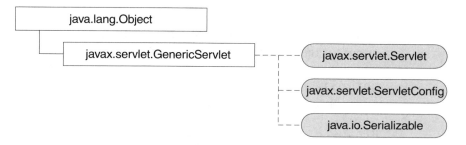

Definition

```
public abstract class GenericServlet implements Servlet,
    ServletConfig, Serializable
```

The GenericServlet class implements the Servlet and ServletConfig interfaces. This class is provided to give the servlet developer a basic framework from which to start. The GenericServlet class implements the init() and destroy() methods as well as the methods defined by ServletConfig. It also provides a log() method for logging significant events. By extending the GenericServlet class, a functional servlet can be built by overriding only the service() method. However, it is a good practice to always override the getServletInfo() method as well.

Constructors

GenericServlet

```
public GenericServlet()
```

Default constructor. Performs no work.

Methods

destroy

```
public void destroy()
```

Called automatically by the server when the servlet is unloaded. This method can be used to free any resources held by the servlet. The servlet destruction is noted in the log file.

getInitParameter

```
public String getInitParameter(String name)
```

Returns a `String` containing the value of the specified initialization parameter or `null` if the parameter does not exist.

getInitParameterNames

```
public Enumeration getInitParameterNames()
```

Returns an `Enumeration` of `String` objects containing the names of the servlet's initialization parameters or `null` if no initialization parameters exist.

getServletConfig

```
public ServletConfig getServletConfig()
```

Returns a `ServletConfig` object which contains servlet initialization parameters and other server configuration settings.

getServletContext

```
public ServletContext getServletContext()
```

Returns a `ServletContext` object containing information about the environment in which the servlet is running.

getServletInfo

```
public String getServletInfo()
```

Returns a `String` object containing a brief description of the servlet.

init

```
public void init(ServletConfig config) throws ServletException
```

Called by the servlet engine when the servlet is first loaded. Performs servlet initialization tasks and notes the servlet initialization in the log file. Returns nothing.

```
public void init() throws ServletException
```

Convenience method that frees the developer from having to store the `ServletConfig` object (and implement the `getServletConfig()` method) or call `super.init(config)` (to pass the `ServletConfig` object to the parent class). This method is actually called by the `init(ServletConfig)` method above. Returns nothing.

log

```
public void log(String msg)
```

Writes the class name of the servlet and the specified message to the servlet log file. The name and location of this file are server specific. Returns nothing.

```
public void log(String message, Throwable t)
```

Writes the class name of the servlet, the specified message, and the stack trace to the servlet log file. The name and location of this file are server specific. Returns nothing.

service

```
public abstract void service(ServletRequest req, ServletResponse
    res) throws ServletException, IOException
```

Called for each client request. The servlet engine passes objects that represent the client's request and the server's response to this method. Returns nothing.

Class ServletInputStream

Definition

public abstract class ServletInputStream extends InputStream

The ServletInputStream class is an abstract class that is implemented by the servlet engine. This class provides a readLine() method to allow servlets to read data from the client request.

Constructors

ServletInputStream

protected ServletInputStream()

Default constructor. Performs no work.

Methods

readLine

public int readLine(byte b[], int off, int len) throws
    IOException

Returns an integer value indicating the number of bytes read or -1 if the end of the stream was reached. Starting at the offset (off), this method reads the specified number of bytes (len) into a byte array (b). It stops reading when the end of the stream is reached or a linefeed ("\n") is encountered (the linefeed is read into the array).

Class ServletOutputStream

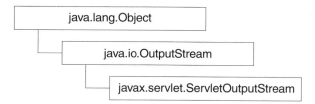

Definition

```
public abstract class ServletOutputStream
```

The ServletOutputStream class is an abstract class that is implemented by the servlet engine. This class provides many variations of print() and println() methods that write information to the output stream.

Constructors

ServletOutputStream

```
protected ServletOutputStream()
```

Default constructor. Performs no work.

Methods

print

```
public void print(boolean b) throws IOException
```

Prints a boolean value to the output stream. Returns nothing.

```
public void print(char c) throws IOException
```

Prints a character value to the output stream. Returns nothing.

```
public void print(double d) throws IOException
```

Prints a double value to the output stream. Returns nothing.

```
public void print(float f) throws IOException
```

Prints a float value to the output stream. Returns nothing.

```
public void print(int i) throws IOException
```

Prints an integer value to the output stream. Returns nothing.

```
    public void print(long l) throws IOException
```

Prints a `long` value to the output stream. Returns nothing.

```
    public void print(String s) throws IOException
```

Prints a `String` value to the output stream. Returns nothing.

println

```
    public void println() throws IOException
```

Prints a carriage return/linefeed (CRLF) to the output stream. Returns nothing.

```
    public void println(boolean b) throws IOException
```

Prints a `boolean` value followed by a CRLF to the output stream. Returns nothing.

```
    public void println(char c) throws IOException
```

Prints a character value followed by a CRLF to the output stream. Returns nothing.

```
    public void println(double d) throws IOException
```

Prints a `double` value followed by a CRLF to the output stream. Returns nothing.

```
    public void println(float f) throws IOException
```

Prints a `float` value followed by a CRLF to the output stream. Returns nothing.

```
    public void println(int i) throws IOException
```

Prints an integer value followed by a CRLF to the output stream. Returns nothing.

```
    public void println(long l) throws IOException
```

Prints a `long` value followed by a CRLF to the output stream. Returns nothing.

```
    public void println(String s) throws IOException
```

Prints a `String` value followed by a CRLF to the output stream. Returns nothing.

Class ServletException

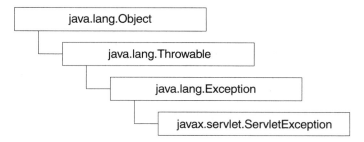

```
java.lang.Object
    java.lang.Throwable
        java.lang.Exception
            javax.servlet.ServletException
```

Definition

    javax.servlet.ServletException extends Exception

The ServletException exception is thrown by the servlet to indicate some problem. The problem should be described by the message parameter passed to the ServletException object's constructor.

Constructors

ServletException

    public ServletException()

Creates a new ServletException object.

    public ServletException(String message)

Creates a new ServletException object using the specified message.

    public ServletException(String message, Throwable rootCause)

Creates a new ServletException object using the specified message and root cause.

    public ServletException(Throwable rootCause)

Creates a new ServletException object using the root cause.

Methods

    public Throwable getRootCause()

Returns the root cause of this servlet exception.

Class `UnavailableException`

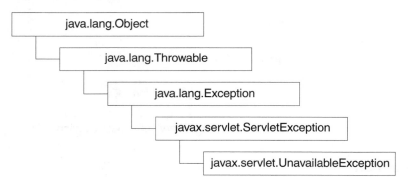

Definition

        public class UnavailableException extends ServletException

A servlet throws an `UnavailableException` exception to indicate that it is not available for some reason. The servlet may be permanently unavailable (e.g., the servlet is misconfigured or contains an error) or temporarily unavailable (e.g., network traffic is too high or server load is too great). The problem should be described by the message parameter passed to the `Unavailable-Exception` object's constructor.

Constructors

`UnavailableException`

        public UnavailableException(int seconds, Servlet servlet, String
           msg)

Constructs a new `UnavailableException` that includes a description of the problem, a reference to the current servlet, and an estimate of how long, in seconds, it will be unavailable (if zero or negative, no estimate is available). Since `UnavailableException` is thrown by the servlet itself, simply pass "`this`" for the servlet parameter to reference the current servlet.

        public UnavailableException(Servlet servlet, String msg)

Constructor used when servlet is permanently unavailable. Constructs a new `UnavailableException` that includes a description of the problem and a reference to the current servlet. Since `UnavailableException` is thrown by the servlet itself, simply pass "`this`" for the servlet parameter to reference the current servlet.

Methods

getServlet

```
public Servlet getServlet()
```

Returns a reference to the Servlet object that is unavailable.

getUnavailableSeconds

```
public int getUnavailableSeconds()
```

Returns an integer indicating the number of seconds the servlet estimated it would be unavailable. If no estimate is available, a negative number is returned.

isPermanent

```
public boolean isPermanent()
```

Returns a boolean value indicating whether the server is permanently unavailable. A permanently unavailable condition requires some administrative action to be taken in order to correct the problem.

CHAPTER 21

`javax.servlet.http` *Package*

The `javax.servlet.http` package contains interfaces and classes that simplify the process of writing servlets that use the HTTP protocol. This package defines and implements much of the functionality required to communicate via HTTP. Cookie, HTTP redirect, and session management support are just a few examples of the functionality that is provided by the `javax.servlet.http` package. The `javax.servlet.http` package contains the interfaces and classes shown in Table 21.1.

Table 21.1 Interfaces and Classes of the `javax.servlet.http` Package

Interfaces	HttpServletRequest
	HttpServletResponse
	HttpSession
	HttpSessionBindingListener
Classes	Cookie
	HttpServlet
	HttpSessionBindingEvent
	HttpUtils

Interface HttpServletRequest

Definition

> public interface HttpServletRequest extends ServletRequest

The HttpServletRequest interface encapsulates vital information pertaining to an HTTP service request. Much of its functionality is inherited from the ServletRequest interface which it extends. The HttpServletRequest interface is implemented by the servlet engine and passed as a parameter into the servlet's service(), doGet(), and doPost() methods.

Some of the request information contained in the HttpServletRequest object includes HTTP header information, requested URL, content type, content length, Web variables, and cookies. In addition, the HttpServletRequest object provides a handle to the client's input stream via the getReader() or getInputStream() method inherited from ServletRequest.

Methods

getAuthType

> public abstract String getAuthType()

Returns a String object describing the authentication scheme used by this request.

getCookies

> public abstract Cookie[] getCookies()

Returns an array of Cookie objects. Returns a Cookie object for every cookie included in the request.

getDateHeader

> public abstract long getDateHeader(String name)

Returns a long representing the date value of the specified HTTP header. If the specified header cannot be converted to a date, an IllegalArgumentException is thrown. A -1 is returned if the specified header does not exist. The name parameter is not case-sensitive.

getHeader

```
public abstract String getHeader(String name)
```

Returns the String value of the specified HTTP header. A -1 is returned if the specified header does not exist. The name parameter is not case-sensitive.

getHeaderNames

```
public abstract Enumeration getHeaderNames()
```

Returns an Enumeration of String objects representing the names of each HTTP header field in the request.

getIntHeader

```
public abstract int getIntHeader(String name)
```

Returns the integer value of the specified HTTP header. If the specified header cannot be converted to an integer, a NumberFormatException is thrown. A -1 is returned if the specified header does not exist. The name parameter is not case-sensitive.

getMethod

```
public abstract String getMethod()
```

Returns a String object describing the HTTP method used by this request (e.g., GET, POST, PUT, HEAD).

getPathInfo

```
public abstract String getPathInfo()
```

Returns a String object representing the portion of the URL path immediately following the servlet path but prior to the query string. Returns null if no extra path information exists in the URL.

getPathTranslated

```
public abstract String getPathTranslated()
```

Converts the portion of the URL path immediately following the servlet path but prior to the query string to a real path (as it exists in the file system) and returns the real path as a `String`. Returns `null` if no extra path information exists in the URL.

getQueryString

```
public abstract String getQueryString()
```

Returns a `String` object containing the query string portion of the URL. Returns `null` if URL does not contain a query string.

getRemoteUser

```
public abstract String getRemoteUser()
```

Returns a `String` object containing the name of the user that issued this request. The name is sent in an HTTP authentication header field. Returns `null` if unknown.

getRequestedSessionId

```
public abstract String getRequestedSessionId()
```

Returns a `String` object containing the session ID included in this request. If the request contains an invalid session ID, this method will create a new session and return a new session ID. Returns `null` if the request does not have a session associated with it.

getRequestURI

```
public abstract String getRequestURI()
```

Returns a `String` object containing the complete URI excluding the query string.

getServletPath

```
public abstract String getServletPath()
```

Returns a `String` consisting of the portion of the URL that contains the servlet path.

getSession

```
public abstract HttpSession getSession()
```

Returns an `HttpSession` object representing the current valid session. If the request is not associated with a valid session, a new session is created and returned.

```
public abstract HttpSession getSession(boolean create)
```

Returns an HttpSession object representing the current valid session. If the request is not associated with a valid session and the create parameter is true, a new session is created and returned. If create is false and no valid session exists, null is returned.

isRequestedSessionIdFromCookie

```
public abstract boolean isRequestedSessionIdFromCookie()
```

Returns a boolean value indicating if the request's session ID was passed in a cookie. Returns true if a cookie was used, otherwise false.

isRequestedSessionIdFromURL

```
public abstract boolean isRequestedSessionIdFromURL()
```

Returns a boolean value indicating if the request's session ID was passed as part of the URL. Returns true if the session ID was passed in the URL, otherwise false.

isRequestedSessionIdValid

```
public abstract boolean isRequestedSessionIdValid()
```

Returns a boolean value indicating if the request's session ID is valid. An invalid session ID usually indicates that the session has expired. Returns true if the session ID is valid, otherwise false.

Interface **HttpServletResponse**

Definition

```
public interface HttpServletResponse extends ServletResponse
```

The HttpServletResponse interface encapsulates information and functionality pertaining to an HTTP response. Much of its functionality is inherited from the ServletResponse interface which it extends. The HttpServletResponse interface is implemented by the server and passed as a parameter into the servlet's service(), doGet(), and doPost() methods. Some of the functionality implemented by the HttpServletResponse object includes adding cookies, sending redirects, setting headers, and retrieving a handle to the output stream (in order to return data to the client).

Methods

addCookie

```
public abstract void addCookie(Cookie cookie)
```

Adds the specified cookie to the server response. Returns nothing.

containsHeader

```
public abstract boolean containsHeader(String name)
```

Returns a boolean value indicating whether the request contains the specified header. Returns true if the header exists, otherwise false.

encodeRedirectURL

```
public abstract String encodeRedirectURL(String url)
```

Returns a String object that encodes the specified URL to include the session ID for use with the sendRedirect() method. If no encoding is necessary, this method will return the URL unchanged.

encodeURL

```
public abstract String encodeURL(String url)
```

Returns a String object that encodes the specified URL to include the session ID. If no encoding is necessary, this method will return the URL unchanged.

sendError

```
public abstract void sendError(int sc) throws IOException
```

Generates an error response using the specified status code and a default message. Returns nothing.

```
public abstract void sendError(int sc, String msg) throws
    IOException
```

Generates an error response using the specified status code and message. Returns nothing.

sendRedirect

```
public abstract void sendRedirect(String location) throws
    IOException
```

Generates a temporary redirect response using the specified redirect location. Returns nothing.

setDateHeader

```
public abstract void setDateHeader(String name, long date)
```

Adds a field of the specified name and date value to the response header. Returns nothing.

setHeader

```
public abstract void setHeader(String name, String value)
```

Adds a field of the specified name and value to the response header. Returns nothing.

setIntHeader

```
public abstract void setIntHeader(String name, int value)
```

Adds a field of the specified name and integer value to the response header. Returns nothing.

setStatus

```
public abstract void setStatus(int sc)
```

Sets the response status code. Returns nothing.

```
public abstract void setStatus(int sc, String sm)
```

Sets the status code and message for the response. Returns nothing.

Variables

SC_ACCEPTED

```
public static final int SC_ACCEPTED
```

Integer variable representing HTTP status code 202. Indicates that the request has been received and is currently being processed.

SC_BAD_GATEWAY

```
public static final int SC_BAD_GATEWAY
```

Integer variable representing HTTP status code 502. Indicates that the server received an invalid response from a gateway to which it forwarded the request.

SC_BAD_REQUEST

```
public static final int SC_BAD_REQUEST
```

Integer variable representing HTTP status code 400. Indicates that the request used invalid syntax and should not be repeated without modification.

SC_CONFLICT

```
public static final int SC_CONFLICT
```

Integer variable representing HTTP status code 409. Indicates that the request cannot be serviced due to a resource conflict.

SC_CONTINUE

```
public static final int SC_CONTINUE
```

Integer variable representing HTTP status code 100. Indicates that the client may continue to make requests.

SC_CREATED

```
public static final int SC_CREATED
```

Integer variable representing HTTP status code 201. Indicates that the request was fulfilled successfully and resulted in the creation of a new resource.

SC_FORBIDDEN

```
public static final int SC_FORBIDDEN
```

Integer variable representing HTTP status code 403. Indicates that the server understood the request but refuses to fulfill it.

SC_GATEWAY_TIMEOUT

```
public static final int SC_GATEWAY_TIMEOUT
```

Integer variable representing HTTP status code 504. Indicates that the server did not receive a timely response from a server to which it forwarded the request.

SC_GONE

```
public static final int SC_GONE
```

Integer variable representing HTTP status code 410. Indicates that the requested resource is no longer available.

SC_HTTP_VERSION_NOT_SUPPORTED

```
public static final int SC_HTTP_VERSION_NOT_SUPPORTED
```

Integer variable representing HTTP status code 505. Indicates that the server does not support the HTTP version used by the request.

SC_INTERNAL_SERVER_ERROR

```
public static final int SC_INTERNAL_SERVER_ERROR
```

Integer variable representing HTTP status code 500. Indicates that the server encountered an unexpected condition that prevented it from fulfilling the request.

SC_LENGTH_REQUIRED

```
public static final int SC_LENGTH_REQUIRED
```

Integer variable representing HTTP status code 411. Indicates that the request cannot be serviced unless a Content-Length header is included in the request.

SC_METHOD_NOT_ALLOWED

```
public static final int SC_METHOD_NOT_ALLOWED
```

Integer variable representing HTTP status code 405. Indicates that the method defined by the Request-Line header cannot be performed on the requested resource.

SC_MOVED_PERMANENTLY

```
public static final int SC_MOVED_PERMANENTLY
```

Integer variable representing HTTP status code 301. Indicates that the resource has been moved permanently.

SC_MOVED_TEMPORARILY

```
public static final int SC_MOVED_TEMPORARILY
```

Integer variable representing HTTP status code 302. Indicates that the resource has been moved temporarily.

SC_MULTIPLE_CHOICES

```
public static final int SC_MULTIPLE_CHOICES
```

Integer variable representing HTTP status code 300. Indicates that the resource is available from multiple locations.

SC_NO_CONTENT

```
public static final int SC_NO_CONTENT
```

Integer variable representing HTTP status code 204. Indicates that the server has fulfilled the request but there is no new information to return.

SC_NON_AUTHORITATIVE_INFORMATION

```
public static final int SC_NON_AUTHORITATIVE_INFORMATION
```

Integer variable representing HTTP status code 203. Indicates that the meta information sent in the client request was not created by the server.

SC_NOT_ACCEPTABLE

```
public static final int SC_NOT_ACCEPTABLE
```

Integer variable representing HTTP status code 406. The requested resource consists of a format that the client request did not include in the `Accepts` header.

SC_NOT_FOUND

```
public static final int SC_NOT_FOUND
```

Integer variable representing HTTP status code 404. Indicates that no resource matching the requested URL exists on the server.

SC_NOT_IMPLEMENTED

```
public static final int SC_NOT_IMPLEMENTED
```

Integer variable representing HTTP status code 501. Indicates that the server does not implement the functionality required to fulfill the request.

SC_NOT_MODIFIED

```
public static final int SC_NOT_MODIFIED
```

Integer variable representing HTTP status code 304. Indicates that the Web client issued a `GET` request with an `If-Modified-Since` header and the resource has not changed since the specified date.

SC_OK

```
public static final int SC_OK
```

Integer variable representing HTTP status code 200. Indicates that the request succeeded.

SC_PARTIAL_CONTENT

```
public static final int SC_PARTIAL_CONTENT
```

Integer variable representing HTTP status code 206. Indicates that the request was partially fulfilled.

SC_PAYMENT_REQUIRED

```
public static final int SC_PAYMENT_REQUIRED
```

Integer variable representing HTTP status code 402. Reserved for future use.

SC_PRECONDITION_FAILED

```
public static final int SC_PRECONDITION_FAILED
```

Integer variable representing HTTP status code 412. The precondition defined in one or more of the request header fields failed when evaluated by the server.

SC_PROXY_AUTHENTICATION_REQUIRED

```
public static final int SC_PROXY_AUTHENTICATION_REQUIRED
```

Integer variable representing HTTP status code 407. Indicates that the client must first be authenticated by the proxy server.

SC_REQUEST_ENTITY_TOO_LARGE

```
public static final int SC_REQUEST_ENTITY_TOO_LARGE
```

Integer variable representing HTTP status code 413. Indicates that the server refuses to service the request because the requested resource is too large.

SC_REQUEST_TIMEOUT

```
public static final int SC_REQUEST_TIMEOUT
```

Integer variable representing HTTP status code 408. Indicates that the client did not issue a request within a predefined timeout period.

SC_REQUEST_URI_TOO_LONG

```
public static final int SC_REQUEST_URI_TOO_LONG
```

Integer variable representing HTTP status code 414. Indicates that the server refuses to service the request because the requested URI is too long.

SC_RESET_CONTENT

```
public static final int SC_RESET_CONTENT
```

Integer variable representing HTTP status code 205. Indicates that the client should reset the document view.

SC_SEE_OTHER

```
public static final int SC_SEE_OTHER
```

Integer variable representing HTTP status code 303. Indicates that the resource can be located at a different location.

SC_SERVICE_UNAVAILABLE

```
public static final int SC_SERVICE_UNAVAILABLE
```

Integer variable representing HTTP status code 503. Indicates that the server is temporarily unable to fulfill the request.

SC_SWITCHING_PROTOCOLS

```
public static final int SC_SWITCHING_PROTOCOLS
```

Integer variable representing HTTP status code 101. Indicates that the server is changing protocols as declared in the Upgrade header.

SC_UNAUTHORIZED

```
public static final int SC_UNAUTHORIZED
```

Integer variable representing HTTP status code 401. Indicates that authorization is required to access this resource, such as username and password.

SC_UNSUPPORTED_MEDIA_TYPE

```
public static final int SC_UNSUPPORTED_MEDIA_TYPE
```

Integer variable representing HTTP status code 415. Indicates that the server is refusing to service the request because the body of the request is in a format that is not supported by the requested resource.

SC_USE_PROXY

```
public static final int SC_USE_PROXY
```

Integer variable representing HTTP status code 305. Indicates that the requested resource can only be accessed through the proxy server described by the Location header.

Interface `HttpSession`

> javax.servlet.http.HttpSession

Definition

```
public interface HttpSession
```

The `HttpSession` interface encapsulates information pertaining to an HTTP session. This interface is implemented and returned by the server when the `getSession()` method of `HttpServletRequest` is called. The `HttpSession` object provides methods to read, add, and remove various session data.

Methods

getCreationTime

```
public abstract long getCreationTime()
```

Returns a `long` representing the time this session was created. The time is expressed as the number of milliseconds since January 1, 1970 UTC.

getId

```
public abstract String getId()
```

Returns a `String` object containing the session ID used to uniquely identify this session.

getLastAccessedTime

```
public abstract long getLastAccessedTime()
```

Returns a `long` representing the time the client last issued a request that contained this session's ID. The time is expressed as the number of milliseconds since January 1, 1970 UTC.

getMaxInactiveInterval

```
public abstract int getMaxInactiveInterval()
```

Returns the maximum number of seconds that a session is guaranteed to be valid without a request from the client. After the maximum inactive interval expires, the session may be expired by the servlet engine. If the session never expires, a -1 is returned.

getValue

```
public abstract Object getValue(String name)
```

Returns an Object corresponding to the specified name. Returns null if the specified object does not exist.

getValueNames

```
public abstract String[] getValueNames()
```

Returns a String array containing the object names contained in this session.

invalidate

```
public abstract void invalidate()
```

Invalidates (i.e., expires) this HTTP session. Returns nothing.

isNew

```
public abstract boolean isNew()
```

Returns a boolean value indicating if this session is new, meaning that it was just created by the server and has not yet been returned to the client.

putValue

```
public abstract void putValue(String name, Object value)
```

Stores the specified Object under the given name and binds it to this session. If an object of the specified name already exists in this session, it is replaced. Returns nothing.

removeValue

```
public abstract void removeValue(String name)
```

Removes the object of the specified name from memory. If no such object exists, no work is performed. Returns nothing.

setMaxInactiveInterval

```
public abstract void setMaxInactiveInterval(int interval)
```

Sets the maximum number of seconds that a session is guaranteed to be valid without a request from the client. After the maximum inactive interval expires, the session may be expired by the servlet engine.

Interface `HttpSessionBindingListener`

(javax.servlet.http.HttpSessionBindingListener)

Definition

```
public interface HttpSessionBindingListener extends EventListener
```

The `HttpSessionBindingListener` interface is implemented by objects that wish to be notified when they are being bound or unbound to an HTTP session. `HttpSessionBindingListener` extends `EventListener`.

Methods

`valueBound`

```
public abstract void valueBound(HttpSessionBindingEvent event)
```

Notifies the listening object that it is being bound to an HTTP session. Returns nothing.

`valueUnbound`

```
public abstract void valueUnbound(HttpSessionBindingEvent event)
```

Notifies the listening object that it is being unbound from an HTTP session. Returns nothing.

Class Cookie

Definition

```
public class Cookie implements Cloneable
```

The Cookie class represents a cookie as originally defined by Netscape in addition to the updated cookie specification, RFC 2109. Cookies are used to store small amounts of state information on the client in the form of a name/value pair. This state information is returned to the server with every client request. Once a Cookie object is created, it is passed to the client using the HttpServletResponse object's addCookie() method.

Constructors

Cookie

```
public Cookie(String name, String value)
```

Constructor that creates a Cookie object using the specified name and value.

Methods

clone

```
public Object clone()
```

Returns an Object that is an exact copy of this cookie.

getComment

```
public String getComment()
```

Returns a String object containing a comment that describes the purpose of this cookie. If no comment exists, returns null.

getDomain

```
public String getDomain()
```

Returns a String object containing the domain to which this cookie will be returned.

getMaxAge

```
public int getMaxAge()
```

Returns an `integer` value indicating the maximum age (in seconds) that this cookie remains valid. A negative value indicates that the cookie expires when the client agent is closed.

getName

```
public String getName()
```

Returns a `String` object containing the name of this cookie.

getPath

```
public String getPath()
```

Returns a `String` object containing all URL prefixes to which this cookie is valid.

getSecure

```
public boolean getSecure()
```

Returns a `boolean` value indicating if this cookie should only be returned across a secure connection. A `true` value indicates that the cookie should only be returned if the connection is secure, otherwise `false`.

getValue

```
public String getValue()
```

Returns a `String` object containing the value of this cookie.

getVersion

```
public int getVersion()
```

Returns an integer value indicating the version of the cookie protocol currently in use. A zero (0) value indicates this cookie is using the original cookie specification defined by Netscape. A one (1) value indicates this cookie is using the updated cookie specification defined by RFC 2109.

setComment

```
public void setComment(String purpose)
```

Adds a comment to this cookie that describes its purpose to the client agent. If the client's browser has been configured to issue a warning when cookies are received, this comment will be displayed to the user. Returns nothing.

setDomain

```
public void setDomain(String pattern)
```

Sets the domain pattern for which this cookie is valid. This cookie should only be returned to domains that match the specified pattern. For more information on the syntax of this pattern, see RFC 2109. Returns nothing.

setMaxAge

```
public void setMaxAge(int expire)
```

Sets the maximum age, specified in seconds, that this cookie is valid. A negative value indicates the Cookie object's default behavior—the cookie expires when the client agent is closed. Setting a zero (0) value indicates that the cookie should be deleted. Returns nothing.

setPath

```
public void setPath(String uri)
```

This cookie should be returned only when the requested resource begins with the specified URI. Returns nothing.

setSecure

```
public void setSecure(boolean flag)
```

Indicates whether the cookie should only be returned across a secure connection. A true value indicates that the cookie should only be returned if the connection is secure, otherwise false. Returns nothing.

setValue

```
public void setValue(String newValue)
```

Sets the cookie's value. Returns nothing.

setVersion

```
public void setVersion(int v)
```

Sets the version of the cookie protocol used by this cookie. A zero (0) value indicates this cookie is using the original cookie specification defined by Netscape. A one (1) value indicates this cookie is using the updated cookie specification defined by RFC 2109. Returns nothing.

Class **HttpServlet**

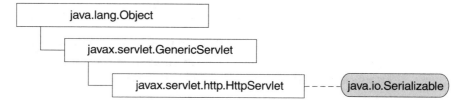

Definition

```
public abstract class HttpServlet extends GenericServlet
```

HttpServlet is an abstract class that can be extended and implemented by servlet developers. This class simplifies servlet development by providing a framework for supporting the HTTP protocol. HttpServlet extends the GenericServlet class.

Constructors

HttpServlet

```
public HttpServlet()
```

Default constructor. Performs no work.

Methods

doDelete

```
protected void doDelete(HttpServletRequest req,
    HttpServletResponse resp) throws ServletException, IOException
```

Called in response to an HTTP DELETE request. The DELETE operation allows the client to request that a resource be removed from the server. Returns nothing.

doGet

```
protected void doGet(HttpServletRequest req, HttpServletResponse
    resp) throws ServletException, IOException
```

Called in response to an HTTP GET request. The GET operation requests a server resource. Returns nothing.

doOptions

```
protected void doOptions(HttpServletRequest req,
    HttpServletResponse resp) throws ServletException, IOException
```

Called in response to an HTTP OPTIONS request. The OPTIONS operation allows the client to request the HTTP methods that are supported by the server. The supported methods are returned in the Allow header field. Returns nothing.

doPost

```
protected void doPost(HttpServletRequest req,
    HttpServletResponse resp) throws ServletException, IOException
```

Called in response to an HTTP POST request. The POST operation allows the client to transmit information to the server and specify the resource that should process this data. Returns nothing.

doPut

```
protected void doPut(HttpServletRequest req, HttpServletResponse
    resp) throws ServletException, IOException
```

Called in response to an HTTP PUT request. The PUT operation requests that a new resource be created on the server at the specified URL using the data included in the request. Typically used for file uploads. Returns nothing.

doTrace

```
protected void doTrace(HttpServletRequest req,
    HttpServletResponse resp) throws ServletException, IOException
```

Called in response to an HTTP TRACE request. The TRACE operation returns the request back to the client for debugging purposes, and thus allows the client to see the request received by the server at the end of the calling chain. This information can be useful for testing or diagnostic purposes. Returns nothing.

getLastModified

```
protected long getLastModified(HttpServletRequest req)
```

Returns a long indicating when the specified resource was last updated. This information is useful for caching information on the client. Often used in conjunction with the If-Modified-Since header. A negative value indicates that a last modified time is not available.

service

```
protected void service(HttpServletRequest req,
    HttpServletResponse resp) throws ServletException, IOException
```

Called in response to any request directed to this servlet. Adds HTTP-specific functionality by overriding the service() method defined by GenericServlet. Returns nothing.

```
public void service(ServletRequest req, ServletResponse res)
    throws ServletException, IOException
```

Called in response to any request directed to this servlet. This is the basic service() method defined by the GenericServlet class.

Class HttpSessionBindingEvent

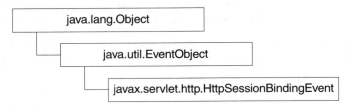

Definition

```
public class HttpSessionBindingEvent extends EventObject
```

The HttpSessionBindingEvent object is passed to an HttpSessionBinding-Listener whenever the listener is bound or unbound using the putValue() and removeValue() methods of the HttpSession object. The HttpSessionBindingEvent class extends java.util.EventObject.

Constructors

HttpSessionBindingEvent

```
public HttpSessionBindingEvent(HttpSession session, String name)
```

Constructor that creates a new HttpSessionBindingEvent object using the specified HttpSession and name.

Methods

getName

```
public String getName()
```

Returns a String object containing the name of the object to which listener is being bound or unbound. Returns nothing.

getSession

```
public HttpSession getSession()
```

Returns the HttpSession object to which listener is being bound or unbound. Returns nothing.

Class HttpUtils

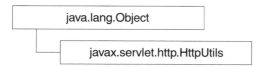

Definition

```
public class HttpUtils
```

The HttpUtils class consists of three static utility methods.

Constructors

```
public HttpUtils()
```

Default constructor. Performs no work.

Methods

getRequestURL

```
public static StringBuffer getRequestURL(HttpServletRequest req)
```

Returns a StringBuffer containing the URL requested by the client excluding any query string.

parsePostData

```
public static Hashtable parsePostData(int len,
    ServletInputStream in)
```

Returns a HashTable containing the name/value pairs posted to the server. The parameters indicate the length of the request's data and the input stream from which the data can be read.

parseQueryString

```
public static Hashtable parseQueryString(String s)
```

Returns a HashTable containing the name/value pairs transmitted to the server in the query string. The parameter is the query string to be parsed.

PART VI

Appendices

APPENDIX A

Common Well-Known Port Assignments

Name	Port	Description
echo	7	Echo is used to test the connection between hosts. Any data sent to port 7 is echoed back to the sender.
daytime	13	Responds to any connection with the time of day on the server.
ftp	21	Used for transferring files.
telnet	23	Allows for remote login to a host machine.
smtp	25	Simple Mail Transport Protocol for sending e-mail.
whois	43	A directory service for looking up names of users on a remote server.
gopher	70	A distributed document retrieval application.
finger	79	Displays information about a user or all users logged in to a server.
http	80	Responds to HyperText Transfer Protocol requests. HTTP is the protocol used for communicating on the World Wide Web.
pop3	110	Post Office Protocol 3 allows users to retrieve stored e-mail messages.
nntp	119	Network News Transfer Protocol provides access to thousands of news groups for the exchange of information. Commonly known as "USENET."
https	443	Secure HTTP protocol. This is the HTTP protocol running on top of the Secure Sockets Layer (SSL) for encrypted HTTP transmissions.

APPENDIX B

Java Port Scanner

The Java Port Scanner scans a range of TCP/IP ports on a remote host and indicates whether a server is responding on each port. The Port Scanner program accepts the IP address or hostname as a command-line parameter or, if absent, defaults to the localhost.

```java
import java.io.*;
import java.net.*;

/**
 * Port Scanner
 *
 * Scans for servers listening on a range of ports.
 *
 * @author Dustin R. Callaway
 * @version 1.0, 01/09/98
 */
public class PortScanner
{
  final static int LOW_RANGE = 0; //scan reserved ports
  final static int HIGH_RANGE = 1023;

  public static void main(String[] args)
  {
    Socket connect=null;
    String host = "localhost"; //defaults to local host

    if (args.length > 0)
    {
      host = args[0]; //sets host to command-line parameter
    }
    for (int iCount = LOW_RANGE; iCount < HIGH_RANGE; iCount++)
    {
```

```
      System.out.print("Checking port " + iCount + "...");
      try
      {
        connect = new Socket(host, iCount);
        System.out.println("Server responding on port " +
          iCount + " of " + host);
      }
      catch (UnknownHostException e)
      {
        System.err.println("Host is invalid.");
        break;
      }
      catch (IOException e)
      {
        System.out.println("No server found");
      }
      finally
      {
        try
        {
          connect.close(); //close socket connection
        }
        catch (Exception e) {}
      }
    }
  }
}
```

This small portion of the output shows a server listening on port 7.

```
C:\>java PortScanner
Checking port 0...No server found
Checking port 1...No server found
Checking port 2...No server found
Checking port 3...No server found
Checking port 4...No server found
Checking port 5...No server found
Checking port 6...No server found
Checking port 7...Server found on port 7 of localhost
Checking port 8...No server found
Checking port 9...No server found
Checking port 10...No server found
```

APPENDIX C

The Internet Standardization Process

Who is responsible for managing the Internet standardization process? In the past, that has been a difficult question to answer. However, today the answer is the Internet Engineering Task Force (IETF) and the Internet Engineering Steering Group (IESG). The IETF is a self-organized volunteer group with representatives from around the world. It describes itself as "the principal body engaged in the development of new Internet standard specifications." The IETF is primarily responsible for providing a forum for standards discussion and submitting standards proposals to the IESG.

The IESG, on the other hand, is responsible for overseeing the activities of the IETF and the standards process. The IESG "is directly responsible for the actions associated with entry into and movement along the Internet 'standards track,' including final approval of specifications as Internet Standards." For more information on the IETF and the IESG, see:

http://www.ietf.org

Before a new standard is proposed, a working document called an *Internet Draft* (ID) is prepared and placed in the IETF's "internet-drafts" directory (*ftp://ftp.ietf.org/internet-drafts/*). Placing the document in this directory does not "publish" it, but rather makes it available for informal review and comment by other interested parties. The Internet Draft is a "working document" because it is constantly evolving as the specification is developed. Due to its informal nature, an ID should never be quoted or referenced in a formal document. An unrevised Internet Draft remains in the *internet-draft* directory for a maximum of six months. This policy ensures that an ID is constantly being refined and does not grow stale. Eventually, either every Internet Draft will be promoted to an RFC or it will be deleted.

When those involved in developing the new specification agree that it is complete, the document is submitted to the IESG. If approved, the document becomes an official Internet RFC (*Request for Comment)*. The IESG then determines whether to place the document on the Standards Track, the Non-Standards Track, or to reject the document. Within the two tracks, each RFC is designated as being at a particular stage, or *maturity level*, in the standardization process.

For the Standards Track the stages include "Proposed Standard," "Draft Standard," and "Standard." As the specification is refined, it may garner additional community support and move through the stages until it becomes a Standard. However, chances are good that it will never get past the Proposed Standard stage or perhaps even be retracted from the Standards Track. Many popular protocols are still Proposed Standards or not even on the Standards Track.

For the Non-Standards Track, the levels are "Prototype," "Experimental," "Informational," and "Historic." Although it may seem that Non-Standards Track RFCs would not be very useful, there are many extremely important protocols relegated to this track. For instance, the RFC specification for HTTP 1.0 (the protocol supported by practically every Web browser in existence) is designated as Informational! Not only is it not an Internet Standard, it is not even on the Standards Track. This is due to the fact that when the original HTTP specification was developed, it did not follow the accepted Internet standardization process. On the other hand, its successor, HTTP 1.1, followed the process and is currently designated as a Proposed Standard. For a detailed description of the entire standardization process, see RFC 1602 entitled "The Internet Standards Process."

APPENDIX D

URL Syntax for Common Protocols

The following table shows the URL format for many common protocols. For more detailed information, see RFC 1738.

Protocol	Default Port	URL Syntax and Description
http	80	`http://host[:port]/path/filename[#section]` `[?query string]` Hypertext Transfer Protocol for communicating with Web servers.
ftp	21	`ftp://username:password@host[:port]/path` File transfer protocol for transferring files to and from an FTP server.
gopher	70	`gopher://host[:port]/gopher-path` The Gopher protocol used for document retrieval.
mailto		`mailto:email_address` Sends mail to the specified e-mail address (address must conform to the format specified in RFC 822).
news		`news:newsgroup_name` Used to access USENET newsgroups as specified in RFC 1036.
nntp	119	`nntp://host[:port]/newsgroup_name/article_` `number` Used to access USENET news on NNTP servers.
telnet	23	`telnet://[user:password@]host[:port]/` Used to establish remote login sessions.

Protocol	Default Port	URL Syntax and Description
wais	210	`wais://host[:port]/database` Used to access databases on WAIS servers.
file		`file://host/path/filename` Specifies a file accessible from the local machine (such as a file on the local hard drive).
prospero	1525	`prospero://host[:port]/object_name` Specifies resources accessed via the Prospero Directory Service. Prospero is used by Archie to search FTP archives.

APPENDIX E

Meaning of URL Special Characters

The following table describes the meaning of each of the special characters in the URL specification. For more information, see RFC 1738.

Character	Meaning/Examples

:	`http://www.awl.com`
	Separates the protocol (or scheme) from the rest of the URL.
	
	`http://www.sourcestream.com:80`
	Separates the port from the host.
	
	`ftp://guest:password@ftp.sun.com/`
	Separates the username from the password.

//	`http://www.awl.com` The double slash indicates that the URL uses the Common Internet Scheme Syntax defined in RFC 1738.
@	`ftp://guest:password@ftp.sun.com/` The "at" symbol is used to separate the host from the name and password.

/	`http://www.awl.com/index.html`
	Separates the host and port from the path.
	
	`http://www.awl.com/documents/public_html/index.html`
	Separates directories and the filename in a resource path.

%	`http://www.awl.com/Inside%20Java%20Servlets` Indicates the beginning of a URL-encoded character.

Character	Meaning/Example
+	`http://www.awl.com/Inside+Java+Servlets` Used in place of spaces.

?	`http://www.webcrawler.com/cgi-bin/WebQuery?searchText=`
	`    servlets`
	Separates a query string from the rest of the URL.

=	`http://www.webcrawler.com/cgi-bin/WebQuery?searchText=`
	`servlets`
	Used in a query string to separate the key from the value.

&	`http://www.mysearch.com/?searchText=servlets&order=`
	`Ascending`
	Used in query strings to separate key/value pairs.

~	`http://www.isp.com/~dustin` Normally used to indicate the user's home directory.

APPENDIX F

US-ASCII Encoding for Unsafe URL Characters

The following table shows the US-ASCII encoding for many unsafe or unprintable URL characters. (See Chapter 2 for information about URL encoding.)

Hex	Character	Hex	Character	Hex	Character	Hex	Character
08	Backspace	26	&	3A	:	5E	^
09	Tab	27	'	3B	;	5F	_
0A	Linefeed	28	(	3C	<	60	`
0D	Carriage Return	29	)	3D	=	7B	{
20	Space	2A	*	3E	>	7C	|
21	!	2B	+	3F	?	7D	}
22	"	2C	,	40	@	7E	~
23	#	2D	-	5B	[	7F	.
24	$	2E	.	5C	\		
25	%	2F	/	5D	]		

APPENDIX G

Java HTTP Server

The following code implements a generic HTTP server. This simple server accepts only GET and HEAD requests from the client and returns HTML files and image data. Adding a "-v" command-line parameter will enable verbose mode which displays all connections in the HTTP server's console window.

```java
import java.io.*;
import java.net.*;
import java.util.StringTokenizer;
import java.util.Date;

/**
 * Java HTTP Server
 *
 * This simple HTTP server supports GET and HEAD requests.
 *
 * @author Dustin R. Callaway
 * @version 1.0, 02/09/98
 */
public class HttpServer implements Runnable
{
  //static constants
  //HttpServer root is the current directory
  static final File WEB_ROOT = new File(".");
  static final String DEFAULT_FILE = "index.html";
  static final int PORT = 8080; //default port

  //static variables
  static boolean verbose=false;

  //instance variables
  Socket connect;
```

```
//constructor
public HttpServer(Socket connect)
{
  this.connect = connect;
}


/**
 * main method creates a new HttpServer instance for each
 * request and starts it running in a separate thread
 */
public static void main(String[] args)
{
  ServerSocket serverConnect=null;

  if (args.length > 0)
  {
    if (args[0].equals("-v") || args[0].equals("-verbose"))
    {
      verbose = true; //print status to standard out
    }
    else if (args[0].equals("-?") || args[0].equals("-help"))
    {
      //print instructions to standard out
      String instructions =
        "usage: java HttpServer [-options]\n\n" +
        "where options include:\n" +
        "     -? -help\t print out this message\n" +
        "     -v -verbose\t turn on verbose mode";

      System.out.println(instructions);
      return;
    }
  }

  try
  {
    serverConnect = new ServerSocket(PORT); //listen on port
    System.out.println("\nListening for connections on port "
      + PORT + "...\n");
    while (true) //listen until user halts execution
    {
      HttpServer server = new HttpServer(
        serverConnect.accept()); //instantiate HttpServer
      if (verbose)
      {
        System.out.println("Connection opened. (" +
          new Date() + ")");
      }
      //create new thread
      Thread threadRunner = new Thread(server);
      threadRunner.start(); //start thread
    }
```

```
    }
    catch (IOException e)
    {
      System.err.println("Server error: " + e);
    }
}


/**
 * run method services each request in a separate thread
 */
public void run()
{
  try
  {
    //get character input stream from client
    BufferedReader in = new BufferedReader(new
      InputStreamReader(connect.getInputStream()));
    //get character output stream to client (for headers)
    PrintWriter out = new PrintWriter(
      connect.getOutputStream());
    //get binary output stream to client (for requested data)
    BufferedOutputStream dataOut = new BufferedOutputStream(
      connect.getOutputStream());

    //get first line of request from client
    String input = in.readLine();
    //create StringTokenizer to parse request
    StringTokenizer parse = new StringTokenizer(input);
    //parse out method
    String method = parse.nextToken().toUpperCase();
    //parse out file requested
    String fileRequested = parse.nextToken().toLowerCase();

    //methods other than GET and HEAD are not implemented
    if (!method.equals("GET") && !method.equals("HEAD"))
    {
      if (verbose)
      {
        System.out.println("501 Not Implemented: " + method +
          " method.");
      }

      //send Not Implemented message to client
      out.println("HTTP/1.0 501 Not Implemented");
      out.println("Server: HttpServer 1.0");
      out.println("Date: " + new Date());
      out.println("Content-Type: text/html");
      out.println(); //blank line between headers and content
      out.println("<HTML>");
      out.println("<HEAD><TITLE>Not Implemented</TITLE>" +
        "</HEAD>");
      out.println("<BODY>");
```

```java
            out.println("<H2>501 Not Implemented: " + method +
              " method.</H2>");
            out.println("</BODY></HTML>");
            out.flush();
            out.close(); //close output stream
            connect.close(); //close socket connection

            if (verbose)
            {
              System.out.println("Connection closed.\n");
            }

            return;
          }

          //If we get to here, request method is GET or HEAD

          if (fileRequested.endsWith("/"))
          {
            //append default file name to request
            fileRequested += DEFAULT_FILE;
          }

          try
          {
            //create file object
            File file = new File(WEB_ROOT, fileRequested);
            //get length of file
            int fileLength = (int)file.length();

            //get the file's MIME content type
            String content = getContentType(fileRequested);

            //generate HTTP headers
            out.println("HTTP/1.0 200 OK");
            out.println("Server: HttpServer 1.0");
            out.println("Date: " + new Date());
            out.println("Content-type: " + content);
            out.println("Content-length: " + file.length());
            out.println(); //blank line between headers and content
            out.flush(); //flush character output stream buffer

            //if request is a GET, send the file content
            if (method.equals("GET"))
            {
              //open input stream from file
              FileInputStream fileIn = new FileInputStream(file);
              //create byte array to store file data
              byte[] fileData = new byte[fileLength];
              //read file into byte array
              fileIn.read(fileData);
              fileIn.close(); //close file input stream
```

```
          dataOut.write(fileData,0,fileLength); //write file
          dataOut.flush(); //flush binary output stream buffer
        }

        if (verbose)
        {
          System.out.println("File " + fileRequested +
            " of type " + content + " returned.");
        }

        out.close(); //close character output stream
        dataOut.close(); //close binary output stream
        connect.close(); //close socket connection
        if (verbose)
        {
          System.out.println("Connection closed.\n");
        }
      }
      catch (IOException e)
      {
        //inform client file doesn't exist
        fileNotFound(out, fileRequested);

        out.close();
        connect.close();
        if (verbose)
        {
          System.out.println("Connection closed.\n");
        }
      }
    }
    catch (IOException e)
    {
      System.err.println("Server Error: " + e);
    }
  }


  /**
   * fileNotFound informs client that requested file does not
   * exist.
   *
   * @param out Client output stream
   * @param file File requested by client
   */
  private void fileNotFound(PrintWriter out, String file)
    throws IOException
  {
    out.println("HTTP/1.0 404 File Not Found");
    out.println("Server: HttpServer 1.0");
    out.println("Date: " + new Date());
    out.println("Content-Type: text/html");
    out.println();
```

```java
    out.println("<HTML>");
    out.println("<HEAD><TITLE>File Not Found</TITLE></HEAD>");
    out.println("<BODY>");
    out.println("<H2>404 File Not Found: " + file + "</H2>");
    out.println("</BODY>");
    out.println("</HTML>");
    if (verbose)
    {
      System.out.println("404 File Not Found: " + file);
    }
  }


  /**
   * getContentType returns the proper MIME content type
   * according to the requested file's extension
   *
   * @param fileRequested File requested by client
   */
  private String getContentType(String fileRequested)
  {
    if (fileRequested.endsWith(".htm") ||
      fileRequested.endsWith(".html"))
    {
      return "text/html";
    }
    else if (fileRequested.endsWith(".gif"))
    {
      return "image/gif";
    }
    else if (fileRequested.endsWith(".jpg") ||
      fileRequested.endsWith(".jpeg"))
    {
      return "image/jpeg";
    }
    else if (fileRequested.endsWith(".class") ||
      fileRequested.endsWith(".jar"))
    {
      return "applicaton/octet-stream";
    }
    else
    {
      return "text/plain";
    }
  }
}
```

APPENDIX H

HTTP Response Status Codes

Table H.1 describes the meaning behind the varying HTTP/1.0 status code ranges. For more information, see RFC 1945. Table H.2 describes the status codes defined by HTTP/1.0.

Table H.1

Code Range	Category	Description
1xx	Informational	A provisional status code for use in experimental applications only. HTTP/1.0 does not define any Informational status codes; however, HTTP/1.1 does.
2xx	Successful	The request was successfully received, understood, and accepted.
3xx	Redirection	The server is requesting the Web client to redirect to another URL. The Web client can automatically redirect only in response to a GET or HEAD request. Redirection of a POST request requires user confirmation. A client should never automatically redirect more than five times.
4xx	Client Error	The request is improperly formatted or cannot be fulfilled. Unless responding to a HEAD request, the server should return information describing the error and whether it is a temporary or permanent condition in the response body. The client must immediately stop sending requests to the server.
5xx	Server Error	A valid request was received but the server cannot fulfill it. Unless responding to a HEAD request, the server should return information describing the error and whether it is a temporary or permanent condition in the response body.

Table H.2

Status Code	Description
200 OK	The request succeeded. The information returned in the response depends on the request method, as follows: GET—Returns the information corresponding to the requested resource. HEAD—Response contains header information only. The body portion of the response is empty. POST—A message describing the results of the action is returned.
201 Created	The request was fulfilled successfully and resulted in the creation of a new resource. The URL to the new resource is specified in the body portion of the response. Of the HTTP/1.0 methods, only a POST request can create a resource. (There is, however, another method specified in HTTP/1.1 that can create a resource. For more information, see the PUT method described in Chapter 3.)
202 Accepted	A noncommittal response conveying that the request has been received and is currently being processed. The body of the response should indicate the current status of the request and either an estimate of when the processing will be complete or a pointer to a status monitor.
204 No Content	The server has fulfilled the request but there is no new information to return. The client should maintain its current view. If desired, additional meta information can be included in the response headers.
300 Multiple Choices	Indicates that the resource is available from multiple locations. The body of the response should include a list of locations where the resource can be found. If a particular location is preferred, the server can specify a URL in the Location header of the response. The Web client may automatically redirect to this new location.
301 Moved Permanently	The resource has been moved permanently. The Location header field specifies the new location. The Web client should automatically redirect to the new URL and update any bookmarks pointing to the old location. Unless a HEAD request has been issued, the body of the response should include a short message explaining the move and a hyperlink to the new location. This message is useful for older browsers that do not automatically redirect. If received in response to a request using the POST method, the Web client must confirm the redirection request with the user.
302 Moved Temporarily	The requested resource has moved temporarily. The Location header field specifies the temporary location. The Web client should automatically redirect to the new URL but bookmarks should not be updated. Unless a HEAD request has been issued, the body of the response should include a short message explaining the temporary move and a hyperlink to the temporary location. This message is useful for older browsers that do not automatically redirect. If received in response to a request using the POST method, the Web client must confirm the redirection request with the user.

Status Code	Description
304 Not Modified	Returned if the Web client issued a GET request with an If-Modified-Since header and the resource has not changed since the specified date. The body of the response is empty and the page should be loaded from the browser's cache.
400 Bad Request	The request used invalid syntax and should not be repeated without modification.
401 Unauthorized	Authorization is required to access this resource, such as username and password. A WWW-Authenticate header field containing an authorization challenge is returned with the response. Normally, upon receiving this challenge, the Web browser will display a username/password dialog box to the user. If the request has already included authorization information, this response indicates that authorization has been refused for those credentials. If authorization is denied a second time for the same credentials, the browser should display the body of the response. This may help the user diagnose the problem.
403 Forbidden	The server understood the request but refuses to fulfill it. Authorization will not help and the same request should not be repeated. If the request was not HEAD and the server chooses to explain the refusal, it may include an explanation in the body of the response.
404 Not Found	No resource matching the requested URL exists on the server. If the server does not wish to divulge the absence of a resource, it may choose to respond with status code 403 instead.
500 Internal Server Error	The server encountered an unexpected condition that prevented it from fulfilling the request.
501 Not Implemented	The server does not implement the functionality required to fulfill the request. Returned if the server does not recognize the method in the request or is not capable of servicing the request method.
502 Bad Gateway	The server received an invalid response from a gateway to which it forwarded the request.
503 Service Unavailable	The server is temporarily unable to service the request, possibly because of overloading or maintenance.

APPENDIX I

Common HTTP Request Header Fields

The HTTP/1.0 and 1.1 specifications define many header fields that are valid in an HTTP request. These fields convey a wide variety of information and/or instructions to the server. The syntax of all HTTP request headers consists of the header name, followed immediately by a colon (":"), a single space, and the field value as illustrated here:

```
<Header>": "<Value>
```

The table that follows shows many of the most common request headers. For more information, see RFC 1945.

Header	Description
Allow	Communicates to the client the HTTP methods that are supported by the requested resource. See example: Allow: GET, HEAD
Authorization	Contains authentication information required by the server.
Content-Encoding	Indicates the encoding scheme that was used, in addition to the MIME encoding, to package the data. See example: Content-Encoding: x-tar
Content-Length	Indicates the length of the request's data portion. See example: Content-Length: 1234
Content-Type	Indicates the MIME type of the request's data. See example: Content-Type: text/html

Header	Description
Date	Indicates the date and time the request was generated. See example: `Date: Sat, 08 Aug 1998 11:35:15 GMT`
Expires	Indicates the date after which the resource should be considered invalid. See example: `Expires: Sat, 08 Aug 1998 11:35:15 GMT`
From	Indicates the Internet e-mail address of the client generating the request. See example: `From: callaway@sourcestream.com`
If-Modified-Since	Indicates that the requested resource should be returned only if it has been modified since the date contained in this header field. See example: `If-Modified-Since: Sat, 08 Aug 1998 11:35:15 GMT`
Last-Modified	Indicates the date and time the requested resource was last modified. See example: `Last-Modified: Sat, 08 Aug 1998 11:35:15 GMT`
Location	Indicates the location of a server resource. Used in conjunction with 3xx responses to redirect the client to a different URL. See example: `Location: www.sourcestream.com/index.html`
Pragma	Communicates implementation directives to the client. This example informs the client that the response should not be cached. `Pragma: no-cache`
Referer	Indicates the address that contained the reference (or hyperlink) to the currently requested resource. In essence, this header indicates the HTML page that referred the client to the requested resource. Useful for determining where the client came from. See example: `Referer: http://www.sourcestream.com/login.html`
Server	Indicates the name and version of the server software. See example: `Server: Apache/1.2.5`
User-Agent	Indicates the type and version of the user's browser. See example: `User-Agent: Mozilla/4.03 [en] (Win95; I)`

APPENDIX J

BrowserRequest HTTP Viewer

The *BrowserRequest* program presented here is a useful utility for examining the HTTP request transmitted by a browser. The program listens for a request on a specified port and returns the HTTP headers and form data (in the case of a POST request) to the browser. In addition, the entire request is printed to the console screen where *BrowserRequest* is running. Note that the program accepts an optional command-line parameter indicating the port on which the server will listen. Port 80 is the default.

```java
import java.io.*;
import java.net.*;

/**
 * BrowserRequest
 *
 * This application echoes an HTTP request back to the browser
 * and prints it to standard out.
 *
 * @author Dustin R. Callaway
 * @version 1.0, 02/15/98
 */
public class BrowserRequest
{
  /**
   * main listens for a request from a client. When receieved,
   * it echoes the request back to the client and prints it to
   * standard out.
   */
  public static void main(String[] args)
  {
    String line; //single line from request
    Socket mySocket; //socket opened to client
    StringBuffer request; //stores request
    ServerSocket serverSocket=null; //gets client connection
```

```
int port=80; //port number defaults to 80

//check for command-line arguments
if (args.length > 0)
{
  try
  {
    port = Integer.parseInt(args[0]); //set port
  }
  catch (Exception e)
  {
    port = 80; //if error, set port to default
  }
}

try
{
  //create ServerSocket
  serverSocket = new ServerSocket(port);
}
 catch (IOException e)
{
  System.out.println("Error: " + e);
  System.exit(0);
}

while (true)
{
  try
  {
    System.out.println("\nListening on port " + port +
      "...");
    //block until connection received
    mySocket = serverSocket.accept();
    System.out.println("Connection established...\n");
    //open input stream
    BufferedReader in = new BufferedReader(
      new InputStreamReader(mySocket.getInputStream()));

    request = new StringBuffer(); //stores entire request

    while (true) //loop through all lines of request
    {
      line = in.readLine(); //read line from request
      System.out.println(line); //print to standard out
      request.append(line + "\n"); //add to string buffer

      if (line.equals("")) //blank line, header complete
      {
        //stores form data passed with a POST request
        StringBuffer formData=new StringBuffer();
        while (in.ready()) //POST request has one more line
        {
```

```
                        //for POST, read content body following empty line
                          char c = (char)in.read();
                          formData.append(c); //add to form data buffer
                        }
                        //print form data to standard out
                        System.out.println(formData.toString());
                        //add form data to request buffer
                        request.append(formData.toString());
                        break; //request is complete, exit while loop
                    }
                }

                //open output stream
                PrintWriter out = new PrintWriter(
                  mySocket.getOutputStream());
                //send HTTP headers for browser to read
                out.println("HTTP/1.0 200 OK");
                //output will be plain text
                out.println("Content-Type: text/plain");
                out.println(); //blank line between headers and content
                out.print(request.toString()); //print browser's request
                out.flush(); //flush output stream
                out.close(); //close output stream
                mySocket.close(); //close socket connection
            }
            catch (IOException e)
            {
                System.err.println("Error: " + e);
                break;
            }
        }
      }
    }
}
```

The following is a sample of the console output and browser display generated when a local browser requests the resource at *http://localhost:8080*.

```
C:\>java BrowserRequest 8080

Listening on port 8080...
Connection established...

GET / HTTP/1.0
Connection: Keep-Alive
User-Agent: Mozilla/4.5 [en] (WinNT; I)
Host: localhost:8080
```

```
Accept: image/gif, image/x-xbitmap, image/jpeg, image/pjpeg, */*
Accept-Encoding: gzip
Accept-Language: en
Accept-Charset: iso-8859-1,*,utf-8

Listening on port 8080...
```

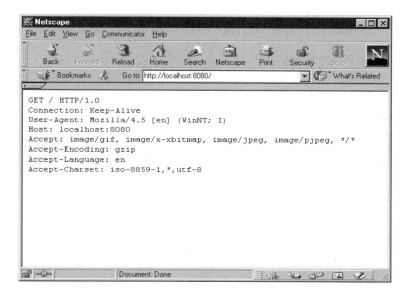

APPENDIX K

Common MIME Types

The following table describes the main areas into which MIME types are categorized as well as specific subtypes. The format of the MIME content type identifier is *type/subtype*. For instance, the MIME type for an HTML document is text/html, and for a JPEG file, it is image/jpeg.

Type	Subtype	Description
application		Binary data that is read or executed by another program
	java	Java byte-code file (.class)
	mac-binhex40	Binary Macintosh file
	msword	Microsoft Word document
	octet-stream	Arbitrary binary data that can be executed or used within another program (sometimes used for Java .class files)
	pdf	Adobe Acrobat file
	postscript	Adobe PostScript file
	rtf	Rich Text Format document
	x-compress	UNIX compress file
	x-dvi	Device independent file
	x-framemaker	FrameMaker document
	x-gtar	GNU tar archive file
	x-gzip	Compressed UNIX gzip file
	x-latex	LaTeX document
	x-mif	FrameMaker MIF document
	x-sd	Session directory announcement for MBONE events

Type	Subtype	Description
	x-shar	Self-extracting UNIX shell file
	x-tar	UNIX `tar` archive file
	x-tcl	Tool Command Language program
	x-tex	TeX document
	x-texinfo	GNU texinfo document
	x-troff	UNIX troff document
	x-wais-source	Wide Area Information Servers source file
	zip	Compressed `zip` file
audio		Sound file that can be played by another program
	basic	Standard audio format used by `.au` and `.snd` files
	x-aiff	AIFF audio format
	x-wav	Microsoft WAV format
image		Picture file that can be displayed by another program
	gif	GIF image
	jpeg	JPEG image
	tiff	TIFF image
	x-bitmap	Bitmap image
	x-fits	Flexible Image Transport System image used by the astronomy community
	x-macpict	Macintosh PICT image
	x-pict	Macintosh PICT image
	x-pbm	Portable bitmap image
	x-pgm	PGM image
	x-portable-bitmap	Portable bitmap image
	x-portable-greymap	Portable greymap image
	x-portable-pixmap	Portable pixmap image
	x-xbitmap	X Window bitmap image
	x-xpixmap	X Window pixmap image
message		Encapsulated mail message
	external-body	Headers of an e-mail message with a reference to the message body located elsewhere
	news	News article
	partial	Part of a fragmented message
	rfc822	RFC822-compliant e-mail message

Type	Subtype	Description
multipart		Data consisting of multiple, possibly heterogenous, parts
	alternative	Multiple formats of the same message (allows the client to choose)
	digest	Message formed by merging many e-mail messages
	mixed	Mixed formats within the same message
	parallel	Multipart message containing parts that should be viewed simultaneously
text		Data consisting of printable text
	html	Hypertext Markup Language document
	plain	Plain ASCII text without any formatting
	richtext	Rich Text Format document (includes formatting codes in standard ASCII text)
	tab-separated-values	Popular file format for exchanging data between spreadsheets and databases. Fields are separated by tabs and records are separated by carriage return/linefeeds.
video		Video file that can be played by another program
	mpeg	Moving Pictures Experts Group video file
	quicktime	Apple QuickTime video file
	x-msvideo	Microsoft AVI (Audio Video Interleave) video file
	x-sgi-movie	Silicon Graphics video file
x-world		Experimental data types
	x-vrml	Virtual Reality Markup Language document

APPENDIX L

printStackTrace() *to* String

The printStackTrace() method of the java.lang.Exception object (inherited from the Throwable object) is a very useful debugging function. This method prints the stack trace to standard error or to a specified output stream (PrintStream or PrintWriter). However, there may be times when you would prefer to write the stack trace to an error log or send it to the client. Unfortunately, it is not immediately apparent how the output produced by the printStackTrace() method can be converted to a String for easy use. The following code demonstrates how this can be accomplished.

```
catch (Exception e)
{
   StringWriter swError = new StringWriter();
   PrintWriter pwError = new PrintWriter(swError);
   e.printStackTrace(pwError);
   String sError = swError.toString();

   // The printStackTrace output is stored in the String
   // variable, sError, and can now be written to a file
   // or returned to the client.
}
```

APPENDIX M

Servlet API Class Hierarchy Diagram

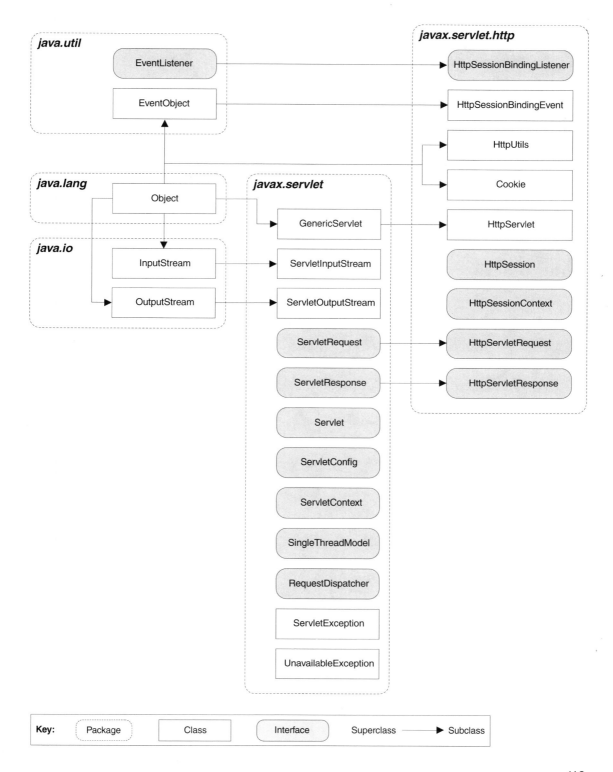

INDEX

CD-ROM WARRANTY

Java™ Technology from Addison-Wesley

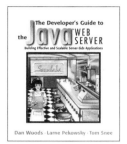

ISBN 0-201-37949-X

ISBN 0-201-37963-5

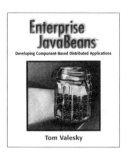

ISBN 0-201-60446-9

ISBN 0-201-43329-X

ISBN 0-201-48543-5

ISBN 0-201-61563-0

ISBN 0-201-30972-6

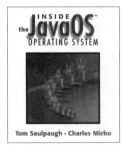

ISBN 0-201-18393-5

ISBN 0-201-32573-X

ISBN 0-201-32582-9

http://www.awl.com/cseng
Addison-Wesley